Nights That Shook the Stage

Nights That Shook the Stage

Forty Pivotal Events in Theater History

DWAYNE BRENNA

McFarland & Company, Inc., Publishers
Jefferson, North Carolina

ISBN (print) 978-1-4766-8978-4
ISBN (ebook) 978-1-4766-5014-2

LIBRARY OF CONGRESS AND BRITISH LIBRARY
CATALOGUING DATA ARE AVAILABLE

Library of Congress Control Number 2023019346

© 2023 Dwayne Brenna. All rights reserved

*No part of this book may be reproduced or transmitted in any form
or by any means, electronic or mechanical, including photocopying
or recording, or by any information storage and retrieval system,
without permission in writing from the publisher.*

On the cover: *shown from left*: Diana Sands and Sidney Poitier
in *A Raisin in the Sun*, (1959–1960 Broadway) play by Lorraine Hansberry,
directed by Lloyd Richards (Photofest); *background* frame © Shutterstock

Printed in the United States of America

*McFarland & Company, Inc., Publishers
Box 611, Jefferson, North Carolina 28640
www.mcfarlandpub.com*

For Don Kerr, Henry Woolf, and Ronald "Bingo" Mavor,
three wise men who in some way or another
inspired the writing of this book

Table of Contents

Preface

This is a book about some of the most raucous evenings in the history of theater. It consists of 40 essays (chapters) about specific evenings when theater makers changed the course of theatrical, and sometimes world, history. What were the reactions of the critics and the public? What was the inside story? Who were the key players? Why do these events still resound with us today?

Several of the essays in the book focus on opening nights when new theatrical developments infuriated or delighted audiences. The Paris opening of Alfred Jarry's *Ubu Roi* was one such evening, with the audience jeering and catcalling for ten minutes after the play's first scatological word was spoken. Several other openings were not particularly auspicious. Predictions were dire when *The Seagull* and *The Glass Menagerie* premiered. When Sophocles' great tragedy *Oedipus Tyrannus* opened in Athens in 427 BC, it was part of a trilogy that won second prize at the City Dionysia. The trilogy that won first prize is now long lost and forgotten, while Sophocles' work has become a standard bearer for excellence in the tragic mode.

Other essays will not necessarily deal with opening nights. The Burbages' systematic tearing down of their theater in North London on December 28, 1598, while their landlord was tucking into his holiday meal, and the subsequent rebuilding of the theater in Southwark, is worthy of attention. Their hasty act of dismantling and rebuilding led to a renaissance in the lively arts in London; they reopened their theater in Southwark, calling it the Globe, with William Shakespeare as their lead playwright. The Old Price riots of 1806 were occasioned by the re-opening of Covent Garden Theatre, after a fire. Disturbances in the theater began on an opening night but continued over a period of several months. The rioting would have occurred no matter what play was opening that autumn. Also noteworthy, although not an opening night, is the evening in 1865 on which John Wilkes Booth assassinated Abraham Lincoln during a performance of *Our American Cousin*.

Still other noteworthy evenings did not occur inside the theater at all.

1

Konstantin Stanislavsky's meeting with Vladimir Nemirovich-Danchenko at the Slavyanski Bazar in 1896 was not an evening of theatergoing, but it did result in an all-night conversation that triggered a new more realistic style of acting and the founding of the Moscow Art Theatre. Similarly, the most important events surrounding the Astor Place riots in New York happened outside the theater where William Charles Macready was preparing for a performance. The chapter on William Terriss focuses on what happened in Maiden Lane, outside the stage door of London's Adelphi Theatre, on November 17, 1897. "The Theatre of Neptune," the first European play ever produced in the New World, did not see the inside of a theater at all; it was performed in the waters off what is now Acadia.

The organization of this book has much to do with a theater history course I've taught at the University of Saskatchewan over the past twenty years. Over the years, I've noticed that one of the best ways to engage young scholars is to begin with a detailed story about one specific event and to expand from there, demonstrating how that event illustrates some important facet of theater history. This technique has allowed me to relate what has gone on inside and outside theaters to larger social or political events. It has also enabled me to tell the human stories of theater makers struggling against poverty, racism, and the theatrical establishment. Students are often excited to learn that Henry Irving left his wife on the night *The Bells* opened in London's West End, that Molière was accused by his competitors of incest, or that Shakespeare retired at the age of 49 after a fire at the Globe. Because the manuscript is largely based on lecture notes compiled over two decades, it has been a painstaking effort as well as a labor of love to adequately acknowledge source materials used over that period. All quotations have been carefully cited and, in the interests of readability and reaching a wide audience, included at the end of the book is a chapter-by-chapter bibliography of works I've consulted (or quoted from) in this endeavor.

Lastly, I've attempted to cover a wide range of international theater events, through a vast swath of theater history, in this book. Chapters are set in Athens, Paris, Moscow, Oslo, London, New Delhi, Seoul, Toronto, Washington, Chicago, and New York. Some deal with Indigenous theater or with plays written by African American playwrights. The time scheme of the chapters takes the reader from Greece in 427 BC to London in 1598 to Toronto in 1986 to New York City in 2021. The book is not organized chronologically but on the basis of theme, largely because that method provides the reader with a quick start and with a more exciting view of theater history. Furthermore, a thematic organization has allowed me to relate historical events to more modern occurrences, illustrating their relevance to a modern reader; it has enabled me to demonstrate how certain themes and ideas have appeared and reappeared in theaters through the ages.

In this book, I deal with theatrical events that had a resounding effect both nationally and internationally. Only in the epilogue do I offer a brief reflection about my own personal favorite night in the theater, an evening not nearly as important as all the other evenings discussed here but an example of how one minor premiere might remain in an actor's memory for a good long time.

I would like to thank the University of Saskatchewan for providing me with a sabbatical leave so that this book could be written. Particular thanks go to several colleagues at the University of Saskatchewan—Professors Henry Woolf, Garry Gable, and Kristina Fagan Bidwell—for reading, and providing comment on, various chapters. Professor Emerita Moira Day, my former colleague at the University of Saskatchewan, has been particularly gracious and meticulous in her comments on the manuscript. Robert Langdon Lloyd was exceptionally generous in allowing me to interview him about his work on *Marat/Sade* with Peter Brook. I also owe a debt of gratitude to Professor Noushad Mohamed, at the University of Hyderabad, and to Professor Ae Ran Jeong, Director of the Publications Committee in the Research, Documentation and Promotion Division at the International Theatre Institute (ITI) Korea Centre, for their immensely helpful suggestions. Special thanks go to my student assistant, James Miller, who researched and applied for copyright clearance for all the photographs included in this book. My writers' group, consisting of Don Kerr, David Carpenter, and David Margoshes, has been extremely supportive during this venture.

And thank you, as always, to Beverley Brenna and to my sons Wilson, Eric, and Connor for their love and encouragement during the writing of this book.

Of Murder
and Premonitions

Murder and self-murder have long been the subject of theatrical exploration. Sophocles dealt with murder in *Oedipus Rex*, which is set in the aftermath of Oedipus' slaying of King Laius on a road outside the city. Shakespeare made a living off plays about murder and self-murder, including *Hamlet*, *Macbeth*, and *Titus Andronicus*, while his contemporaries composed Jacobean revenge tragedies with reckless abandon. Nineteenth-century melodramas, like George Dibdin Pitt's *The String of Pearls*, in which a serial-killing barber dispatches his victims with a razor and a trick chair, were often full of murder. Given the violence of the 20th century, it is perhaps not surprising that the tradition of writing good plays about murder, some of them based on real-life cases, has continued. The murder of celebrated architect Francis Rattenbury was the basis for Terence Rattigan's *Cause Célèbre*. Agatha Christie's murder-riddled play *The Mousetrap* was in 2023 the longest running show in London's West End.

Like *Cause Célèbre*, one of the plays discussed here is about a real murder case. It is included because the real-life murder and the onstage representation of it were so close in time that the sordid details of the real event kept audiences away from the theater. There are other reasons, though, to include Sophie Treadwell's play *Machinal* in this book. One is that Treadwell was among the first female playwrights of the 20th century to have a series of full-length plays produced on Broadway. Female playwrights were even more under-represented on the Broadway stage in the 1920s, when Treadwell was writing, than they are now. Another reason is that *Machinal* is a brilliant play.

Sometimes murders in the theater have not been restricted to the onstage action. The remainder of the theatrical events in this section are famous for their connection to real cases of murder. In "Who Is Dead in the White House?," perhaps the most famous theatrical murder of all—the

5

assassination of a sitting president of the United States—is dealt with in some detail. In "A Night at the Adelphi," I chronicle the sad case of matinee idol William Terriss, murdered by a madman at the stage door of the Adelphi Theatre. "All Hell Broke Loose" is about Safdar Hashmi, a brilliant street performer who was bludgeoned to death by political thugs in a public street in Jhandapur, India.

CHAPTER 1

Who Is Dead in the White House?

Our American Cousin, *Ford's Theatre, Washington, April 14, 1865*

The theater can be a cozy place, warm and dark and overflowing with good humor. At least it must have seemed so to Abraham Lincoln, President of the United States, as he sat in a private box above the stage at Ford's Theatre on April 14, 1865. He'd embarrassed his wife that evening by holding her hand a little too obviously. Mary Lincoln was concerned that their guests, Miss Clara Harris and her beau Major Henry Rathbone, also sitting in the box, might see the President fawning over her. It was after ten o'clock that evening, and Lincoln was chuckling at a laugh line spoken by one of the company's leading actors. Little did Lincoln know that a derringer was aimed at the back of his head, three feet away.

The play they were watching was Tom Taylor's comedy *Our American Cousin*, about a boorish but goodhearted Vermont rustic named Asa Trenchard who travels to England to claim the family estate. While in England, Asa meets his cousin Florence Trenchard who lives at Trenchard Manor. Florence loves Harry Vernon of the Royal Navy, but the estate agent Richard Coyle falsely declares that the family will face bankruptcy unless Florence agrees to marry him. In the course of the play, Asa Trenchard displays his backwoods kindness and knowhow by giving up his claim to the manor and by breaking into Coyle's office and finding papers that prove Florence Trenchard is not in debt.

Our American Cousin had been a hit on both sides of the Atlantic. It had premiered with great success in New York City in 1858, at Laura Keene's theater. Keene toured the production to Washington in 1865, with herself in the role of Florence Trenchard and with Harry Hawk as Asa Trenchard. The play had also enjoyed a successful run in London after its 1861 opening and, even though it became inextricably associated with Lincoln's death, it remained a popular piece until the end of the 19th century.

Laura Keene was an interesting and successful actor-manager at a time when female actor-managers were few. Keene was a stage name that she took to avoid calumny because it was considered socially unacceptable at the time for a woman with children but no husband to be acting upon the stage. She had been born Mary Frances Moss in Winchester, England, and she had decided to become an actress to support herself and her two daughters after her first husband, a tavern owner, was transported to Australia for alleged criminal behavior. Before moving to the United States, she had trained with Madame Vestris, another trail-blazing female actor-manager, at Covent Garden Theatre. Keene was lured to the New York stage when James William Wallack invited her to be the leading lady in his stock company at Wallack's Lyceum. She soon left Wallack's company and entered into theater management. She toured Australia as Edwin Booth's leading lady in 1854–55, and she returned to New York City soon afterwards, where she found investors and built a new theater which was named Laura Keene's Theatre.

Lincoln's assassin, John Wilkes Booth, was a well-known actor from a prominent theatrical family. His father Junius Brutus Booth had been an actor of note in England but had run off to America with a London flower girl, leaving his homeland and his wife and infant son. He began a new life in Baltimore. Several of Junius Brutus Booth's children would eventually become prominent actors in the United States, following in their father's footsteps. Edwin Booth became the leading American actor of his generation, mostly known for playing Shakespearean tragedy. Quiet, thoughtful, and naturalistic, Edwin Booth was considered one of the best Hamlets of his time. Together with John Sleeper Clarke, who was married to his sister Asia, Edwin Booth would eventually buy an interest in the Winter Garden Theatre in New York City. At the time of Lincoln's assassination, John Wilkes Booth was also a rising star. Of lesser note as an actor was his brother Junius Brutus Booth Junior.

The Booths were a politically opinionated bunch. Junius Brutus Booth, Sr., had written an angry, drunken letter to President Andrew Jackson, back in the 1830s, threatening to cut the President's throat.[1] Edwin Booth was a staunch Unionist during the Civil War, but his brother John Wilkes Booth supported the Southern Confederacy. A segregationist, John Wilkes Booth was incensed by Lincoln's suggestion that African Americans should have voting rights. As the Confederacy collapsed in the dying days of the Civil War, Booth had plotted with other conspirators to abduct the President. The plotted abduction had failed because Lincoln changed his plans at the last minute and was no longer in a position to be abducted.

Much has been written about Lincoln's premonitions of assassination and about warnings he'd received not to attend *Our American Cousin* on April 14, 1865. Only a few days before his death, Lincoln narrated to his wife a disturbing dream he'd had of walking through the White House, looking for the source of keening voices:

> I went from room to room; no living person was in sight, but the same mournful sounds of distress met me as I passed along. It was light in all the rooms; every object was familiar to me; but where were all the people who were grieving as if their hearts would break? I was puzzled and alarmed. What could be the meaning of all this? Determined to find the cause of a state of things so mysterious and so shocking, I kept on until I arrived at the East Room, which I entered. There I met with a sickening surprise. Before me was a catafalque, on which rested a corpse wrapped in funeral vestments. Around it were stationed soldiers who were acting as guards; and there was a throng of people, gazing mournfully upon the corpse, whose face was covered, others weeping pitifully. "Who is dead in the White House?" I demanded of one of the soldiers. "The President," was his answer; "he was killed by an assassin."[2]

Lincoln's fears of assassination were understandable. He was not an entirely popular president, even in the North, and there had been at least one other attempt on his life. The bullet hole in one of his hats was proof of that. Others, including War Secretary Edward Stanton, thought that Lincoln's predilection for attending the theater was dangerous folly. Even Lincoln's footman had warned him not to go.

Although he had premonitions and warnings of assassination, Lincoln could hardly have suspected that John Wilkes Booth would be his assassin. Lincoln had seen Booth perform at Ford's Theatre in 1863 and had admired his performance. He had repeatedly invited John Wilkes Booth to the White House on social occasions. After attending Lincoln's second inauguration on March 4, 1865, John Wilkes Booth wrote in his diary, "What an excellent chance I had, if I wished, to kill the President on Inauguration day."[3] Lincoln loved the theater and admired theater folk. As Edward Steers, Jr., writes, he had attended plays at Ford's Theatre on at least 13 occasions prior to April 14. So comfortable was Lincoln in that playhouse that he usually attended plays there with no military escort and with a minimum number of bodyguards.

In fact, President Lincoln had been in an extraordinarily good mood all morning on April 14. His son Robert, who served on General Ulysses S. Grant's staff, had just arrived in Washington. "Well, my son, you have returned safely from the front," rejoiced Lincoln. "The war is now closed and we soon will live in peace with the brave men that have been fighting against us."[4] The Civil War was almost over, Grant having defeated the Confederate army at Appomattox. Lincoln was waiting to hear if General Joseph E. Johnston had also surrendered in North Carolina. With his son home and much of the war behind him, Lincoln abandoned his formerly morose demeanor. He spent some part of the day pardoning captured Confederate soldiers who might otherwise have been imprisoned or executed.

After the cabinet meeting that morning, Edwin Stanton remarked on how happy and spruce the President looked, his face clean-shaven, his clothes neatly pressed—not at all the way he had looked in the months previous. In the afternoon, Lincoln and his wife Mary visited the *Montauk*, an ironclad ship that was resting at anchor in the naval yards. Mary Lincoln described her husband's joyous demeanor in a letter written seven months later. "He was almost boyish, in his mirth & reminded me, of his original nature," she wrote, "what I had always remembered of him, in our own home—free from care...."⁵

In celebration of the war's coming to an end, Lincoln had invited General Grant, newly returned to Washington after accepting Robert E. Lee's surrender at Appomattox, and his wife Julia, to accompany the Lincolns to the theater that evening. General Grant had at first accepted and then refused Lincoln's invitation to join him in a private box at Ford's Theatre. Some historians have attributed Grant's eventual refusal to an antagonism between Julia Grant and Mary Lincoln, but it is also true that Grant had not seen his own children for several weeks and that he chose to catch an early train to New Jersey so that he could visit with them.⁶

John Wilkes Booth had, in the meantime, hatched a conspiracy that was meant to render the Unionist government rudderless. At 10:15 that evening, he would assassinate the President as he sat in his box at Ford's Theatre. Simultaneously, his co-conspirator Lewis Powell was to eliminate Secretary of State William Henry Seward, who was recuperating at home from a near-fatal fall from his horse-drawn carriage. Also at 10:15, Confederate sympathizer George Atzerodt would kill Vice President Andrew Johnson at the Kirkwood Hotel, where Johnson was staying until arrangements could be made for more permanent accommodation. Booth's assassination of Lincoln was the only part of the plot that went as planned. Powell stabbed Seward in his bed but did not manage to kill him. Atzerodt lost his nerve altogether and did not attempt to murder Johnson.

The Lincolns arrived late at Ford's Theatre, sometime between 8:20 and 8:30. As they entered their private box, the orchestra played "Hail to the Chief." The audience stood and applauded. Lincoln waved. The decorations in Lincoln's private box had been arranged by Harry Ford, brother and business partner of impresario John T. Ford, who owned the theater. Earlier that day, Harry Ford had placed three velvet covered chairs, six cane chairs, and a sofa in the box, and a rocking chair for the President to sit in. He'd festooned the balustrade with American flags and hung a blue Treasury Guard flag from a center post.⁷ *The Washington Evening Star* and *The National Intelligencer* had reported that the Lincolns would be in attendance that evening, so one of the lines in the play was altered in deference to the President. When the heroine, played by Laura Keene, asked for a seat away from a drafty corner, the original retort had been "Well, you're not the only one that wants to escape the draft." The revised line, on that evening, was "The draft has already been stopped by order of the President."[8]

Because Lincoln's bodyguard William Crook was off duty that evening, a policeman named John Parker had been assigned to protect the President. Parker and Lincoln's valet, Charles Forbes, left the theater at intermission and went to a nearby tavern. Booth, who was well-known to the theater's stagehands, had free rein to walk its corridors. He entered the presidential box and used a piece of wood to prop the outer door shut. He knew the play by heart and waited for a big laugh line to fire his single-shot derringer. As Asa Trenchard, the actor Harry Hawk was dressing down the pompous Mrs. Marchessington. "Well, I guess I know enough to turn you inside out, old gal," he declaimed; "you sockdologizing old mantrap!"[9] The crowd roared with laughter, and Booth fired his pistol. The bullet struck the President behind his left ear and lodged near the front of his skull. Lincoln slumped forward in his chair.

Major Rathbone attempted to subdue Booth, who slashed him, elbow to shoulder, with a knife. Leaping over the railing of the private box onto the stage—a drop of fifteen feet—Booth caught the spur of his riding boot on the Treasury Guard flag decorating the box. He landed awkwardly on his knees, breaking one of his legs. At first, the audience thought it was all part of the evening's entertainment. Booth got to his feet, brandishing the bloody knife, and shouted "Sic semper tyrannis!" ("Such to all tyrants!") He stumbled across the stage and exited the theater through a side door. Outside a horse was waiting, held by the unwitting Joseph Burroughs (a "general do-all around the theater" who would later be handed a life sentence for his part in the escape, only to have it commuted).[10] Booth struck Burroughs with the handle of his knife and galloped away into the night.

The show did not go on. The 23-year-old army surgeon Charles Leale, in the audience that evening, rushed to the presidential box but found the door jammed shut. The injured Major Rathbone noticed the brace Booth had used to secure the door and removed it. Leale and others shifted Lincoln to the floor. The actress Lincoln had come to see, Laura Keene, cradled the President's head in her lap. Two other doctors arrived in the box. Conferring with each other, the doctors decided it would be too dangerous to transport the President back to the White House and opted to take him to a boarding house down the street from the theater.

In William Petersen's boarding house, the exceptionally tall Lincoln had to be placed diagonally across a bed. An army of surgeons arrived, including Lincoln's personal doctor Robert K. Stone and Surgeon General Joseph K. Barnes. It soon became apparent that the President would not survive. Barnes probed the wound and found where the bullet was lodged. As the hemorrhaging continued, the doctors decided that the best course of action was to remove blood clots as they occurred, to relieve pressure on the brain. Lincoln's wife Mary became so distraught that she had to be banished from the room. She was not told that her husband's death was imminent until 7 o'clock the next morning when she was invited to return to his side. Lincoln died at 7:22 a.m. on April 15, the day before Easter Sunday.

Under the cloak of night, John Wilkes Booth had crossed the Navy Yard Bridge into Maryland where he met with co-conspirator David Herold and retrieved a cache of weaponry at Mary Surratt's tavern. Booth and Herold knocked on the door of Dr. Samuel A. Mudd, who splinted Booth's leg and made him a pair of crutches. From Surrattsville, the conspirators travelled to Zehiah Swamp, where they hid for a few days. On April 24, they arrived at Richard Garrett's tobacco farm in Virginia.

Edwin Stanton offered a 50,000 dollar reward for the capture of John Wilkes Booth, and a desperate manhunt was taking place. When he heard reports of the public reaction to the assassination of Lincoln, Booth was dismayed. He thought he would be celebrated as a national hero. On April 26, Union soldiers surrounded Garrett's barn, where Booth and Herold were sleeping. When the soldiers lit fire to the barn, Booth scrambled to the back door with a rifle and a pistol. Although he had been cautioned to take Booth alive, one of the soldiers crept up behind him and shot him in the back of the head. Booth died on the porch of Garrett's farmhouse two hours later.

The assassination of Lincoln left a series of calamities in its wake. Plunged into a deep depression, Lincoln's wife Mary would later be declared insane and institutionalized. The gallant Major Rathbone, who had shared the presidential box with the Lincolns on that fateful night, would never recover from the trauma. He would later murder his wife (the former Miss Harris) in a fit of insanity. Rathbone attempted suicide but was unsuccessful. He spent the last thirty years of his life in an insane asylum. When John T. Ford attempted to re-open Ford's Theatre in the summer of 1865, Stanton dispatched soldiers to prevent the entertainments from taking place. The United States government eventually purchased Ford's Theatre, gutting the building and converting it to War Department Offices. In 1893, the upper floors of the former theatre collapsed, killing 22 federal employees.

Booth's co-conspirators Lewis Powell, George Atzerodt, and David Herold were all sentenced to be hanged. Mary Surratt, at whose tavern the conspirators had stockpiled weapons, was also sentenced to death. She was the first woman ever to be hanged by the U.S. government.

After Lincoln's assassination, the stigma associated with the Booth family name forced Edwin Booth off the stage for several months. He made a triumphant return, as Hamlet, at the Winter Garden Theatre in 1866. When the Winter Garden Theatre was damaged by fire in 1867, Edwin Booth opened Booth's Theatre in Manhattan in 1869, playing Romeo in its inaugural production. Booth's Theatre went bankrupt in 1873, but Edwin Booth managed to regain his fortune by embarking on an international theater tour. In 1888, he founded The Players, a private club for literary, visual, and performing artists, in New York. Through dint of hard work, he recovered his career nicely in the aftermath of the assassination.

Laura Keene continued to work as an actormanager for several years following Lincoln's death. She died of tuberculosis in 1873 at the age of 47.

Broadside for the capture of John Wilkes Booth, John Surratt, and David Herold (this file was donated to Wikimedia Commons as part of a project by the Metropolitan Museum of Art).

The sleeve of the dress she wore on April 14, 1865, stained with Lincoln's blood, is now on display in the National Museum of American History in Washington.

In 1956, an elderly Samuel James Seymour appeared on the CBS television game show *I've Got a Secret*. After contestants guessed his

connection to the Civil War and to Lincoln, Seymour recounted the scene
at Ford's Theatre where he had come to see *Our American Cousin* on April
14, 1865. He was five years old at the time, brought to the theater by his
godmother. Seymour saw the President as he entered the theater and witnessed the aftermath of the assassination. "All of a sudden a shot rang
out—a shot that will always be remembered—and someone in the President's box screamed," he'd said in an earlier interview. "I saw Lincoln
slumped forward in his seat."[11] The 96-year-old Seymour was the last man
alive to have witnessed Lincoln's assassination. What he remembered of
the event, though, was his immediate sympathy for the actor Booth, who
had so obviously hurt himself while tumbling out of the presidential box.

CHAPTER 2

A Night at the Adelphi

Secret Service, *Adelphi Theatre,* *London, December 16, 1897*

On the evening of December 16, 1897, matinee idol William Terriss arrived at the stage door of the Adelphi Theatre in London. He was to star in William Gillette's play *Secret Service* that evening, opposite his usual co-star (and likely his mistress) Jessie Millward. As Terriss exited the hansom cab he'd shared with his friend John Henry Graves, a thin man in a cape was lurking in the shadows of a shop entrance across the street. Terriss was greeted at the stage door of the Adelphi by the theatrical manager Gilbert Tate. The two men conversed for a moment, and Terriss reached into his pocket for the pass key. At that instant, the thin man emerged from the shadows, with malice in his heart, and approached the great actor.

Terriss had led an adventurous life to that point, though perhaps not as adventurous as the lives of the swashbuckling heroes he tended to play. Born in 1847 in trendy St. John's Wood, the son of a barrister, he received a first-rate education but left university without taking a degree. Terriss (whose real name was William Charles James Lewin) served briefly in the merchant navy, worked for a short time as a tree planter in Bengal, and then found employment in the London hospital where his brother was a surgeon. Having found some success in amateur theatricals, Terriss decided to try his luck on the professional stage. His first professional role was Chouser in *The Flying Scud*, performed at the Prince of Wales Theatre in Birmingham in 1868.

In 1870, he made his first London appearance, playing a small role in Tom Robertson's *Society*. Also in that year, he married the actress Isabel Lewis. Restless still, he journeyed to South America with his new wife, eventually trying his hand at sheep farming in the Falkland Islands. He returned to London in 1871 and had a success in *Robin Hood* at Drury Lane. Seeking to make his fortune, he then emigrated to the United States,

15

setting up a horse breeding operation there. When that venture failed, in 1873, he returned to London and committed himself to the acting profession.

Over the next few years, Terriss managed to establish himself as a matinee idol. A handsome man with a strong voice, he specialized in swashbuckling melodramatic roles. In theatrical circles, he became known as "Breezy Bill." He had success in *The Belle's Stratagem* at the Strand and as Romeo at Drury Lane. In 1880, he joined Henry Irving's company at the Lyceum. Terriss played leading roles in Shakespeare's plays at the Lyceum, performing Don Pedro in the American tour of *Much Ado About Nothing* in 1883–84. By that time, he'd become close friends with Henry Irving and George Bernard Shaw.

In 1885, Terriss starred in *The Harbour Lights*, which ran for 513 performances. His co-star was the 24-year-old Jessie Millward. From that year on, Terriss and Millward played romantic leads at the Lyceum and elsewhere. The pair were acting almost exclusively at the Adelphi Theatre after 1894, with Terriss becoming famous for his roles in *The Swordsman's Daughter* and *One of the Best*. A writer for the *New York Daily Mirror* suggested that Terriss was "one of the greatest and next to Henry Irving undoubtedly the most popular actor in England."[1]

Terriss was also a generous man. He'd befriended a struggling young actor named Richard Archer Prince, sending him small amounts of money through the Actors' Benevolent Fund and continually trying to find him work. Prince had made himself largely unemployable because of the bad behavior that resulted from his alcohol abuse. Nicknamed "Mad Archer" due to his erratic behavior, Prince had been reduced to working as a stage-hand on those rare occasions when he could find employment. On December 13, 1897, he was thrown out of the lobby of the Vaudeville Theatre. The next evening, he was heard arguing with Terriss in Terriss' dressing room at the Adelphi. On December 16, Prince unsuccessfully appealed for money at the Benevolent Fund office. When his request was denied, he walked across the street and concealed himself in a shop doorway in Maiden Lane. According to Millward's autobiography, Prince "had been strutting about the Strand boasting that in a few days his name would be on everybody's lips."[2]

On the morning of the incident in Maiden Lane, Terriss' understudy, Frederick Lane, arrived for rehearsal at the Adelphi with a story to tell. He'd had a terrible dream, he said, and he narrated that dream to anyone who would listen. In his dream, Terriss was lying on the landing inside the stage door. The handsome actor was surrounded by a crowd of people, and he was raving. "[I]t was a horrible dream," Lane later said, "and I couldn't tell what it meant."[3] Others in the theatrical company later verified that Lane had told them about his dream before the murder took place. The

Jessie Millward and William Terriss in *Harbour Lights* **(Wikimedia Commons).**

actress Olive Haygate remembered Lane laughing about the dream, not entirely sure what it meant, before the rehearsal on the morning of the 16th. Another actor, Carter Bligh, related how Lane had told him, "in a jocular and chafing way (*not believing it for an instant*), how he probably would be called upon to play Captain Thomas, that night...."[4] The dream proved uncanny.

The audience had already begun to assemble at seven o'clock on December 16, when William Terriss inserted his key in the stage door lock. As Terriss attempted to gain access to the theater, Richard Archer Prince darted from his hiding place. Without warning, he stabbed Terriss twice, blows that appeared to onlookers as little more than a hearty clap on the back. When Terriss turned to confront his assailant, Prince plunged the blade deep into Terriss' chest. At that point, bystanders stepped in to prevent Prince from striking again. Jessie Millward, who had seen Richard Archer Prince when she'd entered the theater earlier in the evening, testified later that she'd heard the key enter the lock, followed by a strange silence. "Something has happened!" she said to her maid Lottie, who then rushed down to the stage door. When Lottie saw Terriss, he was leaning against a wall near the door. "Here are my keys, Lottie," he said calmly. "Catch that man!"[5]

Terriss was carried inside the theater and laid on the stairwell near the stage door. Jessie Millward rushed down the stairs to comfort him, placing his head on her lap. A Doctor Hayward arrived from nearby Charing Cross Hospital. He later described the scene at the coroner's hearing. "I found Mr. Terriss just inside the door, where he was lying with Miss Millward supporting his head," Hayward testified. "His vest and undergarments were opened, and there was a large piece of ice on the wound directly over the heart. He was breathing heavily. After I examined the wound I saw there was no hope and that death must ensue almost immediately from the extensive internal hemorrhage."[6] Millward described the moment of Terriss' death in her autobiography. "He opened his eyes, and faintly squeezed my hand. 'Sis! Sis!' he whispered. And that was all."[7]

Prince made no attempt to escape. Instead, he sat quietly, with Miss Millward's maid Lottie clinging to him, and waited for the police to arrive. When he was told that Terriss was dead, he replied that he had "meant to kill Miss Millward, too."[8] Constable Bragg arrived from nearby Bow Street and took Prince into custody. Inside the theater, the acting manager Herbert Budd was tasked with announcing that the evening's performance would be cancelled. His announcement, which did not mention the murder, was published in *The Daily Telegraph* a day later:

> Ladies and gentlemen, I am deeply grieved and pained to announce to you a serious, nay terrible, accident which will render the performance of *Secret Service* this evening quite impossible. I will also ask you to pass out into the street as quietly as possible. It is hardly necessary for me to add that your money will be returned on application at the pay-boxes.[9]

When the murderer was transported to Bow Street, an angry mob followed the carriage to the police station. At the station, Prince produced the murder weapon which he'd concealed under his cape. "That's what I stabbed him with," Prince said calmly. "He had due warning."[10] Arraigned in court the next morning, Prince heard the onlookers hissing as he was led away by two jailers.

Millward was a close friend of William Terriss' children Tom and Ellaline, who were both active in London's theater scene at the time. Tom Terriss escorted Millward to St. Martin's Church the morning after the arraignment. William Terriss' corpse was lying in the mortuary. Millward placed a bunch of lilies between his folded hands. Terriss had been accustomed to sending Millward lilies while he was alive, as a token of his affection for her. At the church, Millward took comfort in the "wonderful and majestic peace" emanating from Terriss' face. "As I gazed my last on my comrade, my friend," she later wrote, "I thought of the last lines he spoke on the stage in 'Secret Service' the night before his death: '...Until we meet again.'"[11]

The funeral, on December 21, was a magnificent affair. According to Millward, one newspaper estimated the graveside gathering at Brompton Cemetery, where Terriss was buried, at ten thousand people. Henry Irving attended, as did Terriss' son-in-law Seymour Hicks, and Lillie Langtry. The funeral procession consisted of more than a hundred carriages. The Prince of Wales sent an opulent wreath of white lilies and orchids. In order to carry all the flower tributes, two horse-drawn hearses had to be hired in addition to the one carrying the coffin.

A newspaperman's description of the event was focused on the figure of Jessie Millward. "Miss Millward, clothed in deepest black and leaning on the arm of Sir Henry Irving, was the most conspicuous figure at the funeral of William Terriss at Brompton Cemetery to-day," the story read. "She was one of the dead actor's oldest and closest friends, and her parting kiss was the last thing he felt before he lost consciousness. She has neither slept nor cried, and has hardly eaten or spoken...."[12]

As George Rowell writes, Irving's gesture in accompanying Millward might have been made "to protect her from the malice of theatrical gossip and the resentment of the Terriss family." Rowell also asserts that Victorian funerals were essentially male occasions "which even the closest female relatives did not usually attend."[13] Only two other women were included in the official list of mourners, and Terriss' wife Isabel, who had been ill, was not among them. *Punch* magazine later published a poetic tribute to Terriss that ended with the following stanza: "Why did they love him? The assassin's knife,/ With one fell blow, mangled a loyal life,/ They loved him for his honour! Splendid Will!/ That made a hero of our 'Breezy Bill'!"[14]

The murder left chaos in its wake. William Terriss' wife Isabel, who had been in poor health for some time before the murder, was devastated.

George Rowell quotes the notes from Tom Terriss' unfinished autobiography: "Later that winter, along towards the end of it, Tom goes with his Mother to Algeria, realizing she is not in very good health.... Upon returning from Algeria, Tom's Mother dies within a few months—during the summer of that year." Isabel died in 1898; as Rowell writes, she had "lost the will to survive her partner."[15]

After William Terriss' funeral, Jessie Millward suffered what George Rowell calls "almost total collapse."[16] She spent some time in Italy, trying to recover from the shock of Terriss' death. When she returned to England, she vowed to give up acting, but an offer from American theatrical manager Charles Frohman changed all that. She accepted a five-year contract with Frohman and was acting in an adaptation of Anthony Hope's novel *Phroso* at the Empire Theatre in New York about a year after Terriss' death. In 1907, she married the Scots actor John Glendinning. Millward retired from the theater in 1913 and penned her autobiography ten years later. She died in 1932.

Richard Archer Prince was pronounced guilty of the murder of William Terriss after a trial, on January 14, 1898. Spared hanging "by reason of insanity," Prince was committed to Broadmoor Prison for the Criminally Insane, where he spent the next 39 years and where he died at the age of 79. While at Broadmoor, Prince was, according to some accounts, involved in creating entertainments for his fellow prisoners and in conducting the prison orchestra.[17] The sentence, perceived at the time as lenient, was evidence to some of the lowly worth of an actor, even an actor so beloved as Terriss.

Henry Irving was quoted as saying that his friend "was an actor, so his murderer will not be executed"—a statement that led to Prince issuing a death threat against Irving from his insane asylum ward.[18] Perhaps, though, the murder of William Terriss, and the subsequent funeral, did make the upper classes aware of how highly actors were valued. His friend Henry Irving had become the first theatrical knight in 1895, and the 20th century saw a number of actors and actresses afforded similar honors. In the years after Terriss' death, the monarchy and the aristocracy have made the resounding pronouncement that actors' lives clearly count for something.

Theater folk love a good ghost story. In the years since Terriss' murder, there have been several reported sightings of the actor's ghost, usually dressed in Victorian apparel, at the Adelphi Theatre and the Covent Garden Tube Station. The first documented sighting at the Adelphi occurred in 1928, when a young actress fell asleep in her dressing room before a performance. She awoke when the couch she was sleeping on began to shake. She saw a greenish mist, and then something grabbed her arms and held her down to the couch. There were two knocks on the door, after which the spirit departed, leaving the actress breathless and terrified. Apparently Terriss had been in the habit of knocking on that same door twice with his cane before entering. The actress' arms were bruised for several days after the sighting.[19]

The sightings at the Covent Garden Tube Station are even more difficult to believe, especially since the Covent Garden Tube Station did not exist when Terriss died in 1897. The first reported sighting there occurred in 1955 and involved a ticket taker named Jack Hayden. According to Hayden, the ghost was wearing an opera cloak and gloves. It was holding a cane. The ticket taker claimed that the apparition had "a very, very sad face and sunken cheeks."[20] Paranormalist websites offer several theories about why Terriss' ghost might haunt a tube station. The most convincing is that Terriss had been fond of a bakery which stood on the site of the tube station in the 1890s and that his spirit continues to be lured there by the thought of a tasty mince pie.

CHAPTER 3

A Beauty That Cannot Be Conveyed

Machinal, *Plymouth Theatre, New York, September 7, 1928*

When Sophie Treadwell's *Machinal* premiered in New York on September 7, 1928, it was clear in the reviews that the play was among the best examples of American expressionism. In his review for *Theatre Magazine*, Perriton Maxwell wrote, "Not since Eugene O'Neill's masterpiece, *Strange Interlude*, rose like an effulgent sun over the miasmic lowlands of Theatredom has the American stage seen so truly a work of dramatic art and sincerity as *Machinal*, the forceful, beautiful, thrilling play written by Sophie Treadwell, and produced by Arthur Hopkins."

Word that the play was based on the sordid murder of Albert Snyder by his wife Ruth had leaked out before the opening, a fact which Maxwell lamented. "*Machinal* transcends the drab drama of the police court," he wrote; "it has a quality one finds it difficult to define, a beauty that cannot be conveyed in words, an aliveness and reality tinctured with poetic pathos which lift it to the realm of great art, greatly conceived and greatly presented." Maxwell went on to single out the lead performance of Zita Johann as A Young Woman for "portraying the protagonist with a simplicity, power, delicacy, and understanding that charms, thrills, and impresses her personality upon one." He also commended Arthur Hopkins for his outstanding direction.[1] Not mentioned in the review is the performance of a young actor named Clark Gable, who played the role of A Man.

The real-life murder on which *Machinal* is based was a sordid affair indeed. Born in 1895, Ruth Brown was the daughter of impoverished Scandinavian immigrants. She met her future husband Albert Snyder when she accidentally called the *Motor Boating* magazine offices, where Albert worked as an art director. Unhappy that a prank caller had disrupted his busy workday, Albert responded rudely over the phone. Later, to atone for his rudeness, he agreed to meet Ruth Brown in person so that he could properly apologize. Although Albert was somewhat older than Ruth, the two soon fell in love.

Prior to their marriage, Ruth was apparently not aware of how deeply Albert Snyder had been attached to his former fiancée, one Jessie Guischard, who had died unexpectedly some years earlier. After marrying Ruth, Albert insisted on displaying photographs of Jessie Guischard around their family home in the New York City borough of Queens. He wore a lapel pin on his coat, bearing the initials of his former fiancée. This behavior infuriated Ruth, and she caused great dissension when she took down a large portrait of Jessie Guischard that had hung in the family living room. The birth of a daughter, Lorraine, did not quell the unhappiness. Albert didn't relish the idea of becoming a father at an advanced age.

The relationship was further strained when Ruth's mother moved into the household to help care for the new baby. Taking advantage of her mother's presence, Ruth began to frequent nightclubs and restaurants, eventually meeting a young corset salesman named Judd Gray. Despite an extremely religious upbringing (and having served for some time as a Sunday School teacher), Gray became Ruth Snyder's lover. Seeking a way out of her unhappy marriage, Ruth took out three separate insurance policies on her husband's life. Each of these policies featured double indemnity clauses, which would pay out double if her husband's death was categorized as an accident. Ruth attempted to murder Albert, and to make the murder look like an accident, on a number of occasions. On one of those occasions, Ruth rigged an automobile jack to collapse while Albert was working under his car. Sensing danger, Albert wheeled out from under the car moments before it crashed to the cement floor of his garage. On another occasion, Ruth brought Albert a drink laced with sleeping powder while he was again working on his vehicle. Albert fell asleep with the engine running and the garage door closed, but woke up and escaped the enclosed space and the noxious carbon monoxide fumes.[2]

In his book *The "Double Indemnity" Murder*, Landis MacKellar describes another murder attempt that took place in an afternoon in July 1926, when Ruth left the house to do some shopping while her husband napped. When she returned from the store an hour later, Albert was staggering around the garden, nearly overcome by gas fumes. He did recover, and Ruth later "professed horror," saying she must have accidentally kicked the glass tube off the gas line. "When an almost identical incident occurred in January or February 1927," MacKellar writes, "Albert Snyder joked at a ... family gathering that his wife had twice barely escaped widowhood by way of gas."[3]

On March 19, 1927, after a party at a neighbor's house, Ruth again administered a sleeping powder to one of Albert Snyder's drinks. Albert managed to climb the stairs and was fast asleep in his bedroom when Ruth went back downstairs to meet her lover. Judd Gray had gained access to the house through an unlocked door. The two lovers returned to the upstairs bedroom. Gray struck the sleeping Albert on the head with a weighty object, thinking that the force of one blow would finish him off. When Albert woke up and fought back, Ruth was ready with a cloth soaked in chloroform. She held the cloth over Albert's nose and mouth, and he quickly lost consciousness. The two lovers then found some picture hanging wire and strangled their unconscious victim.

Ruth Snyder and Judd Gray had not settled on an alibi beforehand. In the heat of the moment, they decided to make the murder look like a botched robbery. They hid some of Ruth's jewelry under a bed. Gray tied Ruth's hands and feet to a chair and stuffed a gag in her mouth before leaving the house. Ruth waited for some time for her nine-year old daughter to wake up and find her. Upon waking, Lorraine Snyder removed the gag from her mother's mouth and ran to the neighbors for help.

When the police arrived and studied the murder scene, their suspicions were aroused. Ruth told them that the thieves has stolen some of her jewelry, but the officers quickly located the jewelry where it had been hidden, under the bed. They found Albert's lapel pin with the initials "J.G." upon it. These were the initials of Jessie Guischard but also, coincidentally, of Judd Gray. They found a check book with a receipt for two hundred dollars made out to Gray.

When she was called into the police station and confronted with the evidence a few days later, Ruth Snyder was quick to confess. She blamed Gray for plotting the murder. When he was located for questioning, Gray in turn blamed Ruth Snyder for conceiving the plot, arguing that he was an unsuspecting dupe in the crime.

In court and outside of it, the lovers were vicious in their incriminations of one another. In a statement to the press, Judd Gray warned all men about bad liquor and evil women. "If I had not taken to drink," he wrote, "I would never have met the woman who has placed me in the position I am now in."[4] Ruth Snyder blamed Gray for the killing in her own 600-word statement:

> I know Judd Gray as well as any woman knows a man. I know him better now than I ever did before. I know that he is a coward, a low, cringing, sneak-
> ing jackal, the murderer of my husband, who is now trying to hide behind my skirts to drag me down into the stinking pit that he himself willingly wallowed in; to brand me as a woman who killed her husband.[5]

Both were sentenced to death. They were executed in Sing Sing prison on January 12, 1928. So insatiable was the media for news of the murder and the murderers' fate that one enterprising reporter for the *New York Daily News* managed to smuggle a camera, strapped to his ankle, into the execution chamber. The photographic image of Ruth Snyder dying, as the electrical current entered her body, was broadcast in newspapers around the world. After the execution, Ruth Snyder was buried in New York's Woodlawn Cemetery, under a grave marker that read "May R. Died 1–13–1928."[6]

Landis MacKellar notes that the Snyder-Gray murder case has inspired stage plays, novellas, and motion pictures. As a journalist, Sophie Treadwell had covered the case for the *Herald Tribune*, and she was quick to adapt the real-life events into an expressionistic drama. "*Machinal* is not, to say the least, a cheery vision of American capitalism," writes MacKellar, "the American moral landscape, or the American suburban middle-class household."[7] Another play, written by William Styron and John Phillips and entitled *Dead! A Love Story*, was first staged in 1986 at the HB Playwrights Foundation and Theatre in Greenwich Village.

In 1936, James M. Cain used the murder case as the basis of his novella *Double Indemnity*, which was serialized in *Liberty* magazine. Billy Wilder adapted Cain's novella into a movie in 1944. In the cinematic adaptation, Barbara Stanwyck played Ruth Snyder who, as MacKellar writes, "was in real life more drab, more neurotic, and much less intelligent" than in Stanwyck's portrayal.[8] Stanwyck was nevertheless nominated for an Oscar for her work in the film. The 1981 movie *Body Heat*, starring William Hurt and Kathleen Turner, was also based on the Snyder-Gray case. According to MacKellar, *Body Heat* is notable "in large part for the amount of sex it managed to pack in while hanging on to an R rating."[9]

Treadwell's play is based on the real-life murder case, but it goes much further than that in its creation of an expressionistic, machine-age world. The play might be compared to other early pieces of American expressionism, including Patrick Kearney's adaptation of *An American Tragedy* (which both Ruth Snyder and Judd Gray had seen on Broadway) and Elmer Rice's *The Adding Machine* but, as Perriton Maxwell writes, "she has outstripped them in power and beauty."[10] None of the characters in the play are provided with names, a choice that emphasizes the universality of the story. The unnamed heroine works as a stenographer as the play begins.

Whereas Ruth Snyder doesn't seem to have been likeable or sympathetic (at least as she was portrayed in the press), Treadwell's Young Woman is far more fragile, vulnerable, and confused than her real-life counterpart. She tries to live by a code of conduct that society expects from her but has trouble doing so. She marries her repulsive boss to gain financial stability and quickly begins an affair with a younger man. Together the lovers plot the murder of the husband and, after the murder, the Young Woman is executed. What makes *Machinal* especially interesting is its adherence to expressionistic theatrical techniques. Whether witnessing the impersonal, mechanized stenographers' pool in its tap tap tap splendor or the oppressive courtroom later on, the audience is treated to a tour of the Young Woman's mind. We are encouraged to experience life from her point-of-view.

The play capitalizes on Sophie Treadwell's two major preoccupations: journalism and theater. While studying French at the University of California in Berkeley, the young Sophie had immersed herself in theater and journalism. She'd served as the University's correspondent to the *San Francisco Examiner* and, in 1910, had married the sportswriter William O. McGeehan. Following her husband when his career took him to New York, Treadwell took classes in acting from Richard Boleslavsky and began writing plays.

Influenced by the first wave of the feminist movement that grew up after the First World War, Sophie Treadwell was determined to succeed in a male-dominated theater community. The thing that set her apart from many of her contemporary female playwrights was her insistence on getting her plays produced on Broadway—and the number of plays she had produced there. Between 1921 and 1942, seven of Treadwell's plays opened on Broadway, beginning with *Gringo* and ending with *Hope for the Harvest*. Her contemporary Susan Glaspell, also a product of the first wave of the feminist movement in the United States and a prolific writer, was one of a few other female playwrights who had a string of Broadway credits in that era. Treadwell had much in common with Glaspell. Among other things, Glaspell's most famous play, *Trifles*, was also based on a real-life murder committed by an abused housewife. Both Glaspell and Treadwell can be seen as predecessors to later female playwrights who wanted success on Broadway. They broke new ground for playwrights like Lillian Hellman, who had many Broadway successes beginning in the mid–1930s and stretching through the 1940s. When the floodgates opened, there was eventually room for other female playwrights, including Lorraine Hansberry, Lynn Nottage, Marsha Norman, Paula Vogel, and Sarah Ruhl.

By far the most influential of Treadwell's plays, in her own day and afterwards, was *Machinal*. Like Perriton Maxwell, theatrical luminary Brooks Atkinson reviewed the original New York production in glowing terms. The production ensemble had "with great skill managed to retrieve a frail and sombre beauty of character" from the sordid murder case, he argued. "Subdued, monotonous, episodic, occasionally eccentric in its style, *Machinal* is fraught with a beauty unfamiliar to the stage."[11] The play was included in Burns Mantle's *The Best Plays of 1928–29*. It was produced in London, under the title *The Life Machine*, in 1931. Atkinson's and other reviewers' assessments of the play have been vindicated by the fact that the play has had many revivals and that it continues to be produced almost a century later. A revival of the play, produced by Roundabout Theatre, opened on Broadway in 2014. The Almeida Theatre in London also revived the play, directed by Natalie Abrahami, in 2018. Today, *Machinal* is commonly regarded as being among the best works of American expressionism ever written, and Sophie Treadwell is now commonly viewed as being among the best American playwrights—male or female—of the 20th century.

CHAPTER 4

All Hell Broke Loose

Halla Bol, *Janya Natya Manch,*
Jhandapur, India, January 1, 1989

On New Year's Day in 1989, the Janam theater troupe was preparing to perform a play called *Halla Bol* ("Raise Your Voice") in the community of Jhandapur, a short distance from New Delhi. The company met, that morning, in the Center of Indian Trade Unions (CITU) office, had tea and biscuits, and then proceeded to a nearby intersection where they would perform in the open air. The director of the troupe was 34-year-old Safdar Hashmi; he had also written the play they were about to enact. His wife Moloyashree placed the stage properties meticulously around the circular space in the street where the performance would take place. One of the actors, Jogi, played the dholak (a two-headed drum) to begin the show. Sudhanva Deshpande, a troupe member who would not be performing that day, was chosen to say a few introductory words. Jhandapur was in the midst of a municipal election, and Deshpande urged the audience, in his oration, to vote for a left-wing candidate. Then the performance began.

Deshpande and Safdar Hashmi watched the proceedings from a tea shack on the corner. About ten minutes into the show, they heard a loud disturbance coming down the street from the north. A cavalcade arrived, led by an automobile and about a dozen men, walking behind the vehicle and shouting campaign slogans. The men were carrying lathis, heavy bamboo sticks that Indian policemen often use as batons. Hashmi went over and talked to one of the men in the car. "Sir," he said, "we are doing a small play here. Why don't you stop and watch the play? There's only ten minutes to go. You'll enjoy it."[1] The man in the automobile did not want to see the play. "Then why don't you take an alternative route," Hashmi said, "and come back here after a short while? Our play will be over by then."[2] The driver of the car backed up and stopped near a temple less than a block away. Hashmi apologized to the audience, and the actors resumed their performance. "And then," as Deshpande wrote later, "before we knew it, all hell broke loose."[3]

Safdar Hashmi was born in Delhi on April 12, 1954. He studied at St. Stephen's College at Delhi University, where he completed his master's degree in English Literature. While at school, Hashmi became involved with the left-wing Students' Federation of India and also with the Indian People's Theater Association. He co-founded Janya Natya Manch, the People's Theater Front, more popularly known as Janam, in 1973. He produced his street play *Kursi, Kursi, Kursi* ("Chair, Chair, Chair") as a reaction to the controversy surrounding then Indian Prime Minister Indira Gandhi, when she was accused of rigging the 1971 election. In the play, a king seemingly attempts to give up his throne to an elected representative, but the throne persists in following the king wherever he goes. By the time Gandhi declared a state of emergency in India in 1975, in her attempt to restore order after she had been found guilty of dishonest election practices and stripped of her parliamentary seat, Janam had become a political force. During the Emergency, as it was commonly called, it was difficult to produce political theater in India.

Indian politics was volatile in the seventies and eighties. Indira Gandhi continued as Prime Minister until her assassination, on October 31, 1984, at the hands of her two Sikh bodyguards. Her son Rajiv Gandhi was installed as Prime Minister later that same day. In the aftermath of the assassination, organized mobs of National Congress supporters rioted against the Sikh community in Delhi. It is estimated that at least eight thousand members of the Sikh community were murdered in the course of the riots. In the December election that followed, the National Congress Party won a huge majority of votes. Rajiv Gandhi's period in office was nevertheless rocked by conflict and controversy, including the Bhopal disaster, the Kashmir riots, and the reversal of the Maldives coup in 1988. Indian intervention in the Maldives infuriated Tamil secessionists and led, eventually, to the assassination of Rajiv Gandhi by a Tamil suicide bomber.

After the Emergency was lifted in 1977, Hashmi produced a play that was to become his most famous. *Machine*, which he co-wrote in 1978 with Rakesh Saxena, was based on the true story of an incident at Harig India metal factory in Ghaziabad, where six workers were shot dead during a protest gathering. Leading up to the protest, the workers' demands had been small; they wanted management to provide them with a parking lot for their bicycles and a small oven in which to heat their food. Only about thirteen minutes long, *Machine* was performed in the round and in the open air. On November 20, 1978, it was played before an audience of more than 200,000 workers at a trade union meeting. A Narrator sums up the Marxist message of the play:

Yes, my brothers and sisters! Sixty plus three, this machine has been running for the last sixty-three years. The machine turns out things, from needles to guns, without any hesitation. But, there is one issue that upsets my mind so much…. [Some people] keep on growing up to the sky, bagging all the wealth of this land. Whether it is the case of valuable goods in the warehouses, or the possession of fertile fields, or the control over the farmers … nothing is safe from their jaws. And on the other side … there is a crowd of millions and millions of poor people. Those who have built the structures like pyramids and the Taj Mahal. Greatly skilled artisans are they. From this earth to the sky, their fame and footprints are there. But there is no grain in their empty stomachs; they roam around like the destitute.[4]

The divide between the wealthy few and the multitude of skilled artisans who do the work but do not reap the benefits of their labors is a central theme that resonated with the workers in Janam's audience. Even after the play had been performed hundreds of times, Hashmi could not explain the success of *Machine*. "The workers love this play," he said. "I still do not understand, for it's so simple."[5]

The success of *Machine* led to many other plays and street performances. Among Hashmi's other works are *The Determiner of India's Fate*, *Goat*, *Mother*, *We Shall Remain Here*, *Killers*, *Woman*, *Hijacking Culture*, and *The show goes on*. Hashmi's wife Moloyashree acted in *Woman* ("Aurat"), playing three female characters: a child who wants to go to school; a college student; and an old factory worker. Moloyashree performed in the play many times, and her friend Sudhanva Deshpande remembered those performances fondly. "It remains, to my mind, the finest piece of acting I have ever seen in street theatre," he wrote. "Her performance was tender, vulnerable, moving, poetic, powerful, all at the same time. I know that for thousands of young women, just watching such a performance in the open, in a public space, was inspiring and empowering."[6] There were more inspiring and empowering performances to come; Janam continues to produce left-wing street theater into the present day.

Hashmi's final play was *Halla Bol*. After their initial interruption of the performance on New Year's Day, the political thugs returned to the site of the performance with lathis and iron rods. The spectators scattered. Having no weapons of their own, the actors picked up stones and hurled them at their assailants. The call went out to flee and to reconnoiter at the CITU office nearby. When Deshpande arrived there, a woman from the house opposite told him, "One of your men is dying in the street."[7] Deshpande and a comrade ran toward the dying man. It was Hashmi. He was bleeding from his ears, nose, and throat; having been beaten with an iron rod, he had a gaping laceration on his scalp. Deshpande looked down the street. At the spot where they had been performing, two men stood, one with a pistol, the other with an iron rod. The gunman fired his pistol into the air. Deshpande and his friend managed to get Hashmi into a car, and the dying man was eventually transported to Ram Manohar Lohia Hospital in nearby Delhi. On the morning of January 2, a crowd began to gather outside the hospital.

Reports of the incident began to circulate in the news media. It was reported that Hashmi had been injured and that a second man, Ram Bahudar, a migrant factory worker from Nepal, had also been shot, probably for no other reason than to create terror in the citizenry. When it was also reported that one of the attackers was Mukesh Sharma, an Indian National Congress Party leader from Sahibabad, the government of Rajiv Gandhi offered to pay Hashmi's hospital bills. About three hundred actors, artists, and intellectuals gathered at the residence of Buta Singh, the Home Minister, to protest the killing. Later that afternoon, prominent actor and director M.K. Raina spoke to the media:

> We have walked together in processions because of Safdar Hashmi. Because he was a pivotal force in binding artists together. For thirteen years, I have seen his plays. These are plays which are relevant, which question all the time the status quo. Communal harmony, national integration. What more do you want from a citizen? That this kind of poet, artist, intellectual, painter, writer—the kind of work he's done, the potential—can be hit by a goon, and he is to be dead? Just outside Delhi? Only fourteen kilometres distance from here? If it happens to Safdar Hashmi, what is left in this country?[8]

Others spoke, as well. By ten thirty that evening, Safdar Hashmi was dead.

On the third of January, a funeral procession took place. Fifteen

Halla Bol, **January 3, 1989. Moloyashree Hashmi is at the far right (photographer unknown; courtesy of the Janya Natya Manch Archive).**

thousand people watched as Hashmi's body was transported through the streets. Deshpande later described the significance of that occasion. "Already on that day, through my state of shock and grief, I had begun to comprehend that Safdar's killing had touched a raw nerve in the country," Deshpande wrote. "It had become a cause larger than Janam, larger than Safdar, larger than the Left. It seemed to me to crystallize the feeling of dissatisfaction and anger that was to sweep aside the Congress in the upcoming elections."[9] Indeed, Rajiv Gandhi's Indian National Congress Party was voted out of office later that same year.

Moloyashree Hashmi, Sudhanva Deshpande, and the rest of the Janam troupe boarded buses on January 4, 1989. They rode to the intersection in Jhandapur where the attack had taken place three days earlier. They sang. Onlookers began to arrive, many of them, standing and sitting on the street and on the rooftops. Deshpande rose to speak:

> We are here to perform our interrupted play. We are here to fulfil our commitment to our audience. We are here to say that they can kill us, but they can't stop us. We are here to honor Comrade Ram Baduhar. We are here because Comrade Safdar Hashmi is not dead. He lives here, among us, and he lives among countless young women and men all over the country.[10]

And then the play began.

Brave New Theaters

Sometimes the theatrical establishment does not serve the needs of individual practitioners. This can happen when older theater companies, secure in their reputation, no longer feel the need to experiment and to break new ground. It can happen when playwrights, actors and directors find it difficult to get their work produced. It can happen when a group of playwrights, deemed salacious or immoral by the standards of the time, find common ground in their exclusion and decide to resist or fight back. It can also happen when the State becomes involved in the day-to-day running of particular theaters, bogging them down in bureaucratic red tape.

The following chapters are about theater companies that came into existence for some of the reasons listed above. In "Free Theater," the founding of the Théâtre Libre in Paris is discussed, a time when untutored impresario Andre Antoine could find no other way to produce edgy playwrights like Fernand Icre, Émile Zola, Alexey Tolstoy and Henrik Ibsen. "The Slavyanski Bazaar" tells the story of the founding of the Moscow Art Theatre as a reaction to the dreary production standards of larger state-run theaters in Russia. "A Wonderful, Heretical Play" is about the Moscow Art Theatre's 1898 production of Anton Chekhov's *The Seagull* and about the playwright's reticence to have it produced again after a failed production at the Alexandrinsky Theatre a few years earlier. The last chapter in this section, "La Mama," chronicles the arduous journey of Ellen Stewart, who created an Off Off Broadway venue for the production of experimental theater. She did so, in part, because her stepbrother was having trouble getting his plays produced elsewhere, but she eventually became legendary for her battles with civic authorities and for her unwavering support for often untested and edgy young playwrights.

CHAPTER 5

Free Theater

The Serenade, *Théâtre Libre,*
Paris, December 23, 1887

In Jean Jullien's play *The Serenade*, a young tutor named Maxime carries on an affair with the wife of a wealthy Parisian jeweler. He also seduces the jeweler's daughter and makes her pregnant. To keep up appearances, Maxime is forced to marry the daughter. At the wedding, the jeweler's wife sidles close to the new groom and whispers, invitingly, "Sit by me, son-in-law." It's easy to see why the play infuriated Parisian audiences and why it was considered too scandalous and too immoral to be presented in America.

When *The Serenade* opened on December 23, 1887, at the Théâtre Libre in Montmartre, the production heralded the rise of a new genre in French theater called *comédie rosse*. The genre became all the rage at the boulevard theaters in Paris in the late 1880s and 1890s. The term was applied to naturalistic plays that focused on an ignoble character who assumes the guise of respectability. At times, it seemed that playwrights in the genre purposely set out to offend the sensibilities of their spectators in scenes replete with immoral situations and perverse humor. Other writers in the genre included Oscar Méténier and Paul Alexis.

The Serenade might never have been produced had not André Antoine emerged onto the theater scene in Paris. Antoine was an unlikely theatrical reformer. Growing up in Rouen, he had little formal education. He moved to Paris in the 1870s, where he served as a paid clapper at the Comédie-Française and, later, as a supernumerary actor, playing in crowd scenes for on-the-spot remuneration. He attempted to gain acceptance into the actor-training program at the Conservatoire. By his own account, Antoine auditioned using a realistic voice—not the stilted, declamatory voice that was common among leading actors at the time—and his auditors became embroiled in a spirited discussion of the merits of naturalism. While some of his auditors saw in Antoine the future of naturalistic theater, others did not. The naysayers won the day, and Antoine was not admitted to the program. He served in the army for five years. Upon returning to Paris, he found work as a clerk in the Paris Gas Company.[1]

Circles of arts and letters were common among the middle class at the time, and Antoine found his way to the Cercle Gaulois at 98 rue Blanche in Montmartre. Gaining entrance into a cercle signified that one had the leisure and financial stability to involve oneself in what had previously been an upper-class addiction—curiosity about the literary arts, painting, and theater. The Cercle Gaulois was populated with amateur actors who discussed plays and performed them. Their leader was a retired army officer with conservative tastes. Almost as soon as he joined the cercle, Antoine began agitating for a more contemporary, radical program of plays. He suggested new playwrights who were having trouble getting produced in Paris' major theaters, writers like Arthur Byl, Jules Vidal, and Émile Zola (who had already made a name for himself as a writer of naturalistic novels). The Cercle refused to produce a bill of this nature but offered to rent the theater to Antoine so that he could produce a season of provocative drama under another name.

Antoine labeled his company Théâtre Libre, the "Free Theater," thinking that it would be a one-off venture. The company opened its doors on March 30, 1887, with several plays in the naturalistic vein. They included Duranty and Alexis' *Mademoiselle Pomme*, Arthur Byl's *Un Préfet*, Oscar Méténier's *En Famille*, and Auguste Villiers de L'Isle-Adam's *L'Évasion*. Leon Henrique adapted Émile Zola's novel *Jacques d'Amour* for the stage. Because he had almost no money, Antoine was forced to haul set pieces and props through the streets of Montmartre in a wheelbarrow.

Antoine had not envisioned a second season for Théâtre Libre, but his friends urged him on. Luckily, he had friends in high artistic places. Zola became one of Antoine's most ardent supporters, as did Zola's good friend Paul Alexis. If a second season was

André Antoine (Wikimedia Commons).

to materialize, Antoine would need an infusion of money. While Zola and other successful artists could provide some financial support, they could not provide all that was needed. Antoine came up with an ingenious solution. Since his theater was categorized as private, he could not by law charge admission fees for specific performances. He landed on the idea of developing a subscription audience—not an entirely new idea since the Comédie-Française had relied on subscribers for years. What was unique, though, was that subscribers would account for 100 percent of Antoine's audience. He would collect subscriptions to pay for the entire season, and subscriber membership would entitle spectators to attend shows free of charge. A further advantage of this scheme was that it circumvented the censor. Since Théâtre Libre was a private club, members were entitled to watch any play they wanted within the confines of that private space. Suddenly, Parisian audiences could see provocative new plays like Ibsen's *Ghosts* or Tolstoy's *Power of Darkness*, plays which had been banned either in France or in other parts of the world.

Antoine was an intelligent theater manager and director. While his company became associated with *comédie rosse* and naturalism, Antoine refused to let those genres define his theater. He insisted on producing the realists, becoming a purveyor of Ibsen's most scandalous dramas. He dabbled in symbolism, as well, producing Villiers de L'Isle-Adam's work. He devoted endless attention to reshaping stage practices. Attempting to achieve a complete illusion of reality on his stage, he designed settings specifically for each play he produced—not the standard practice in most theaters of the time. For naturalistic dramas, he furnished rooms completely, including bric-a-brac and small props. For Curel's play *The Fossils*, Antoine created three different sets, each one showing the same room from a new angle. For Icre's *The Butchers*, Antoine hauled in real carcasses of beef which added not only to the visual spectacle but also to the olfactory experience.[2]

Having publicly criticized actor training at the Conservatoire, where "stage voice" was taught, Antoine devoted a great deal of care to the realism of his actors. He developed an ensemble of reliable performers, an acting company that in some respects resembled the well-oiled ensemble that was currently all the rage in Saxe-Meiningen. Antoine demanded that his actors seek to live on stage rather than to act; the characters in the plays he directed were viewed as real people in real places. Actors were encouraged to avoid the melodramatic, codified gestures that were characteristic of the Conservatoire and the Comédie-Française.

The Théâtre Libre existed for only a short time, mostly due to recurring financial troubles. During its brief existence, it produced 184 plays by at least 69 different playwrights. Its influence was widely felt and long-lasting. Perhaps the best proof of the durability of Antoine's legacy can be found in the fact that Off Broadway companies in the 1960s were still using Antoine's concept of a subscription-run private theater to avoid censorship and to produce brave, new work.

Antoine's influence can also be seen among his contemporaries in other countries. In Germany, dissatisfaction with the moribund state of theater led to the formation of several artistic collectives in the 1880s. One of these was Jungsdeutschen (Youngest Germans), led by the brothers Julius and Heinrich Hart. Jungsdeutschen demanded a new theater based on subjects chosen from the lives of the working class. Of greater influence was Durch (Through), founded in Berlin in 1886. Among its members was the poet Arno Holz, who was responsible for the famous naturalistic equation "Art = Nature minus x."[3] All of this activism led to the formation of an independent theater in Berlin in 1888. That theater, Freie Bühne, was based on the model of Théâtre Libre but with some differences. A theatrical board, with Otto Brahm at its helm as manager and director, ran the theater, and the company of Freie Bühne produced new plays but not necessarily with new production methods. Freie Bühne became the home of the avant-garde in Germany, with productions of Ibsen's *Ghosts*, Zola's *Thérèse Raquin*, and Hauptmann's *The Weavers*.

England was not far behind, although there had long been murmurings about the sad state of London theater. In his book *About the Theatre* (1886), William Archer had argued that England was lagging behind the continent in matters theatrical. London theater had been reduced to revivals of old plays and foreign adaptations. Few playwrights of note had emerged since Thomas William Robertson's death in 1871.[4] J.T. Grein, a Dutchman living in London, entered the theatrical scene in 1891. He founded the Independent Theatre, again based on Antoine's subscription model, "to give special performances of plays which have a literary and artistic rather than a commercial value."[5] The company's first productions were of Ibsen's *Ghosts* and Zola's *Thérèse Raquin*.

Grein's theater soon attracted the attention of George Bernard Shaw, who was mostly known as a theater critic until that time. Spurred on by Grein and his theater, Shaw launched into a career as a playwright, compiling an impressive list of works through the 1890s and early 1900s. Many of them—including *Major Barbara* (1905) and *Pygmalion* (1913)—have become classics in the tradition of the well-made play. While Shaw considered himself a realist, and while he was a product of the independent theater movement begun by Antoine in the 1880s, he had little patience for transferring naturalistic human behavior directly to the stage. As Oscar Brockett writes, Shaw was never hobbled by the desire to write realistic conversations or characterizations. As Brockett states, "Shaw's is a superrealism in which the essence of life is captured by sharpening and exaggerating carefully chosen elements."[6]

Out of André Antoine's wheelbarrow grew a tradition that would sweep across Europe in the coming years. Little did he know, when he produced *The Serenade*, that he had created a model upon which theaters in Germany and England would be based. Along the way to theatrical reform, Antoine also managed to give voice to some of the most important playwrights of the late 19th century. Writers like Zola, Hauptmann, Ibsen, Pinero, and Shaw came to the stage, and avoided censorship, through the independent theater movement.

CHAPTER 6

The Slavyanski Bazaar

The Moscow Art Theatre, June 22, 1897

On June 22, 1897, two theater impresarios, Konstantin Stanislavsky and Vladimir Nemirovich-Danchenko, had lunch together at the Slavyanski Bazaar, an upscale hotel restaurant near the Kremlin in Moscow. They had met to discuss the debased state of Russian theater and also to devise a new way forward, a way that would take artistic decisions out of the hands of government bureaucrats.

It seemed to Stanislavsky and Nemirovich-Danchenko that there were, in fact, two possible routes to theatrical excellence: they could seize control of the state-run Maly Theatre, which had once been great; or they could create a new enterprise run entirely by artists. If that new enterprise were to flourish, would it rely on the wealth of industrial capitalists in order to continue? Or would it eschew private funding, running on a shoestring out in the country where the costs of producing theater might be much lower?

As Nick Worrall writes, Nemirovich-Danchenko thought that founding the theater using Stanislavsky's family fortune would ensure the survival of the theater in its early years. However, Stanislavsky's money was tied up in other ventures, and Stanislavsky did not have confidence that the theater would produce a financial return on his investment.[1] Both men had a great deal of business acumen, and both had entrenched views about these matters. To find basic areas of agreement was not easy. In the end, they decided to create a public syndicate, a shareholding company of private investors.

They talked for hours, commiserating on the low state of Russian theater which, like most other theaters in most other countries at the time, was mired in melodramatic texts and melodramatic acting styles. "We were in love with one and the same idea," Nemirovich-Danchenko later wrote, "the idea of a new theatre. What it was, neither of us at the time knew. We were just two protestants: we were protesting against everything

39

that was pompous, unnatural and 'theatrical,' against well-thumbed, stereotyped tradition."[2] Both men knew that censorship was also an issue. The great Tolstoy's first important play, *The Power of Darkness*, had initially failed to get past the censor in Russia. It was first produced in 1888 at the Thèâtre Libre in Paris. Next to censorship, the biggest obstacles to high art were antiquated theatrical practices. Schedules were regularly such that the entire cast of a play often did not rehearse together more than three times before an opening. Frequently, actors did not have the opportunity to perform in front of stage scenery until opening night. V.A. Nyelidov, an administrator in the offices of Moscow's Imperial Theaters, described the typical process of receiving and rehearsing a play in the 1880s:

> Having received the play [the director] distributed the parts…. Furthermore, the director wrote the "montirovka" [the staging], i.e., filled out a form with the headings: "Actors, décor, furniture, costumes, wigs, props, effects" (headings 1 to 10). Under the heading of, say, "décor," he wrote: "prison, forest, drawing room," etc., nothing more. Under "furniture," the words "poor" or "rich." Costumes were defined as "metropolitan" or "historical." Wigs were "bald," "grey" or "red-haired." All this was carried out by the office. The director and the actors frequently did not see any of these details before dress rehearsal or even sometimes before opening night, for it was considered that, once they knew the plan of the stage, i.e., that a door would be here and a writing table there, everything was fine. They would arrive on stage with script in hand, read the role from it and "decipher" places, i.e., arrange that "x" stands here and "y" sits there.[3]

Until 1882, state theaters had held a monopoly on theatrical production in larger cities like Moscow and St. Petersburg. Political appointees, more concerned with appeasing their political masters than with producing great art, frequently governed these state theaters. Although this theatrical monopoly was rescinded in 1882, allowing public theaters to expand and flourish, political appointees were still in control of several theaters by the time Stanislavsky and Nemirovich-Danchenko met. This earlier theatrical monopoly was perhaps one reason why exceptionally talented amateurs like Stanislavky had retained their amateur status instead of choosing to become professional actors. An artist-run theater like the Moscow Art Theatre, in which the creation of great theater was paramount to other concerns, was simply not possible in most Russian cities until 1883.

The two men could not have been more different from one another in terms of upbringing, personality, and experience. The son of a wealthy industrialist, Stanislavsky had been born with a silver spoon in his mouth. His real name was Konstantin Alexeyev (he took the name Stanislavsky as an act of homage to a retired Polish actor). His family's wealth could be compared to the wealth of the Rockefellers in the United States. Among his contacts were some of the richest people in Russia, people on whom he could rely when it came to subsidizing his art. In 1888, Stanislavsky became chairman of the Moscow Society of Arts and Letters, which continued to produce plays through the 1890s. His expertise had to do with what happens on stage, directorial techniques and actor training. Stanislavsky had, by that time, secured a sterling reputation in amateur theater; he was considered more forward-looking than many of the country's esteemed professionals. He had become interested in theater early in life and, when on a business trip to Paris as a young man, he had taken advantage of the opportunity to study at the Conservatoire. He was tall and regal (six-foot-six) and abstemious. He did not drink or womanize (although it is well known that he had fathered an illegitimate son when he was about twenty). He was happily married. His worst habit was a love of tobacco.

Nemirovich-Danchenko had a working-class upbringing. His father was an army officer. He distrusted capitalists and would seek to limit their influence in theatrical matters—a fact that was something of a sticking point in his relationship with Stanislavsky. Nemirovich-Danchenko had dropped out of the Moscow State University in 1879 to become a theater critic and playwright. His first play, *Dog-rose*, was staged in 1881 at the Maly Theatre. He'd had a long professional career by the time he met Stanislavsky. In 1891, Nemirovich-Danchenko had taken over the Drama Department at the Philharmonic School, where he had educated star pupils like Olga Knipper and Vsevolod Meyerhold. Knipper would go on to become one of the greatest Russian actresses of her time, helping to found, and devoting much of her career to, the Moscow Art Theatre. Meyerhold would later become a famous director in his own right, founding his own theater school and a method of acting, based on biomechanics, that differed from American preconceptions about Stanislavsky's method.

By the time he and Stanislavsky met, Nemirovich-Danchenko had an established reputation as a professional playwright and director. He was frequently penniless. He was short and stocky. He gambled to excess and was prone to the affections of women other than his wife. In later life, Stanislavsky frequently lent Nemirovich-Danchenko money to cover his gambling debts. If, at the age of 39, Nemirovich-Danchenko felt slightly superior to the 24-year-old Stanislavsky in theatrical matters, that would have been understandable. His résumé was better. A man of letters, Nemirovich-Danchenko sought new playwrights who would move Russian theater away from low melodramas and into the realm of high realism.

The two impresarios had many differences but one thing in common—they were both passionate about the art of theater. They talked for hours at the Slavyansky Bazaar. In the evening, they hopped into a carriage and rode out of the city to Stanislavsky's estate. Their conversation continued, deep into the night. Would their new theater be an artist-run venture, as Nemirovich-Danchenko wanted, or would it rely on wealthy patrons? Would they produce light comedies, which Stanislavsky preferred as a training tool for young actors, or would they produce the serious realistic dramas that Nemirovich-Danchenko admired. If a new theater were to materialize, what would be the division of labor between its two artistic directors? Would Nemirovich-Danchenko be relegated to the position of literary manager while Stanislavsky acted and directed? How would the acting company operate?

By the time Nemirovich-Danchenko climbed again into a carriage, after breakfast on June 23 (and after an 18-hour meeting), the two men had worked out a plan of action. They would create a theater from the ground up, one which would make artistic decisions paramount. They would call this venture the Moscow Public-Accessible Theatre, a title that expressed their intention to provide affordable theater to a broad audience that included spectators of all classes. (The word "Art" was added to the title at the last minute after Nemirovich-Danchenko suggested it. Stanislavsky was initially worried that the inclusion of the word would put too much pressure on the young company.)[4] They would extend rehearsal times in their new theater, ensuring that actors had the opportunity to work with costumes and settings long before opening night. They would eliminate the orchestra pit. More importantly, they would create an acting ensemble, with serious-minded and talented young actors who would work together over months and years to find an acting style befitting the coming century. In case of a disagreement, Stanislavsky would have a veto over matters pertaining to the onstage direction of plays. Nemirovich-Danchenko would have a veto over literary matters such as play selection and play edits.

And so the Moscow Art Theatre was born. The original company consisted of 39 persons, mostly chosen from the Society for Arts and Letters and the Philharmonic Society. With a nod to Nemirovich-Danchenko's vision, the original company lived and rehearsed together in Pushkino, a quaint village thirty miles from Moscow. They rehearsed in a hastily remodeled building that looked like an indoor cricket pavilion. As Nick Worrall writes, "[E]very effort had been made to render the space as much like a theatre and as congenial as possible. The interior walls had been covered with hessian and wallpaper; the exterior boards had been painted and curtains hung at the windows and along the newly constructed, roofed veranda where the actors drank tea and awaited their calls."[5]

Stanislavsky gave a speech at the first rehearsal, on June 14, where he emphasized the newness and the importance of the venture. "Do not forget that we are striving to bring light into the dark lives of the poorer classes," he said, "to give them joyful aesthetic moments amidst the gloom which envelops them."[6] The company rehearsed for four months during that hot summer, in the afternoons and evenings, often working on two different scripts in the same day. In their inaugural season, in 1898, the Moscow Art Theatre prepared Tolstoy's *Tsar Fyodor*, Sophocles' *Antigone*, Shakespeare's *The Merchant of Venice*, and Chekhov's *The Seagull* for performance. Nemirovich-Danchenko had led the way in terms of choosing plays for that first season, while Stanislavsky concerned himself mostly with directorial decisions and with acting.

Then there was the issue of where to perform in Moscow. Stanislavsky had signed a rental agreement with the management of the Hermitage (or Ermitazh) Theatre in Carriage Road, but the Hermitage was in disrepair. As Stanislavsky himself wrote in later life,

> The Ermitazh in Karetnyy ryad was in a terrible state, dusty, uncomfortable, unheated, with the smell of beer and some sort of acid that had remained from the summer use of the building. There was a garden and the public was entertained with various divertissements in the open air, but in inclement weather the entertainment would be carried over into the theatre. The furnishings of the theatre had been intended for garden audiences and were tasteless....
>
> We had to get rid of all this, but we had no money to create an interior that would be bearable for cultured people. We painted all the walls and the posters on them white. We covered the rotten chairs with decent material; we found carpets and spread them in the corridors which bordered on the auditorium, so as to deaden the sound of footsteps which would interfere with the performance.[7]

When the remodeling was complete, the Hermitage was almost unrecognizable, but the costs of refurbishing the theater and rehearsing the plays had been high. The result was that ticket prices could not be kept as low as Stanislavsky and Nemirovich-Danchenko would have liked. During the company's first season, the average cost of tickets was only fractionally lower than ticket costs at the Maly.[8]

As time passed, the rifts between Stanislavsky and Nemirovich-Danchenko became more apparent. Both men directed productions and were responsible for some of the most striking, innovative theater in the world. Eventually, though, the theater moved its operations entirely to Moscow, putting an end to Nemirovich-Danchenko's dream of a theatrical arcadia freed from the temptations of the city and all other restraints. Stanislavsky became more insistent about involving outside moneymen, particularly as the theater had lost a sizeable amount of money in its first season. He brought the railroad magnate Savva Morozov on board to help pay for production costs. Later, Stanislavsky and Nemirovich-Danchenko would squabble over artistic matters. Stanislavsky became increasingly more interested in using the stage as a forum for research into acting techniques; in his view, rehearsals were more important than the creation of a finished product. Nemirovich-Danchenko was more performance-oriented; he grew increasingly impatient with Stanislavsky's stance, and their relationship deteriorated.

When Anton Chekhov died in 1904, the Moscow Art Theatre went into a brief tailspin. Chekhov had hoped that Maxim Gorky would succeed him as the theater's chief playwright, but Stanislavsky and Nemirovich-Danchenko were not enthusiastic about Gorky's most recent work. As a result, Gorky cut his ties with the company, taking Savva Morozov with him. To assuage the financial bleeding, Stanislavsky and Nemirovich-Danchenko took the company on an international tour, with stops in Berlin, Dresden, Frankfurt, Prague, and Vienna. The tour was a huge financial success, but the antagonism between its founders continued to be a problem. Without consulting Nemirovich-Danchenko, Stanislavsky appointed his friends to the management office of the theater. When Nemirovich-Danchenko protested, Stanislavsky resigned from the Board.

The theater suffered further financial setbacks in the twenties and thirties. It was renamed the Maxim Gorky Moscow Art Theatre in 1932. With Stalin in power, the theater began to espouse socialist realism, a move that would negatively affect its artistic standing for years to come. Nemirovich-Danchenko tended to affiliate himself with Stalin and his hard-liners while Stanislavsky had been quietly moving away from his early concentration on realism. Neither Gorky nor Meyerhold fared well in the Stalinist regime.

Although he was an apologist for Stalin through much of his later career, the playwright Gorky died of pneumonia in 1936, while under house arrest in Moscow for (among other things) a speech he had given to the Writers' Union as well as for his stance against state censorship of literature. Stalin and Molotov were among the state officials who carried his urn during the funeral. Meyerhold, who had been critical of Stanislavsky and his method in the 1920s, was invited by an ailing Stanislavsky to run the Stanislavsky and Nemirovich-Danchenko Music Theatre in the late thirties when Meyerhold had fallen out of favor with the authorities. At the time, Stalin was involved in a campaign to bring Russian artists to heel. Meyerhold became increasingly critical of government intervention in Soviet theater and said as much at a conference of theater-makers in 1939. He was almost instantly incarcerated and tortured until he confessed to being a spy for the British and the Japanese. He was shot by firing squad on February 2, 1940.

After the fall of Stalin in the mid–1950s, the Moscow Art Theatre experienced a resurgence. In 1970, a former student of the Moscow Art

Theatre Studios, Oleg Yefremov, began a campaign to reinstate the working principles of Stanislavsky and Nemirovich-Danchenko. As a result, the theater has regained some of the artistic vigor of its early years.

Stanislavsky and Nemirovich-Danchenko continued to be involved, to some degree, with the Moscow Art Theatre well into their old age. The talented amateur Stanislavsky revolutionized the art of acting when he articulated his Method of Physical Actions in his classic texts *An Actor Prepares* and *My Life in Art*. The Moscow Art Theatre tours of the early 1900s, born out of financial need, had done much to spread Stanislavsky's theories and acting methods internationally; they probably also helped to prolong Stanislavsky's life, and bolster his reputation, under the Stalinist regime. Stanislavsky's method remains, to this day, the most thoughtful summation of the actor's process ever written. Some of the most celebrated stage and film actors of the 21st century still credit Stanislavsky for their success. While his relationship with Stanislavsky was never quite as affable as it had been on that day in June 1897 at the Slavyanski Bazar, the seasoned professional Nemirovich-Danchenko continued to direct plays into the 1930s. Because he never managed to articulate his theories of directing and acting in the form of a book, he is often the forgotten partner, even though he helped to found one of the greatest theaters of the 20th century.

CHAPTER 7

A Wonderful, Heretical Play

The Seagull, *Moscow Art Theatre,*
Moscow, December 17, 1898

When his play *The Seagull* opened at the Moscow Art Theatre on December 17, 1898, Anton Chekhov was not in the audience. He didn't have the stomach for it, having witnessed the same play flop two years earlier in another theater. Chekhov thought he was finished writing plays, but Vladimir Nemirovich-Danchenko had other ideas. He'd cajoled Chekhov, flattered him, and made promises until Chekhov allowed one more production of his misunderstood play.

Chekhov had begun his playwriting career after a lengthy apprenticeship spent writing short stories. In fact, he had put himself through medical school with his pen—no mean feat—writing humorous and brief stories for various journals. Later, as a country doctor, Chekhov had purchased a house at Melikhovo, fifty miles south of Moscow, where he began writing plays.

Chekhov began working on *The Seagull* in 1895. "I am writing a play which I shall probably not finish before the end of November," he wrote to a friend in October of that year. "I am writing it not without pleasure, though I swear fearfully at the conventions of the stage."[1] In his play, Chekhov would defy the melodramatic conventions that were so popular in the late 19th century. He would ground his characters' actions and words in subtext and work to keep other symptoms of melodrama off the stage.

The Seagull was first produced at the Alexandrinsky Theatre in Petersburg. During rehearsals for that first, ill-fated production, things looked promising. Vera Komissarzhevskaya, who played Nina, was one of the best actresses in Russia. Chekhov reported that she had moved her acting colleagues to tears during rehearsals. The opening night, however, was an unmitigated disaster. "The play was not a success," Chekhov's friend and publisher Aleksey Suvorin wrote in his diary after the first performance. "The audience was not attentive, not listening, talking all the time, bored. It's a long time since I saw such a dreadful performance."[2] So nervous was she that Komissarzhevskaya lost her voice. During the curtain call, the actors were greeted with booing. Chekhov had sought refuge backstage for the last half of the play. A reviewer in *The Petersburg Gazette* characterized the performance as "a decadent weariness" and maintained that the entire acting ensemble "lacked distinction."[3] Shortly after that first opening night, Chekhov informed Suvorin that he was finished writing plays.

Nemirovich-Danchenko thought that Chekhov was the best hope for the future of Russian theater. After he'd helped create the Moscow Art Theatre, with his friend Stanislavsky, Nemirovich-Danchenko campaigned ceaselessly for Chekhov's permission to revive *The Seagull*. On April 25, 1898, he wrote, in a letter to Chekhov,

> Among contemporary authors I have decided to cultivate only those who are most talented and as yet insufficiently understood…. And Russian theatre-goers still don't know you. You must be presented in a way that only a man of letters with taste, who can appreciate the beauty of your works, and who is at the same time a capable director, can present you. I consider I am such a person.[4]

At first, Chekhov was understandably reticent to put his play forward again and risk further abuse. Nemirovich-Danchenko wrote him another letter on May 12: "If you don't give it to me it will be a real blow as *The Seagull* is the only contemporary play that excites me as a director and you are the only contemporary writer who presents any great interest for a theatre with an educational repertoire."[5] Chekhov continued to balk at the idea until Nemirovich-Danchenko seemed offended. "Your arguments are on the whole inconclusive," he wrote Chekhov later the same day, "unless you are hiding the most basic one—that you don't believe I can do a good production."[6] Chekhov relented on May 16, offering Nemirovich-Danchenko an invitation to visit him at Melikhovo. "I can't tell you how anxious I am to see you," he wrote, "and just for the pleasure of seeing you and talking to you I am ready to give you all my plays."[7]

Rehearsals for the Moscow Art Theatre production began in September 1898. There is a famous photograph of Chekhov reading the play to the cast, as was the usual practice in that period. In the photograph, a handsome and bespectacled Chekhov sits at a table, play in hand. Stanislavsky looks on. The wonderful actress Olga Knipper, who played Arkadina and later became Chekhov's wife, sits, resting her palm on her cheek, at Chekhov's left. Later, in her *Memoirs*, Knipper remembered her first meeting with Chekhov. "Chekhov and I met for the first time on September 9 1898…," she wrote. "We were all captivated by the extraordinarily subtle charm of his personality, his simplicity, his inability to 'teach' or 'demonstrate.'"[8] Vsevolod Meyerhold, who played Treplev, sits at the far left in the photograph. At the far right is Nemirovich-Danchenko.

The rehearsal period was not without growing pains. Stanislavsky and Nemirovich-Danchenko were sorting out a system of co-directing. In total, the production was given an unheard-of 80 hours of rehearsal (which, according to Stanislavsky, was still too little time). The rehearsals were broken down into 24 sessions. Stanislavsky directed in nine sessions while Nemirovich-Danchenko directed in fifteen. To add to the confusion, Stanislavsky was also playing the role of Dorn, the country doctor. In the middle of the rehearsal period, after Chekhov attended a session and complained that the actor playing Trigorin was bloodless and ineffectual, Stanislavsky was persuaded to move into the role.

In advance of the rehearsal period, Stanislavsky had done a great deal of preparatory work on Chekhov's script.[9] He'd drawn up ground plans for each of the play's four acts. He'd contemplated characters' personalities and thought processes, and he'd worked out ways of expressing those thought processes through physical actions. At the end of act one, as Masha confides in her biological father about her unrequited love for Konstantin, Stanislavsky provides the following stage directions that cue the audience to the frenzy within her: "Masha bursts into sobs and, kneeling, buries her head on Dorn's knees. A pause of fifteen seconds. Dorn is stroking Masha's head. The frenzied waltz grows louder, sounds of a tolling church-bell, of a peasant's song, of frogs, of a corncrake, the knocking of the night-watchman, and all sorts of nocturnal sound effects."[10]

Stanislavsky's concern with subtext, and with the intangibles of human experience, changed the public's perception of the play. According to Vsevelod Meyerhold, before the Moscow Art Theatre production, "people had only played the theme in Chekhov and forgot that in his plays the sound of the rain outside the windows, the noise of a falling tub, early morning light through the shudders, mist on the lake were indissolubly linked (as previously in prose) with people's actions."[11]

There was a pervading sense of doom among the Moscow Art Theatre cast on opening night. Several of the actors had to be sedated with valerian drops. Then, in the middle of the first act, the unexpected happened. As one member of the audience wrote, in a letter to Chekhov, afterwards, "In the first act something special started, if you can so describe a mood of excitement in the audience that seemed to grow and grow."[12] As the play came to an end that evening, the audience sat silently, digesting what it had seen, for a long moment before breaking into thunderous applause. Nemirovich-Danchenko later described the sound and emotion of that moment as being similar to a dam breaking.

The critical reception of the play was also extremely favorable. "An excellent production," the reviewer in *Russkiye Vyedomosti (Russian News)* wrote, "the general tone entirely corresponded to the atmosphere of the play and was kept up to the end by the actors." In *Russkaya Mysl (Russian Thought)*, a reviewer argued that the play "was a big success because the actors succeeded in catching the most important thing in it—'the mood'—and conveyed it in absolutely the right and proper way."[13] Chekhov's friend and fellow playwright Maxim Gorky congratulated him before Gorky had even seen the play:

> You know of course about the triumph of *The Seagull*. Yesterday a man who has an excellent knowledge of the theatre and who is on familiar terms with all the leading lights of the theatre, a man who is almost sixty—an expert and a man of taste—said to me with tears in his eyes: "I have been a play-goer for forty years and there isn't much I have not seen, but I never saw such a wonderful, *heretical* play of genius as *The Seagull*."[14]

Clearly, Gorky's friend was not the only theatergoer to have such a glowing opinion of the play.

While Nemirovich-Danchenko felt that their production of *The Seagull* entirely vindicated the play, and while it is widely argued that Stanislavsky's method and Chekhov's words created a perfect marriage, Chekhov's own view of the production was not without reservation. When he finally attended a performance on May 1, 1889, he was unhappy with the actress playing Nina and also with Stanislavsky's performance as Trigorin. "I can't judge the play with equanimity," he wrote, a few days later, to Maxim Gorky, "because the seagull herself gave such an abominable performance—she blubbered loudly throughout—and Trigorin (the writer) walked around the stage and spoke like a paralytic." Despite these reservations, Chekhov still managed to find some good in the production. "It wasn't bad on the whole, though, quite gripping in fact," he wrote. "There were moments when I found it hard to believe I had written it."[15]

The success of the production was sufficient to convince Chekhov to continue writing plays. When he had finished *Uncle Vanya*, the following year, he did not immediately approach Stanislavsky and Nemirovich-Danchenko with the play. Instead, he submitted *Uncle Vanya* to the Maly Theatre, which was also located in Moscow. Only when the Maly rejected the play as being socially irrelevant did Chekhov give the Moscow Art Theatre permission to produce it. Following the success of *Uncle Vanya*, Chekhov's relationship with the Moscow Art Theatre was stable and secure. He would go on to produce two more masterpieces of modern realism, *Three Sisters* (1901) and *The Cherry Orchard* (1904). For future generations, Chekhov's work would be linked with Stanislavsky's theories of psychological realism on the stage.

Unfortunately, Chekhov lived only six more years after the Moscow

Art Theatre opening of *The Seagull*. He died of tuberculosis in the spa town of Badenweiler, Germany, on July 5, 1904. His wife Olga later wrote an account of his death:

> Anton sat up unusually straight and said loudly and clearly (although he knew almost no German): "*Ich sterbe*" ("I'm dying"). The doctor calmed him, took a syringe, gave him an injection of camphor, and ordered champagne. Anton took a full glass, examined it, smiled at me and said: "It's a long time since I drank champagne." He drained it and lay quietly on his left side....[16]

Chekhov and his wife had a longstanding tradition of writing love letters to one another, and Olga Knipper continued to write letters to Chekhov for two months after his death. On September 11, 1904, she wrote:

> Dearest darling sweetheart, it's so long since we had a chat. I've been so unkempt, so overwrought you wouldn't have liked me at all. I feel as though I am on my knees before you, leaning my head against your breast, hearing your heart, and you are tenderly stroking me. Anton, where are you? Are we really never to see each other again? It cannot be.[17]

Although she survived Chekhov by 55 years, Knipper never remarried. Instead, she devoted her life to the theater.

CHAPTER 8

La Mama

One Arm, *Café La Mama,*
New York, July 27, 1962

Ellen Stewart was a woman of mystery, one step ahead of the law and two steps ahead of anyone who wanted to know about her past. She was born in either Illinois or Louisiana, in 1920 or thereabouts, depending upon which of her stories you'd like to believe. Stewart may or may not have been married to one Larry Lebanus Hovell, who died in 1963. We do know that she worked for a time at Saks Fifth Avenue as a brassiere and corset trimmer and later as a fashion designer for Victor Bijou. Although she had no theatrical background or training, she also founded a theater company that became the champion of the avant-garde and that launched the careers of more playwrights than perhaps any other theater in North America.

By her own account, Stewart came to New York City in about 1950, seeking to attend one of the few fashion design schools that would admit African Americans. With 60 dollars in her pocket, she spent her first night in a cheap hotel room in Spanish Harlem. A devout Catholic, she made her way to St. Patrick's Cathedral a day or two later and prayed for divine intervention against her poverty. She found the answer to her prayers in the Saks Fifth Avenue building next door to the church. While a woman of color was not welcome on every design team in the store, Stewart found work with Edith Lances. At first, she was given menial jobs like trimming stray threads off undergarments, but Lances soon recognized Stewart's potential. Lances began to offer Stewart some minor design work and eventually put her in charge of a line of high-end sportswear. According to David Crespy, Stewart's career at Saks was curtailed because of jealousy and racism. Other employees were critical of her. "Adverse reactions came from Saks customers, as well," Crespy writes; "a few bigots were outraged to learn that their expensive clothes had been designed by a black woman, and they canceled their orders."[1] Stewart would never attend the design

51

school of her early dreams; instead, she learned fashion design from the ground up, as an apprentice at Saks.

After she left Saks, Stewart found inspiration in a fabric shop owner from the Lower East Side. "Papa" Abraham Diamonds was a Romanian immigrant who had started his career in fabrics as a pushcart salesman before graduating to a shop of his own. He took Stewart under his wing, advising her that everyone needs a pushcart "to serve others."[2] With this advice in mind, Stewart decided to open a boutique, in which to show her fashion designs, that would become a theater by night. Part of the impetus behind the project was that her foster brother, Fred Lights, was a playwright who was having trouble getting his plays produced.

Her first space was the basement of a building at 321 East 9th Street, in the middle of a white neighborhood. Stewart spent a great deal of time and money renovating the squalid basement, cleaning out garbage, covering the dirt floor with planks from orange crates, plugging ratholes with rags, and installing a sink that was serviced with water through a garden hose. Nine months later, when the basement was ready, theater artists—most of them men—began to frequent the place. Other tenants in the building complained that Stewart seemed to be running a house of prostitution. They reported the issue to the police and to the City's Health Department.

Fortunately, the health inspector was a retired vaudevillian, and he still had a soft spot for the theater. He informed Stewart that it was easier to procure a license to run a café than it was to get a theater license. Taking the health inspector's advice, Stewart called her space Café La Mama, in part because her playwrights were already thinking of her as a beneficent mother-figure. She served coffee and cake during performances and subsidized the theater with her fashion designs. The first production, Andy Milligan's adaptation of Tennessee Williams' short story "One Arm," opened on July 27, 1962.

Not much is remembered about that first production. Reviews are difficult to find because Stewart was extremely protective of her playwrights, actors, and directors. Critics were not usually invited to attend. The La Mama playwrights tended to be at the beginning of their careers, and Stewart did not believe that inexperienced playwrights benefited from harsh criticism. She wanted her theater to be a place where theater practitioners could explore their work collectively, without fear of negative reviews. She coddled her playwrights and directors, sometimes fed and housed them. "I call them my kids," she said in a 1997 interview. "I'm very fortunate. They know they can come to see me whenever they want. They don't need to have appointments."[3] It was this concentration on the artist, and particularly the playwright, that made La Mama unique.

Some details of that first production might be gleaned from what we know of the space. It was a tiny 20 by 30–foot room, with seating for no more than 30 spectators arranged around coffee-house style tables. There was no admission charge. Audiences in the early years usually consisted of five or six people, dragged in from the street by Paul Foster, who functioned as a "kind of street barker."[4] A hat was passed from table to table after the performance, and the artists split the proceeds. The stage was minuscule, as well, and it was encumbered in early years by one set piece—a bed on which much of the action tended to take place. The space was intimate; there was not much room for physical blocking or large production numbers.

Stewart was learning the theater business much as she had learned the fashion business, from the ground up. She was unaware, for example, that theaters were required to procure the rights for a play before producing it. When Harold Pinter found out that she was planning to produce his play "The Room," without first procuring the rights, he made his way to the 9th Street basement with his agent. Stewart apologized to the playwright and asked him to let her go ahead with her plans to produce the play even though she had no money to pay for royalties. She must have been extremely persuasive because Pinter gave Stewart permission to produce the play for no recompense despite his agent's protestations. Years later, when La Mama began touring shows to London, Pinter admitted to the fact that his early play had had an inauspicious and unpaid opening at La Mama.

Troubles with the law plagued Stewart through the first year of her work as a theater impresario. Even after Stewart had obtained a café license, the fire department required various expensive improvements that she could not afford. Between July 1962 and April 1963, La Mama was closed and reopened approximately ten times, usually for infractions against the fire code. Stewart was arrested several times and held at Greenwich Village's Women's House of Detention. New York was readying itself to host the 1964 World's Fair, and the Parks Commissioner was on a mission to clean up the city. City officials had little sympathy for theater companies in squalid basements. Stewart was convicted twice of code violations under her own name and several times under aliases. She feared a third conviction under her own name because such a conviction would have branded her a felon. When, on April 17, 1963, the police threatened another arrest, Stewart decided to cease operations at the 9th Street location.

La Mama's second home was a loft, above a florist's shop, at 82 Second Avenue. Much larger than her former space, the loft could accommodate an audience of 50 people. Its stage was eight feet by 20 feet, and Stewart was able to afford other set pieces besides the bed which had been a relatively permanent fixture at the Ninth Street basement. Stewart's first production in the new space was Ionesco's classic absurd drama *The Bald Soprano*. In the years that followed, La Mama also produced Lanford Wilson's early play *Balm in Gilead*, with its cast of 36 actors. It was during this period that Stewart revised her mission statement, making the decision to produce only new works by emerging playwrights. It was also during this period that Stewart began the practice of ringing a cow bell before each performance, sometimes inside the theater and sometimes out on the street. "Good evening, ladies and gentlemen," she would shout. "Welcome to La Mama—dedicated to the playwright and all aspects of the theater."[5]

Battles with the authorities over code violations continued to haunt Stewart at the Second Avenue location. After the fire department padlocked her doors, Stewart applied for and received a dispensation from the Mayor's Office. The theater would be allowed to run but only as a private, nonprofit theater club, in much the same way that Théàtre Libre had run in Paris almost a century earlier. Stewart acquiesced to the demands, and her theater became known as the La Mama Experimental Theater Club. Legal issues continued to plague Stewart, even though she was operating her theater as a private club. Hoping to keep the authorities away from the premises, Stewart took to advertising her shows in newspapers like *The Village Voice* but not listing an address for the theater.

For the uninitiated, finding the theater was a particularly arduous task. Club members attended the theater in droves, however, and audiences grew. The police were still requiring a Certificate of Occupancy which would have necessitated a $15,000 renovation. It was time to move again. After a performance of Paul Foster's play *Balls*, Stewart requested that audience members pick up chairs, tables, and props so that they could help her move. The assets of the theater company were carried down the block to La Mama's new home at 122 Second Avenue. One audience member, a lady in high heels, carried a table down the street. "Do you do this often?" she asked.[6]

At 122 Second Avenue, some of La Mama's most important work took place. Functioning as an artistic director, Tom O'Horgan directed plays there regularly, infusing his productions with music and modern movement techniques. His production of *Hair*, first produced at Joseph Papp's Public Theatre, soon became a huge Broadway success and catapulted him to stardom. New playwrights like Jean-Claude van Itallie, Lanford Wilson, Rochelle Owens, and Sam Shepard opened plays at La Mama during this time. In September of 1965, 16 La Mama artists took the best plays of the past three years on tour to Europe.

It was an exciting time for the American avant-garde. Stewart and her theater were suddenly bankable. On the backs of her successes, Stewart was able to procure a Rockefeller Foundation Grant of $44,000, which meant that she was no longer having to fund the theater from her own purse. In 1968, when the Ford Foundation also agreed to grant $25,000 for the rehabilitation of a new space, Stewart made her move to 74 4th Street. The 4th Street location proved to be satisfactory; La Mama has continued to operate out of that space since that time. The company has also expanded to other buildings nearby, where it continues to serve new playwrights and performers.

Ellen Stewart died in 2011, probably at the age of 91. Her memorial service was held at St. Patrick's Cathedral, where she had prayed for help more than a half century earlier. In the intervening years since her arrival in New York City, Stewart had introduced many fine playwrights and actors to New York audiences, including Paul Foster, Andrei Serban, Harvey Fierstein, Al Pacino, Robert De Niro, Bernadette Peters, and Bette Midler. She had been inducted into the American Theater Hall of Fame, and she had been appointed an officer of the Ordre des Arts et des Lettres in France. She had come a long way with her little pushcart to serve others, a long way from the holding cells at the Women's House of Detention in Greenwich Village.

Riotous Behavior

A testament to the importance of theaters is that they have been the focal point of riotous activity in past years. Sometimes riots have arisen for reasons that might be termed "political" or out of a sense of nationalism. At other times, the supposed immorality of a play has led citizens into violent protests in theaters. Occasionally, the ideology of an era or a society comes into the mix; if what society views as true and beautiful and good is not reflected on the stage, public unrest can be the result. Sometimes the reasons have been economical; theater patrons have been known to riot over the cost of a ticket.

"Old Price" is an essay about the importance of economics. Especially in London, arguably the first industrialized city in the world, money and class distinctions were at the root of many social problems at the close of the 18th century. While the gap between the rich and the poor was widening, the rich and poor alike thought of affordable theater as something like a right. When John Kemble decided to raise the price of a ticket in the pit at Covent Garden Theatre from three shillings sixpence to four shillings, his decision was seen as a move to keep the lower class out of the theater. The riots that lasted from mid–September almost until Christmas in 1801 were a full-scale class war involving legal disputes, professional fist-fighters, and mock funerals.

"A Cut-Throat Competition" moves forward in time to May 10, 1849, and discusses perhaps the most violent of theatrical riots, one which cost the lives of at least 22 people. The riot stemmed from a nationalistic feud over who was the best actor. Englishman William Charles Macready and American Edwin Forrest were both vying for that distinction. It had been more than fifty years since the United States had emancipated itself from British colonial rule. One fateful evening in New York City, militiamen began to congregate near the Astor Place Opera House where Macready was preparing to perform *Macbeth*. Supporters of Forrest stood across the street and hurled paving stones at the soldiers, who fired a point-blank volley into the crowd.

The riots that attended the Viennese production of Arthur Schnitzler's *La Ronde* in February 1921 were of a more ominous nature. Schnitzler had written the play in 1897 but, because of its controversial content, the work had faced censorship issues both in print and on stage until 1920. Even in 1921 in Vienna, the play and its Jewish author so offended the Christian Socialist Party that young Nazi sympathizers decided to storm the theater. On more than one occasion, they disrupted the performance, shouting anti–Semitic epithets and hurling stink-bombs. When one particular riot resulted in beatings and a flooding of the theater, the police swooped in and closed down the play. The production of *La Ronde* became a focal point for political tensions in pre–World War II Austria. Hard copies of the play would later be incinerated during Joseph Goebbels' series of book burnings in 1933.

In 1969, when *Oh! Calcutta!* had its premiere, the world was changing and not everybody was keeping up. It was an era of free love and political unrest. State censorship had been dealt a blow with the Theatres Act of 1968, when the Lord Chamberlain's Office ceased to operate as censor of plays in Britain in 1968. The Lord Chamberlain's Office had been around since Elizabethan times. It had been delegated the power of theatrical censor in England with the Theatres Act of 1843 and had often dealt heavy-handedly with plays that offended public morality or dealt with current events. By the early 1960s, playwrights like John Osborne and Edward Bond had sometimes found themselves afoul of the Lord Chamberlain's Office. As a last blow against censorship, the creators of the *Oh! Calcutta!* revue put an entirely naked cast onstage. The production raised eyebrows on both sides of the Atlantic, but it was in England where police threatened to bring obscenity charges against the show. While there were no actual riots—except the riot to purchase tickets for the popular show—the revue was considered revolutionary. "People were looking for a revolution," one of the actors said. "And we were part of that."

CHAPTER 9

Old Price

Macbeth, *Covent Garden Theatre,*
London, September 18, 1809.

Theater at the beginning of the 19th century was arguably more vital to the fabric of society than it is today. Partly that vitality was due to the fact that 19th-century theaters did not have to compete with television and motion pictures. Partly it was owing to the fact that theater could be communicated to a broad cross-section of society, to the aristocrats who inhabited the boxes and to the (sometimes illiterate) working men and women who inhabited the stalls. Several life-changing riots occurred in theaters during the 1800s, having to do with issues of nationalism and economics. Although theater has gotten more provocative in the intervening years, playhouses are not typically sites of rioting in the 21st century. Political activists have instead devoted their attention to other methods of mass communication that have the ability to sway the minds of greater and greater swaths of people. "If all the theaters in North America shut down tomorrow," an acting teacher friend of mine used to say, "there would be a smaller outcry than if all the Coca Cola plants ceased to operate."

One gauge of the social importance of a medium has to do with censorship. Theater was censored heavily in 19th-century England, where the Lord Chamberlain banned anything that smacked of immorality or current politics. It is not that censorship of plays was a new phenomenon or that censorship in England was stricter than elsewhere. The Lord Chamberlain's Office had been active since the Elizabethan era. And censorship in other countries was arguably even stricter than in England. In England, though, the censors grew stricter in the 18th century, after the bawdiness of the Restoration Period, both for moral and political reasons, and that new sense of stringency continued well into the 19th century. Censorship was understandable since theater was an avenue for communicating ideas to large crowds, even to large crowds of illiterate men and women. In the 20th century, other methods of mass communication—radio, television, and motion pictures—proved themselves more effective at reaching the masses. Each of these media was almost immediately upon arrival the subject of censorship, at local and national levels. In the 21st century, the Internet has come to the fore, originally without much censorship, but lately the need to control information and misinformation has become the subject of much controversy.

From the early 1700s, the Borough of Westminster had been the location of London's two patent theaters. After an interregnum that followed the beheading of his father and that witnessed the tearing down of venues like the Globe, Charles II decided to allow a small number of theaters to operate once more, under the strict supervision of the monarchy. Only two theaters were permitted to operate. Theatre Royal Drury Lane opened its doors in 1663, managed by Thomas Killigrew. The King's mistress Nell Gwynn performed there in the comedies of Wycherley and Dryden. William Davenant had also been granted a patent in 1662, and he produced successful seasons of plays at Lincoln's Inn Fields until his death in 1668. Later, Davenant's patent was transferred to John Rich, who built the Covent Garden Theatre in 1732. Only one other theater in London had found its way around licensing restrictions. In 1758, Theophilus Cibber was granted a patent to operate the Haymarket as a summer theater only, between the months of May and September.

In the early 1800s, fire swept through both Drury Lane and Covent Garden, leaving London without its two full-time patent playhouses for a brief period. Covent Garden burned down on September 20, 1808, and was rebuilt within a year, thanks to an insurance settlement of £50,000, public subscriptions for £76,000, and a £10,000 gift from the Duke of Northumberland. Unfortunately, these monies covered less than half of the 300,000-pound cost of rebuilding the theater. Drury Lane burned down on February 24, 1809. The playwright Richard Brinsley Sheridan, who managed the theater, drank a glass of wine in Bow Street as he watched the theater burn. "A man may surely be allowed to take a glass of wine by his own fireside," he is reported to have said.[1] The fire ruined Sheridan financially, and he was forced to withdraw from management when the theater was rebuilt, finally, in 1812. For a period of three years after it was re-built, Covent Garden was the only patent theatre in London, and it was not lost on the public that the theatre was benefiting from an artificial monopoly.

As Marc Baer writes, in *Theatre and Disorder in Late Georgian London*, two competing ideologies were at the center of the Old Price riots. The political thinking, at the time, employed by government officials and Kemble's patrician supporters, was user-pay. If the citizens of London wanted access to a beautiful new theater, they would have to pay for it through rising ticket costs. Lower and middle class thinking about the theater was based on tradition. Baer suggests that the OP rioters were "operating within a framework of a competing 'moral economy.'"[2] As far as the theater-going public was concerned, the good citizens of London had a right to affordable theater. Shouldn't Kemble have consulted with his patrons before summarily raising ticket prices?

There was pressure on Kemble to recoup the costs of rebuilding the theater and to make the enterprise more profitable. The newly rebuilt theater in Covent Garden opened on September 18, 1809. It was a grand playhouse, built in a classical style, containing well over 3,000 seats. In the new building, a third tier of dress boxes was replaced by 26 private boxes that, if rented on a seasonal basis, would bring in approximately £15,000 per year. As Baer writes, the upper gallery was considered "far less desirable than in the old theatre, seats there being referred to as 'pigeon holes.'"[3] As befits a grand building, Kemble made its opening a grand affair. Several thousand people gathered on the ancient piazza outside the theater to mark the event. Not all of them were able to purchase a ticket for the evening's entertainment. The theater's manager and part owner, John Phillip Kemble, was to play Macbeth that evening, a role he had famously played in his London debut, back in 1783. Kemble began to speak a prologue but was shouted down by surly spectators. The last few lines of Kemble's oration, probably unheard, were meant to appeal to the audience's sense of patriotism:

> We feel, with glory, all to Britain due,
> And British Artists raised this pile for you;
> While, zealous as our patrons, here we stand,
> To guard the staple genius of our land.
> Solid our building, heavy our expence;
> We rest our claim on your munificence;
> What ardour plans a Nation's taste to raise,
> A Nation's liberality repays.[4]

The uproar continued even after the main piece began, with Kemble taking the stage as Macbeth. After the performance, two magistrates were called in to the theater to read the riot act. The disturbance continued until two in the morning.

Economics and nationalism were at the root of the unrest. To recoup costs, Kemble had raised ticket prices in the pit from three shillings and sixpence to four shillings. Prices of seats in the regular boxes rose from six to seven shillings.[5] Then there was the matter of the new private boxes which were economically out of reach for working class spectators. If the new prices and the private boxes were not enough to raise the ire of the public, the hiring of an Italian soprano named Angelica Catalani at a rate of £75 per night was the tipping point. In the public view, Kemble had been profligate with his spending and had shown a flagrant disregard for his audience.

On September 19, rioters showed up in the theater bearing placards that bore the letters "OP." This abbreviation for "Old Prices" was to become a ubiquitous call-to-action for concerned citizens. Soon, in the streets, people were wearing pins and hatbands with the letters "OP" inscribed on them. Tourists arriving in London during the autumn of 1809 frequently commented, in their journals, on the craze for OP pins and hatbands. "There were hats with O.P. on them," wrote one Swedish visitor. "An O.P. medal was struck which was worn on the breast during the struggle. There were O.P. fans, O.P. waistcoats and caps. O.P. is inscribed on all the walls in London."[6] At the end of the September 19 performance, most of the audience "remained in their seats, hissing and bellowing, 'God Save the King—no Foreigners—no Catalani—no Kemble.'"[7]

The rioting continued for five days, during which time the actors were frequently shouted down inside the theater. Kemble tried to explain the management's position from the stage but was greeted with derision. A new dance was invented and performed in the pit of the theater. Accompanied by marrowbones, cleavers, and a dustman's bell, this carnival-like display was dubbed the OP dance. Rioters banged sticks against the seats, and the sounds of whistles and rattles reverberated throughout the theater. Finally, on September 23, Kemble proposed a truce. The theater would close, he said, until a neutral committee had examined its finances to determine whether the new prices were justified. He then proceeded to stack the committee with members who were sympathetic to the theater's management. In due time, the committee pronounced the new ticket prices entirely justified and reasonable. In the meantime, Madame Catalani, whom the rioters had nicknamed "Madame Cat" and then "Nasty Pussy," was dismissed by the theater on September 24, whereupon she departed to Ireland.[8]

When the theater reopened on October 4, management had made no adjustment to ticket prices. The rioters were still unhappy. They carried a coffin into the theater, at one point, staging a mock funeral. A message, displayed with the coffin, read: "Here lies the body of the new price, which died of the whooping cough on 23 September 1809, aged 6 days." Seeking an end to the conflict, Kemble hired a number of professional boxers (mostly from East London) to control the crowd. The former national champion Daniel Mendoza was the most famous of the pugilists Kemble hired, and his reputation took a downturn among the lower classes as a result. Mendoza's caricature survives in one of Isaac Robert Cruikshank's woodcuts, in which he is portrayed at the center of a disturbance in the theater, uttering the words, "Down down to H--l with all

KILLING no MURDER. as Performing at the Grand National Theatre

Woodcut cartoon of the riot by Isaac Robert Cruikshank (Wikimedia Commons).

Ops & say twas Dan that sent thee there."[9] Thereafter would-be rioters were greeted with a punch in the face. Fistfights broke out in the pit. To outflank the prizefighters, riotous patrons began coming to the theater between eight and nine o'clock in the evenings, when half price admissions kicked in.

The Old Price movement seemed to be losing steam by early November, but another incident inside the theater stoked the fires of unrest. Elderly James Brandon, who had been the doorkeeper at Covent Garden since 1768, charged a patron by the name of Henry Clifford with assault. After the charge had been dismissed in court, Clifford, who was also a well-known London barrister, brought a countersuit against Brandon for false arrest. The story behind these charges became public fare, reported in the newspapers. Rioters appeared in the theater with a renewed willingness to interrupt performances. They threw apples and lemons at the actors. Mock battles and sword fights were staged in the pit.

By mid–December, Kemble's theater had accrued a £12,000 deficit. The actor-manager had little choice but to issue a public apology, and he did so on December 15. By that time, Kemble had dismissed his longstanding doorman. Kemble announced that he would return to the old ticket prices for all seats in the pit. He also promised to drop all charges against the rioters. Having gotten most of what they wanted, the Old Price rioters were happy to give up their riotous ways. Upon hearing Kemble's apology and promise of a return to the old pit prices, they unfurled a banner in the theater that read "WE ARE SATISFIED."[10] The Old Price fiasco had come to an end, and Kemble was able to finish the 1809-10 theatrical season unimpeded.

CHAPTER 10

A Cut-Throat Competition

Macbeth, *Astor Place Opera House, New York, May 10, 1849*

Edwin Forrest and William Charles Macready were comrades-in-arms. Both were celebrated as the foremost actors of their age. The two men had supped together, first at Macready's home in London, then at Forrest's in New York. Both men were Type A personalities, and both were perfectionists. They sought a reputation for excellence and the fame that attends such a reputation. Eventually they found themselves locked in an international debate over which man was the better actor. A cut-throat competition for the hearts of audience members ensued, and ill feelings followed. By May 10, 1849, when the Astor Place riots took place, they had become the bitterest of enemies, engaging in a feud that would result in the deaths of 21 people.

Macready was the undisputed champion of the London stage, both as an actor and as a manager. He served as manager of Covent Garden between 1837 and 1839 and as manager of Drury Lane between 1841 and 1843. Although his tenure as actor-manager in these theaters was not marked by financial success, he did manage to bring a new style of acting and a greater sense of unity to the London stage. Discerning and well educated at a time when most leading men were not, Macready led the charge against the theatrical histrionics of the bombastic Edmund Kean (1787–1833) and his generation. Unlike his predecessor, Kean, who gauged his success in *Hamlet* by the number of women who fainted in the front row of the theater, Macready emphasized subtlety, grace, and textual analysis in his work. In an age when many star actors refused to spend much time rehearsing, the actor-manager Macready insisted on rehearsing all his actors thoroughly so that a unity of acting styles could be attained.

Macready was also moralistic and judgmental of his colleagues, both qualities that are apparent in his well-kept diary. He was sometimes arrogant, refusing to have his name appear on publicity bills with the names of

lesser-known actors. He was known for upstaging others. One of his leading ladies, Mrs. John Drew, testified that Macready was a "dreadful man
to act with."[1] According to one report, a reviewer for *Punch* magazine once
remarked that Macready must have thought his leading lady "had a very
handsome back, for, when on the stage with her, he always managed that
the audience should see it and little else."[2] For his part, Macready often
chastised himself for his own arrogance when writing in his diary after
the fact. After he'd thrown a tantrum, upon seeing his play script in the
dirty hands of the prompter, he reviled himself at length in a diary entry.
But he also asserted, in his diary, that it was "not vanity that makes me
case myself in pride, but a consciousness of not having won a secure title
to distinction."[3]

Edwin Forrest was 13 years Macready's junior. He had been born in
Philadelphia in 1806, the son of a merchandise peddler. A robust, well-
built young man, everything Forrest did on stage emphasized his mas-
culinity and machismo. He was also an ardent nationalist, a colonial boy
with a chip on his shoulder—not surprising since the American Revolution had been fought only sixty years before Macready and Forrest first
met. Forrest harbored political aspirations; he dreamed of one day being
President of the United States. He surrounded himself with elder states-
men, Andrew Jackson among them. Forrest gained renown as an actor,
touring through the States and spawning a playwriting competition in
which he offered the unheard-of sum of $500 for a new play about the
Indigenous people of North America. John Stone's play *Metamora* won the
first such award, and it immediately became part of Forrest's repertoire.

The first time Macready saw the American act in 1826, he was struck
by Forrest's potential and said so in his diary 17 years later. After seeing
Forrest in *King Lear* in 1843, Macready wrote:

> I had a very high opinion of his powers of mind when I saw him exactly sev-
> enteen years ago; I said then, if he would cultivate those powers and really
> study, where, as in England, his taste could be formed, he would make one of
> the very first actors of this day or any day. But I thought he would not do so,
> as his countrymen were, by their extravagant applause, possessing him with
> the idea and with the fact, as far as remuneration was concerned, that it was
> unnecessary.

After 17 years, Macready concluded that Forrest had not lived up to the
promise he had exhibited earlier. "He has great physical power," Macready
admitted to his diary. "But I could discern no imagination, no original
thought, no poetry at all in his acting."[4]

The trouble started in 1836, when Forrest decided to make a foray into
England, Macready's home territory. He appeared at Drury Lane as Spart-
acus in Robert Bird's *The Gladiator*, parading his handsome physique in

a toga. By most accounts, the production was not an unqualified success but, the day after opening, the *London Chronicle's* reviewer gave Forrest a charitable review. "Victory sits perched upon his beaver," the reviewer commented, "and he must and will support her without losing a single feather."[5] The review not only commended Forrest's performance; it also predicted success for the young actor in his future endeavors. A week later, Forrest played Othello, a performance that was lauded by the London critics. Over the next ten months, he also performed in *Macbeth* and *King Lear.* None of this made the competitive Macready particularly happy, but he did summon enough generosity of spirit to invite Forrest to his house for dinner.

Macready toured the United States the following year, appearing in various cities sometimes two or three days before Forrest, also on tour, was scheduled to appear in the same cities. The British star consistently outdrew Forrest in his homeland, although, as Forrest maintained, the market had been saturated in each city before his arrival. Macready's tour was financially successful; he returned to England £5,000 richer. He hadn't particularly enjoyed his stay, however, despite supping with Forrest and Forrest's British wife at their home in New York. He'd found that American audiences were incurably lowbrow, just the sort to enjoy Forrest's style of acting. To top it off, there were repeated comparisons of Forrest's and Macready's Macbeths in the American newspapers, usually offering Forrest the most favorable reviews.

Macready nevertheless returned to America for another tour in 1843 and was still on good enough terms with Forrest to sup with him. "Dined with Forrest; met a very large party, too large for comfort, but it was mostly kindly intended," Macready wrote in his diary on October 3, 1843. "Our day was cheerful; I like all I see of Forrest; very much. He appears a clear-headed, honest, kind man; what can be better?"[6]

When Forrest returned to England in 1845, he found himself playing to houses in London that were rude, hisses and catcalls rising out of the gallery. Certain newspaper critics, known friends of Macready, bestowed filthy reviews upon Forrest. Discouraged by his poor reception in London, Forrest decided to try his luck elsewhere. He applied to perform his stock repertoire in Paris, where an English-speaking theater company was run by one of Macready's friends. When the Parisian company turned him down flat, Forrest deduced that Macready was, in part, responsible for his lack of success. Finally, Forrest decided to tour the British counties, where he received reviews that were more favorable.

Macready was playing in a theater in Edinburgh while Forrest toured the provinces. One evening, in Edinburgh, playing Hamlet, Macready adopted his usual business, waving a white handkerchief and strutting across the stage. One spectator in the audience that night took exception to the handkerchief wave. He hissed. Soon, other audience members did the same thing. Macready was mortified. After the performance, several witnesses asserted that the man who initiated the hiss was none other than Edwin Forrest. A few days later, a local policeman advised the theater company "that it was Mr. Forrest who had hissed on Monday night, and that it was sent down in the report of the night (a practice here) to the police office by the officer on duty, regularly entered among the occurrences of the evening."[7] In a letter to *The Times*, Forrest later admitted that he had indeed hissed at Macready's shallow bit of grandstanding, arguing that it was every man's right to applaud or boo and describing Macready's handkerchief twirling strut as "a desecration of the scene."[8]

Having developed a quick aversion to Americans and America, Macready was also hemorrhaging financially. He needed to make money fast, so he decided in 1848 to tour the United States one last time. The American theater-going public was not ignorant of the dispute going on between the two actors. Their animosity had become the subject of a nationalistic debate. Macready was immediately met with an unfavorable reaction to his performances. American newspapers reviewed him antagonistically. Forrest wrote a letter to the *Philadelphia Public Ledger*, in which he outlined his grievances with Macready. Macready began to include a note in his programs, suggesting that he did not deserve to be blamed for Forrest's poor reception in England. Privately in his diary on September 26, 1848, Macready referred to Forrest as "an ignorant, uneducated man, burning with envy and rancour at my success."[9]

After touring the lesser theater centers, Macready finally arrived in New York. He was contracted to perform Macbeth at the Astor Place Opera House on the same evening that Forrest was performing Macbeth at a larger Broadway theater. Even before Macready's arrival there, the Astor Place Opera House had been the focal point of a dispute between upper class New Yorkers and the working class. The theater had been built at the nexus of Broadway and Lexington, at the edge of the Bowery. The Bowery Boys, as they were called, tended to resent Astor Place's wealthy audience members, who arrived in the theater, wearing kid gloves and smart vests, in smart carriages. These same Bowery lads were partial to Forrest, who had begun his career at the Bowery Theatre, and whose muscular frame made him the darling of the working class.

Three nights before the riot, Forrest's supporters bought hundreds of tickets to sit in the top balcony at the Astor Place Opera House. From this vantage point, they hurled rotten eggs, lemons, apples, and shoes at the stage. Macready's company was forced to end their performance of *Macbeth* in dumb show because they could not be heard over the hissing and booing. After that disastrous evening in the theater, Macready announced that he would leave America on the next boat. Appalled by the behavior of their fellow citizens, 47 wealthy and influential New Yorkers signed a petition in an effort to persuade Macready to stay. Herman Melville and Washington Irving were among the signators. They promised Macready that good sense and a love of order would prevail during the remainder of his scheduled performances. Moved by their petition, Macready decided to perform again at Astor Place on May 10.

A confrontation was brewing. New York's chief of police informed the upper-class Whig mayor, Caleb S. Woodhull, that he didn't have the manpower to quell a possible riot. Woodhull decided to call in the militia. On May 10 in the evening, 350 soldiers gathered in Washington Square Park, along with 100 police officers. Meanwhile, Captain Isaiah Rynders, who was an ardent supporter of both Tammany Hall (a democratic, labor-based political party) and Edwin Forrest, distributed bills across the city with the headline: "Working men. Shall Americans or English rule in this city?"[10] By the time Macready was set to perform, about 10,000 citizens of New York had assembled in the streets around the theater. One of these assemblers was E.Z.C. Judson, better known as Ned Buntline, a dime novelist who was also Rynders' associate. Buntline and his compatriots found curbstones from a construction site nearby and proceeded to pelt the theater. Others tried to set the Astor Place Opera House on fire. Even in those circumstances, Macready managed to finish the show, slipping out of the theater afterwards in disguise.

SCENE OF THE RIOT.

The Astor Place riot (The Miriam and Ira D. Wallach Division of Art, Prints and Photographs: Print Collection; New York Public Library).

The stone throwers injured several policemen in the melee. The militia arrived in front of the theater at 9:15 p.m. and were under attack. After issuing a verbal warning (which was probably unheard), they fired a volley into the air. The second volley was fired point-blank into the crowd, hitting both rioters and innocent bystanders. When the riot was over, at least 21 lay dead, most of them working class men, many of them immigrants. The corpses were laid out in nearby shops and saloons, to be identified and claimed the next morning. At least 50 policemen suffered injury as did 151 militiamen.

Macready got on a ship as soon as he could and sailed back to England. He retired from the profession of acting altogether three years later, disillusioned with the state of theater in his own country and abroad. Upon Macready's retirement, Alfred Tennyson wrote a verse in his honor. It began, "Farewell, Macready, since to-night we part:/ Full-handed thunders have often confessed/ Thy power, well used to move the public breast."

Forrest never recovered after the tragedy at Astor Place, which would be forever associated with his name. He resumed his acting career but with limited success. His personal life suffered, as well. In 1850, he filed for divorce from his wife Catherine, accusing her of having an affair with a fellow actor. The writer Nathaniel Parker Willis leapt to Catherine's defense, an act that led to Forrest publicly beating Willis with a whip in Washington Square Park. Parker Willis later sued Forrest for assault.

Forrest's forays into acting became more and more infrequent. He spoke of an urge to run for Congress but was never successful in doing so. In 1865, after Edwin Booth's assassination of Abraham Lincoln made the American public contemptuous of the acting profession for a time, Forrest opened his summer home in Philadelphia to fellow actors who could no longer find work. He died alone in Philadelphia on December 12, 1872. His heroic style of acting remained influential, however, even as Forrest was not. With the advent of silent movies in the early 1900s, that same heroic acting style could be seen in the work of Douglas Fairbanks and John Barrymore.

CHAPTER 11

Round Dance

La Ronde, *Deutsches Volkstheater,*
Vienna, February 7, 1921

On February 7, 1921, about twenty Nazi youths stormed the Deutsches Volkstheater in Vienna, hurling stink-bombs and shouting anti–Semitic insults. Attempting to stop the performance, they shouted "Phui" and "Schweinerei" at the stage.[1] Instead of sympathizing with them, the audience expressed disdain at the intrusion of the young men. Six of the intruders were arrested, and the performance was allowed to continue.

The occasion of this demonstration was a performance of Arthur Schnitzler's play *Reigen*, or *La Ronde* as it is more popularly known. The play's opening, a week earlier, had elicited much criticism in the press. Left-wing journalists had expressed reservations about the play's frank and possibly immoral descriptions of sexual encounters in 19th-century Vienna. Right-wing journalists had decried the play as pornography and "Jewish literature." The *Reichspost*, a Christian Socialist Party newspaper, had suggested that its readers should interfere with the performance.[2] *La Ronde* became a focal point for political tensions that would result in the rise of the Nazi party over the next twenty years.

Arthur Schnitzler was a medical man with a boundless curiosity for the workings of the human mind. He was born in 1862, the son of a well-known laryngologist. Young Arthur received his medical degree at the University of Vienna, having written a dissertation on hypnotic treatments for neuroses, and he began his career at Vienna's General Hospital. His interest in sexual pathology and psychotherapy led Schnitzler into a parallel path with another noted Viennese specialist, Sigmund Freud. Although the two lived within walking distance from one another and despite having several acquaintances in common, they met only a few times. Schnitzler's brother Julius played cards regularly with Freud on Saturday nights, and his brother-in-law Markus Hajek was the doctor who eventually diagnosed the cancerous growth on Freud's jaw. Although they were not the best of friends, Arthur Schnitzler was a follower of Freud's theories, having read *The Interpretation of Dreams* as soon as the book was published in 1899. Schnitzler wrote a 50th birthday greeting to Freud in 1906, and Freud responded with these kind words:

> I have been aware for several years of the extensive concurrence which exists between your views and mine regarding some psychological and erotic problems.... I have often asked myself in wonder where you could have found this or that secret knowledge which I was able to discover only after arduous examination of the object, and ended up feeling envious of the poet for whom I had always had the deepest admiration. You cannot imagine the pleasure and delight I obtained from your lines in which you tell me that you, on your part, have received inspiration from my writings.[3]

Many years later, on June 16, 1922, Freud invited Schnitzler to dine at his house, and the two met several times after that date. But Schnitzler, who was by that time wary of psychoanalysis, had become increasingly ambivalent in his attitude toward Freud. "His whole character attracted me," Schnitzler wrote in his diary, "and I sense a certain desire to talk with him about all the abysses of my work (and my existence)—but I don't think I will."[4]

Whereas Freud wrote theoretically about the human mind, Schnitzler chose more creative avenues. He recorded his dreams (and other matters) religiously in a diary. In his plays, he was preoccupied with sexuality and death or, more specifically, with what Freud called the life force and the death wish. As Richie Robertson writes, love and death co-exist in Schnitzler's play *Flirtations* (*Leibelei*). Robertson maintains that the male character Fritz "is drawn not only to stormy relationships but to wanton games with danger."[5] The possibility of dying becomes much more likely when an aggrieved husband challenges Fritz to a duel after one of his amorous affairs.

Similarly, death is never far away in *La Ronde*, even though the play is ostensibly about sexual congress. Death is present in the Soldier's remark, early in the play, that falling into the Danube might be his best course of action. It is also there in the Count's observation, late in the play, that post-coital sleep "washes away all differences. Like his brother Death."[6] And, as Robertson writes, any reader in the 1890s would immediately associate promiscuity with the fear of catching syphilis, a disease for which there was, at the time, no real cure.[7]

Schnitzler's plays are reflective of his passion for psychology but also of the hedonism that was prevalent in fin-de-siècle Vienna. According to Carl Mueller, turn-of-the-century Vienna was "a city that still lives the baroque tradition, that set itself apart from modernization, that resisted not only the railroad but the telephone, a city that suffered repression, and compensation for repression, like no place else: Vienna, City of Dreams."[8] Bruce Thompson suggests that the "most vivid and possibly the most accurate presentation of [fin-de-siècle] Viennese life is to be found in the narrative and dramatic works of Schnitzler...."[9]

The playwright's extremely active sex life, which is perhaps quite typical of the time and place in which he lived, is chronicled in vivid detail in his diaries. He was frequently involved in sexual relationships with more than one woman at a time. During his love affair with Jeanette Heeger, he took to recording the number of orgasms he experienced with her and with his other girlfriends. As Robertson writes, these orgasms occasionally numbered eight per evening.[10] While involved with Heeger, Schnitzler also embarked on a sexual relationship with a patient named Marie Glumer and, while still involved with Glumer, he began an affair with the actress Adele Sandrock.

Schnitzler's promiscuity was not uncharacteristic of the Vienna in which he lived, and it is reflected in his characters' similar preoccupations. In none of his other plays is the study of the sex lives of his characters more open and forceful than in *La Ronde*. The play consists of ten interlocking scenes, each of which revolves around a pair of lovers. The first scene, for example, is between a soldier and a prostitute. The second scene is between a soldier and a chambermaid. The third scene is between the chambermaid and her young master. Other characters, from various walks of life, are introduced in subsequent scenes. The prostitute makes her reappearance in the last scene of the play, during her dalliance with the Count. Schnitzler's argument, through the play, is that sex is the great social leveler. It does not recognize or respect class distinctions.

Schnitzler completed *La Ronde* in 1897, but he was never certain that the play should be produced. He had 200 copies of the play printed privately in 1900. These copies he distributed only to his friends, but some of them were shared more broadly, resulting in an increased demand for the play. In 1903, he was persuaded to allow a trade edition to be printed, and the publication was immediately attacked for its immorality. Newspapers refused to review the play as written. In Budapest, an unauthorized production of *La Ronde* was subsequently banned by the police.

When, in 1921, the play was first performed in Berlin, the actors and director were charged with public obscenity. They endured a six-day trial, during which much of the debate focused on moments of sexual congress in each scene when the lights faded and the audience was treated to an orchestral version of Sibelius' "Valse Triste." The prosecution argued that the rhythm of the music imitated closely the rhythm of the sex act, and the defense countered that the composer, and not the actors, should then be prosecuted. In the end, the cast and director of the Berlin production were cleared of all charges.

Furor over the subsequent Vienna production was not limited to one
particular evening. As Otto Schinnerer writes, the most frightening riot
took place on February 16, 1921, in front of a sold-out audience:

> In the first scene there were sharp, penetrating odors, caused by stink-bombs.
> In the fifth scene a mob of about six hundred, many of them students, stormed
> the theatre. Ten policemen were unable to stop the onrush. At this moment
> a stink-bomb of hydrogen sulphide was thrown on the floor and then the
> tumult started. The mob entered, swinging canes. From the boxes they hurled
> paper balls soaked in tar and eggshells filled with tar, and even seats, into the
> auditorium and onto the stage. A panic ensued with scenes that can hardly
> be described. Men trying to defend their escorts were clubbed. Ladies were
> slapped in the face and insulted. The stagehands hurried to the hydrants and
> turned the hose on the invaders. Soon the stage and the dressing rooms were
> flooded. The theatre looked as if it had been wrecked.[11]

A day later, on February 17, the Viennese production was closed down "as a
threat to public order." Vocal critics of the production often referred to the
fact that the playwright was Jewish, and Adolf Hitler himself later referred
to the play as "Jewish filth."[12] *La Ronde*, along with Schnitzler's other plays
and with the works of Freud and Einstein, was publicly incinerated during
Goebbels' book-burning crusade in 1933.

After the 1921 Vienna production, *La Ronde* was not much produced
anywhere in the world, but that changed when Max Ophuls made a popular film version of the play in 1950. There have since been several cinematic adaptations, including Richard Lerner's *Hot Circuit* (1971), Simon
Nuchtern's *New York Nights* (1983), Dean Howell's *Nine Lives* (2004), and
Alexis Lloyd's *30 Beats* (2012). In some of the modern cinematic versions,
the fear of syphilis is replaced with the fear of AIDS. In the theater, playwrights have freely adapted Schnitzler's work to make it more relevant to
modern audiences. In his adaptation entitled *The Blue Room*, David Hare
sets the action in 1990s London. Steven Dietz's *American La Ronde* updates
the characters and brings them to North America, and the playwright also
leaves the gender of all roles at the discretion of any theater that is likely to
produce the play.

CHAPTER 12

Oh, What an Arse You Have!

Oh! Calcutta!, *Eden Theater,*
New York, June 17, 1969

In 1969, Richard Nixon became the 37th President of the United States. Neil Armstrong walked on the moon. John Lennon and Yoko Ono sang "Give Peace a Chance" from a bed in Montreal. Edward Kennedy drove off a bridge at Chappaquiddick. The war in Vietnam raged on. At an Off Broadway theater called the Eden, *Oh! Calcutta!* opened on June 17 of that year.

The late Sixties was a time of upheaval, with the hippy movement advocating peace, free love, utopian socialism, and rock and roll. At the center of it all was a youth movement. The trappings of an older culture were thrown off at every turn. University students in the United States were protesting their country's involvement in an international war. In England, the Lord Chamberlain's Office was divested of its duty as a public censor. In the summer of 1966, British theater critic Kenneth Tynan put forth the idea of creating an erotic revue, eventually called *Oh! Calcutta!*, that would blow the lid off censorship once and for all. He approached Harold Pinter to direct the production, but Pinter wanted none of it. Tynan got luminaries like Jules Feiffer, Sam Shepard, and Samuel Beckett to contribute sketches. Peter Shickele (alias PDQ Bach), Stanley Walden, and Robert Dennis composed music for the extravaganza. The result was a revue that set all sorts of records, eventually running for 1,314 performances on Broadway and for more than 3,900 performances in London.

In the intervening years between Tynan's conception of the idea and its coming to fruition in 1969, a musical entitled *Hair* had captured the public's attention. The musical, written by Jerome Ragni and James Rado with music by Galt McDermott, told the story of a hippy commune in New York City that fights conscription into the Vietnam war. There is also a moment of nudity in Ragni's and Rado's play which excited and sometimes infuriated audiences. Premiered at Joseph Papp's Public Theater on

October 17, 1967, the play featured catchy songs like "Aquarius," "Hair," and "Good Morning Starshine." *Hair* transferred to Broadway on April 29, 1968, under the direction of Tom O'Horgan. The West End opening of the play was delayed until the Theatres Act of 1968 had been passed, and it opened at the Shaftesbury Theatre in London in September of that year. Not as sexually explorative as *Oh! Calcutta!*, *Hair* nevertheless broke new ground in bringing hippy culture, and its preoccupations, to the stage.

    Oh! Calcutta! got its title from a Clovis Trouille painting. It is a pun on "O quell cul t'as!" which is French for "Oh, what an arse you have!"[1] In its inaugural New York staging, the revue began with Samuel Beckett's brief play "Breath" and then proceeded to a scene entitled "Taking Off the Robe," in which the actors danced and disrobed to the opening song. Other scenes in the first act included a scandalous riff on the "Jack and Jill" nursery rhyme. The scene begins with a seemingly benign conversation:

> JILL: I think you're adorable, Jack.
> JACK: What shall we do?
> JILL: I don't know.
> JACK: What would you like to do?
> JILL: Anything you want to do, Jack. After all, you're the boy. It's all up to
>   you. I'm just the girl.[2]

But the scene takes on a more sinister tone when Jack rapes Jill and when, according to a stage direction, she dies. In "Dick and Jane," a sexually repressed young woman was tutored in the art of loosening up. In Act Two, there was a nude interpretive dance entitled "One on One" and a scene called "Four in Hand," written by John Lennon, about four men in a masturbation ring, facing a video screen with their backs to the audience. A character identified only as "1" explains the rules. "Now this (pointing to the screen) is a new kind of machine—a telepathic thought transmitter," he tells the others. "Whatever you think about flashes on the screen. Now the rules of the game are this: all of us think of things to jerk off to—until somebody comes—and the first guy who comes has to stop everybody else from coming."[3] While the other characters imagine the breasts and legs of women, a character named George persists in imagining the Lone Ranger. He puts the other men off their game and, much to their unhappiness, ends up having the first orgasm.

    The revue was a hit on both sides of the Atlantic. It premiered in London at the Roundhouse Theatre on July 27, 1970. The Metro Police's obscenity squad sent two officers to the preview of the initial production. One of the officers returned to see the play two more times before recommending prosecution under the Theatres Act of 1968. The revue transferred to the Royalty Theatre in September of that year and ran there until January 1974. In New York, the musical transferred to the Belasco Theatre on February 17, 1971, and closed there on August 12, 1972. The original New York cast featured Alan Rachins (who later played Douglas Brickman on *L.A. Law*), Margo Sappington, Leon Russom, and Bill Macy (who later became famous playing Beatrice Arthur's husband on the hit television show *Maude*). Jacques Levy, a clinical psychologist and an associate at Joseph Chaikin's Open Theater, directed the production. The 21-year-old Margo Sappington choreographed the dances. A recent set of interviews about the production was published in the *New York Times*.

The revue was created in a haphazard manner. Tynan asked his friends and acquaintances to be involved. Many turned him down. Tennessee Williams and Edna O'Brian both refused to let their work be part of the show. Beckett asked for his play "Breath" to be dropped from the production during the first New York run. "Ken Tynan asked me to contribute," Jules Feiffer said later. "I more or less knew what I was getting into, and couldn't resist the shoddy rock'n'roll glamour of it all."[4] When Jacques Levy became involved, he enlisted his friends from a band called The Open Window to write original music. He asked Michael Bennett to choreograph the revue, but Bennett soon dropped out, recommending Sappington to replace him.

The auditions for the show would never pass muster today. Some were held in a producer's office where actors were required to disrobe. Margo Sappington, whose audition took place in a theater, later described the audition process. Actors were given a "situation." They had recently received good news and had gone for a long, joyful walk in the forest while they were processing this news. Arriving at an imaginary river, the actors were told to go for a swim. They were required to disrobe and wade into the water (which was a sheet of plastic draped across the stage). Near the end of the audition, actors were asked to compose a letter, or talk on the phone, to a loved one, telling them the good news.[5] Actress Nancy Hillman seemingly had little problem with the nude audition. "I dressed in clothes I could easily take off," she said. "A safari dress and red-and-white-striped bikini underwear, no bra…. After I got the job, Jacques said, 'When I saw the red-and-white underwear, I knew I had something special.'"[6] Such cavalier attitudes toward nudity in a first audition were apparently permissible in the sexually liberated sixties, although many actors and actresses would have been wary of producers who needed them to undress before casting them in a play.

The rehearsal period was, according to most participants, quite chaste. There was no casual nudity in the dressing rooms or backstage. Whenever an actor was not working on a scene, she or he was required to wear a robe. One of the writers, Sherman Yellen, later said that the rehearsals for the show were less sexually charged than other rehearsals in which he had been involved.[7] The actors did sensitivity exercises for the first three weeks of the rehearsal period. Then, according to Sappington, director Jacques Levy asked the actors to throw off their robes. They did so, and the first nude rehearsal was characterized by a great deal of laughing and screaming and jumping around until the actors fell into "an exhausted heap." Bill Macy maintained that the nudity did not bother him. In his bio for the program, he wrote, "I was born nude." Another cast member, Alan Rachins, had more difficulty dealing with the nudity. "It was very difficult," he said later. "You're not just naked, you're vulnerable. I felt extremely vulnerable."[8]

At the first preview, the revue was three-and-a-half hours long. Levy and his cast experimented with cutting certain scenes, including a big production number about the history of women's underwear. When the first New York production finally opened, the early reviews were not particularly good. According to composer Stanley Walden, the cast, crew, and producers waited at Sardi's for the *New York Times* review to appear. When Clive Barnes panned the show, the investors began to question their commitment to the project. Their faces were sagging. The show's producer Hilly Elkins climbed onto a chair and said, "Anybody who wants to get their money back, I will buy out their investment here and now."[9] Indeed, Barnes had written in the *New York Times* that the show's humor was "doggedly sophomoric and soporific." Later, in London, critic Irving Wardle saw some redemptive qualities in the revue. "I have seen better revues than *Oh! Calcutta!*" he wrote in *The Times*, "but none based on ideas that strike me as more sympathetic." Wardle concluded his review with a reference to the juvenile subject matter of the show. "In many ways, it is a ghastly show," he wrote, "ill-written, juvenile, and attention-seeking. But it is not a menace."[10]

The producers of the show had higher aims than merely to bring erotica or soft pornography to the stage, but it is also clear that the writing reflected the mores of its age. According to Sherman Yellen, the show was about regarding women as three-dimensional human beings and refusing to objectify them. Yellen maintained that "the lesson of *Oh! Calcutta!* was not nudity. It was an attitude toward women as objects, detaching romance from sexuality." Still, most of the writers and actors involved with *Oh! Calcutta!* would probably regard the show as something particular to its age. "I would never write that [Jack and Jill] sketch today," Yellen said in 2019. "I would never think that a subject which dealt with rape, even peripherally, was a funny one." Revivals of the show have been proposed but none have materialized since the 1980s. As Stanley Walden has argued, so much has changed in the fifty years since *Oh! Calcutta!* was first produced that the thought of a revival of the original revue, with the playscript intact, would be unthinkable. "You'd have to do a completely different show now," he said in his 2019 interview with Alexis Soloski.[11]

The show ended up making its investors a lot of money, both on Broadway and in London's West End. And the 1976 revival of *Oh! Calcutta!* turned out to be the longest running revue in Broadway history. "People were looking for a revolution," cast member Samantha Harper Macy said later. "And we were part of that."[12]

Theatrical Quarrels

Theater practitioners are not normally a quarrelsome lot. When so much of the theatrical enterprise depends on collaboration, a fractious atmosphere can sabotage a project almost before it begins. In a business where personal success depends so much on reputation, however, friction can arise when the participants do not feel respected. Professional jealousy can often muddy the waters of creation. If a playwright decides to write about unhappy events in the life of a friend, that friendship can be broken irreparably. The following chapters are about moments in time when theatrical quarrels occurred during (and sometimes inhibited) groundbreaking work.

Molière was not by nature a quarrelsome man, but he found himself at the center of a major controversy when *The School for Wives* opened in 1662. He was a talented playwright, and others in the theater community were jealous of his talent and success. Rumors of plagiarism began to circulate, and then the attacks became much more personal. The idea that Molière was married to his own daughter entered the rumor mill, and Molière decided to fight back. He did so in a new play called "The Critique of *The School for Wives*." The quarrel soon escalated, and King Louis XIV himself weighed in, supporting Molière but also insisting that he find a way to clear his name.

Professional jealousy was also at the core of Lillian Hellman's relationship with Tallulah Bankhead. Their quarrel, during the Broadway run of *The Little Foxes*, was ostensibly about whether to support the Finns in their resistance of the Soviet invasion in 1939. But more than that, their quarrel was about two people who just didn't like one another. Bankhead was beautiful and Hellman was not. Hellman was politically sophisticated and Bankhead was not. At the height of their tiff, Hellman slammed her purse into Bankhead's lovely jaw in the back seat of a New York cab. Neither Bankhead nor Hellman had much good to say about the other for the remainder of their lives.

Laura Kieler was a Norwegian writer whose life and marriage were the inspiration for Henrik Ibsen's seminal play *A Doll's House*. Kieler had endeared herself to the great playwright by writing a salutary review of his early play *Brand*. In 1873, she had married a schoolteacher who contracted tuberculosis soon after the wedding. Like Nora in *A Doll's House*, Kieler had borrowed money under false pretenses to pay for her husband's restorative trip to Italy. Kieler later became a celebrated novelist, but she never forgave Ibsen for using those incidents from her life as the basis of his controversial play.

"A Mighty Personage" is an essay about the struggle between the symbolists and the realists. Alfred Jarry's first plays about the Ubu character were a schoolboy's prank, and he found himself at the focal point of the struggle between the symbolists and the realists when he premiered *Ubu Roi* at Théâtre de l'Oeuvre in Paris on December 10, 1896. The first word that actor Firmin Gémier uttered, as Ubu, resulted in audience pandemonium. Even W.B. Yeats, who was in the theater that evening, had mixed feelings about the event. "After Stephane Mallarmé, after Paul Verlaine, after Gustav Moreau, after Puvis de Chavannes, after our own verse, after all the subtle colour and nervous rhythm, after the faint mixed tints of Conder, what more is possible?" he asked. "After us the Savage God." The savage god that Yeats wistfully referred to was the god of a literary future that represented a turn away from ordered sophistication and a turn toward chaos and childishness. As James Panero suggests in *The New Criterion*, Jarry had seized upon a vision of defeat in art. "The future of art was uncertain," Panero writes; "art had become uncertain of itself; the Commune of one century was giving way to the Vichy of the next...."[1]

CHAPTER 13

La Querelle

The Rehearsal at Versailles, *The Palace at Versailles, October 14, 1663*

The first night of "The Rehearsal at Versailles," on October 14, 1663, was supposed to signal an ending and a beginning. The play's author Jean-Baptiste Poquelin (better known by his stage name Molière) had proposed a truce with his strident critics or, at least, a refrain from their most personal attacks. He wanted to move on from the insistent accusations of plagiarism and sacrilege that had attended his earlier plays. While it quelled some of the criticism for a time, the opening of "The Rehearsal at Versailles" did not mark the end of Molière's troubles.

Molière's quarrel with his critics began with the opening of an earlier play, *The School for Wives*, in 1662. A satire on May–December marriages and on the limited education upper class families afforded their daughters, *The School for Wives* is now widely considered a masterpiece of the French Renaissance. In its day, however, the play was met with charges of plagiarism and vulgarity. Some of his critics suggested that Molière had plagiarized lines directly from the work of Corneille. According to Michael James Foulkes, Molière was unlikely to have plagiarized Corneille's work because he frequently produced Corneille's plays and an act of plagiarism would have made further collaborations impossible.[1] Others noticed the similarities between Molière's plot and the plot of Scarron's *Précaution Inutile*. Others criticized the implausibility of the setting in *The School for Wives*. Like the ancient comedies of Plautus, Molière's play was set in a public square where, critics argued, intimate dialogues were unlikely to occur. Some found the scene in which the aging Arnolphe explains the maxims of marriage to his virginal wife Agnes to be sacrilegious.

The critics were also quick to seize upon the fact that the Arnolphe-Agnes relationship, in the play, resembled the real-life relationship of Molière and his new wife Armande Béjart. Armande was reputed to be the much younger sister of Molière's long-time theatrical partner Madeleine

Béjart, but it is more likely that Armande was Madeleine's illegitimate daughter, perhaps the result of a liaison with the Duke of Modena. There had long been hearsay that Madeleine Béjart and Molière, who were roughly the same age, had also been involved in a romantic affair. When Molière married the 17-year-old Armande in 1662, rumors began to swirl through Paris to the effect that he had incestuously wed his own daughter.[2] While none of the rumors were baldly stated in print (because to do so might have been libelous), they were certainly bandied about in theater stalls and rehearsal spaces.

One of Molière's most strident critics was the writer Jean Donneau de Visé, the founder of a literary gazette called *Le Mercure Galant.* De Vise's first criticisms of Molière were printed in 1663, under the title *Nouvelles nouvelles.* In the *Nouvelles,* de Vise offered his readership a discussion of Molière's recent rise to fame. The discussion was tempered and seemingly fair; it commended Molière on his strengths as a writer and revealed his supposed weaknesses, attributing Molière's fame more to the "fashion" of the time than to literary genius.[3]

Molière had no doubt heard the criticisms of *The School for Wives,* and he had read de Vise's *Nouvelles.* He decided to answer the criticisms from the stage, writing a new play entitled "The Critique of *The School for Wives.*" This new play opened in Paris on June 1, 1663. In "The Critique," Molière presented his audience with an after-theater dinner party. Three characters in the play are supportive of Molière's work and three are not.

A character named Lysidas lists several objections to *The School for Wives,* and a character named Dorante responds to each objection. Lysidas argues that the play ignores Aristotelian rules (which, as we know, were paramount among the neoclassicists of the age), but Dorante suggests that it is more important to be entertaining than correct. While Lysidas asserts that there is not enough action in the play, Dorante responds that Scene Six is full of comedic horseplay. Lysidas condemns the play's vulgarity, but Dorante argues that Arnolphe is, in fact, tricked by the innocence of the other characters, and not by their hypocrisy or evil intentions. Lysidas criticizes Arnolphe's apparent attack on religion, and Dorante argues that Arnolphe's excessive language is justified because the character is habitually excessive.

By satirizing the audience of *The School for Wives,* Molière seemed to be suggesting that the morality of the spectators was no more pristine than the play's characters. Dorante argues that Molière was simply reverting to neoclassical maxims. *The School for Wives,* he asserts, holds the mirror up to nature for the purpose of educating the audience.

Two months later, de Vise published his own one-act play, *Zelinde.*[4] On the surface a love story, *Zelinde* quickly becomes a vehicle for criticizing both *The School for Wives* and "The Critique of *The School for Wives.*" In *Zelinde*, Melante is waiting for her lover Oriane to meet her in Agrimont's fabric shop. While she waits, Melante discusses Molière's plays with the shop owner and some of his other customers. When he arrives, Oriane offers the occasional, weak defense of Molière's work, but the other characters have no sympathy for him or for his arguments. They criticize Molière's titles, his settings, the behaviors of his commedia-based servants, and the character of Lysidas in "The Critique." Agrimont himself mouths the strongest arguments against Molière's work. He criticizes *The School for Wives* for its impropriety (the line where Agnes tells her aging husband that her suitor "took something from her" had been singled out by Molière's critics), and he focuses on the improbable behavior of the suitor Horace.

Two months after the opening of *Zelinde*, Edmé Boursault launched his own attack on Molière with a play entitled *Le Portrait du Peintre*. Boursault had strong literary connections; he was friends with Pierre Corneille and other successful writers. He was also under the impression that Molière had based the character of Lysidas, in "The Critique," on Boursault himself. *Le Portrait* mirrored the structure of Molière's "The Critique."[5] It is set at the beginning of a dinner party, and the pre-dinner discussion centers on Molière's work. As in "The Critique," there are three characters who support Molière's work and three who criticize it. The criticizers argue that Molière is a plagiarist.

In the stage production of Boursault's play, there was apparently a scandalous song about Madeleine Béjart, focusing on her sexual appetite and her age. There were likely other references to Molière's personal life, and to the personal lives of his acting company, but these were deleted from published versions of the play. Molière himself attended a performance of *Le Portrait* that October. While other spectators reported that Molière appeared to enjoy the performance, he was not much amused.[6]

Molière had many enemies, some of them in high places, who did not like his politics or his personal life. Included among them were the Parti de Dévots, a religious group self-appointed to oversee the morality of the nation, the Prince of Conti (who had once been Molière's friend), and the Jansenists who waged a religious war against depravity. Luckily for Molière, he had one strong supporter, Louis XIV, the King of France, who had granted him a pension and who had agreed to be godfather of Molière's first son. The King supported Molière through la querelle, but he also wanted Molière to clear his name.

"The Rehearsal at Versailles" was staged a month after Boursault's play appeared, at the request of the King. It was first performed in the palace at Versailles. The little-known one-act play offers a glimpse of

Molière's company in rehearsal. It shows us something of the company's rehearsal methods, although the rehearsal is continually interrupted. Courtiers burst in to flirt with the actresses. Molière appears as a character in the play, wasting valuable time during rehearsals by doing impressions of various actors at the Hôtel de Bourgogne, a rival company. He also attacks Edmé Boursault but pronounces his name wrong in order to make the point that Boursault and his criticisms are inconsequential. Molière uses the play to announce his retirement from la querelle, suggesting that he is open to any valid criticism of his writing but also that critics should refrain from commenting on his private life. When, at the end of "The Rehearsal," it is apparent that the company is in need of more rehearsal time, the King magnanimously demonstrates his goodwill toward Molière by sending a messenger to tell him that his company will be excused from performing on that particular evening.

Molière would later be reconciled with de Vise and Boursault, but the criticisms did not go away. The Hôtel de Bourgogne mounted its own response with a play entitled *The Rehearsal at the Hôtel de Conde*. Montfleury fils, who had earlier made accusations of an incestuous relationship between Molière and Armande Béjart, was the Bourgogne play's author. In 1664, the Théâtre du Marais entered the fray with Chevalier's play *Les Amours de Cantonin*, which was largely supportive of Molière's work. Also in 1664, Molière produced another masterpiece, this one focused on religious hypocrisy. The play was entitled *Tartuffe,* and it created even greater scandals in Molière's life. Having re-offended both the Jansenists and the Parti de Dévots, Molière became the object of their unmitigated wrath. Almost immediately after the King had enjoyed its first performance at Versailles, he bowed to public pressure and *Tartuffe* was banned from further performances in France.[7] A proposed production of *Tartuffe* in New France thirty years later also caused the Archbishop of the Catholic Church to ban the play and virtually all theater in that region for decades to come—a ban that lasted until the Fall of Quebec in 1763.

CHAPTER 14

Nora's Incomprehensible Act

A Doll's House, *Royal Theatre,* *Copenhagen, December 21, 1879*

Henrik Ibsen's famous play *A Doll's House* premiered at the Royal Theatre in Copenhagen, Denmark on December 21, 1879. In the cast were Bette Hennings as Nora and Emile Paulsen as Torvald. The run of the play was entirely sold out. Other successful productions followed, in Sweden and in Ibsen's homeland, Norway, even though reviewers were critical of the play's stance on the institution of marriage. The most controversial opening of *A Doll's House* occurred several months later, in February 1880, when the play opened in Flensburg, Germany, with a new final scene that Ibsen was forced to write. Why that opening was so controversial is the subject of this chapter.

A Doll's House is based on a true story. Ibsen's friend and fellow writer Laura Kieler had met with scandal when she procured an illegal (and secret) loan to pay for her husband Victor's tuberculosis treatments. She later approached Ibsen for a letter of recommendation to his publisher, in the hope that a book deal and subsequent sales might help her repay the loan, but the manuscript had been written hurriedly and was not, in Ibsen's estimation, publishable. Sensing that Kieler was troubled by personal issues, Ibsen advised the young writer to confide in her husband, but Kieler's husband was even harder on her than Torvald would eventually be with Nora. When the truth was found out, Kieler suffered a nervous breakdown. Her husband divorced her and had her committed to an asylum. She survived the ordeal, eventually recuperated, and returned to her husband and children two years later.[1]

Kieler became a well-known author in her own right—her subsequent novels included *Silhouetter* (1887) and *Sten Stensen til Stensbo* (1904)—but she never forgave Ibsen for using her life as the raw material for a play. For his part, Ibsen was shaken by Kieler's husband's response and also by the role he had inadvertently played in the tragedy by refusing to support her manuscript and then by counselling Keiler to confide in her husband. *A Doll's House* was written, after a long gestation period, from a place of soul searching, sadness, and concern.

Kieler's life was the inspiration for Ibsen's play, but he added many details that could not have come directly from his knowledge of her. In the play, Nora Helmer's husband is not a schoolteacher, as Kieler's husband Victor was, but a prospective bank manager in a rural Norwegian town. The play revolves around themes of fate and free will, money and reputation, and the lot of women in 19th-century Norway. Most scandalous of all is the final scene of the play, where Nora decides to walk away from her marriage and her children. The shutting of the door behind her, as she leaves the familial home, was the door slam that was heard around the world.

Ibsen wrote the play when he was 51 years old. Had he died young or abandoned playwriting in his late forties, his literary output would have been limited to a couple of early plays, a closet drama entitled *Brand*, and his folk play *Peer Gynt*. He would have been remembered today as a minor playwright of the 19th century. *A Doll's House* was the play that changed all that, securing Ibsen an international reputation and a degree of immortality as the father of realism.

His life to that point had been a rollercoaster of poverty and limited success. Ibsen was born into an affluent family in the coastal town of Skien. His grandfather had been a wealthy ship's captain, but his parents' financial situation had taken a downturn when Ibsen was a boy. At the age of 15, Ibsen was forced to leave school. He apprenticed as a pharmacist in the neighboring village of Grimstad. When he was 18, Ibsen formed a romantic liaison with a local girl, engendering a child. Despite his low wage, Ibsen helped to pay for the child's upbringing for the next 14 years. In the meantime, he moved to Christiania (which is now called Oslo) in the hope of attending the university there.

While at the university, he wrote prolifically but not successfully for the stage, including a tragedy entitled *Catalina* and a folk play entitled *The Burial Mound*. These first theatrical stirrings of Ibsen's youth, while not commercial successes, got the attention of the artistic director of the Norwegian National Theatre, Ole Bull (who was also a celebrated violinist). Bull invited the young Ibsen to assume the position of stage manager at the theater in Bergen. It was at the National Theatre that Ibsen served his apprenticeship, keeping records of the staging of all the plays produced there for a five-year period.

Ibsen remained in Bergen until 1858, when he moved back to Christiania to become creative director of a theater there. He got married and became a father again, all the while living in abject poverty. When the

Norwegian government granted him a pension for his artistic service a few years later, Ibsen emigrated to Italy almost immediately. He did not return to live in Norway until 27 years later, but he wrote unceasingly about his homeland during that period.[2]

Henrik Ibsen (Wikimedia Commons).

Ibsen's gestation period, between the time he started thinking about a play and the time he began writing it, was long. He became interested in the Laura Kieler story in May 1878 but did not begin a first draft of *A Doll's House* until a year later. Once he began putting pen to paper, Ibsen wrote quickly. He sent a fair copy of the manuscript to his publisher on September 15, 1879.

One prominent characteristic of Ibsen's plays, at least at this point in his career, was his allegiance to the model of the well-made play, as characterized by the work of Eugene Scribe. The Scribean well-made play features a late point-of-attack and a great deal of exposition. Reversals of fortune, from bad to good and from good to bad, are sudden and common. Dramatic entrances and exits and the arrival of important letters change the direction of the protagonist's trajectory. Each scene mirrors the entire play by increasing tension and rising to a climax.

The influence of the well-made play on Ibsen's work can be seen in the immense amount of exposition buried beneath the opening scene. (An old professor of mine used to draw an iceberg on the blackboard, with 10 percent of the iceberg above sea level. The other 90 percent, he said, was the exposition in any of Ibsen's plays.) The death of Nora's father, her forging of the cheque, Helmer's illness, and the trip to Italy are all gracefully in the background. The reversal, after Helmer has repudiated Nora and when Krogstad's letter arrives to announce that he has given up on the blackmail, is one of the most dramatic in theater history. But it is Nora's reaction, after the letter is received and the threat of blackmail is removed, and her refusal to reconcile with Helmer, that takes the play to an unexpected and radical place.

Why was the play so scandalous? European society—and especially Norwegian society—was heavily invested in patriarchy in the 19th century. Marriage was considered a sacred institution, ordained by the Church, and husbands were traditionally the overseers of the family's finances and its moral wellbeing. If a family faltered, in either category, the husband was to blame. It is not surprising, then, that Torvald refers to his Nora as a small woodland creature in the first act of the play, or that he is affronted when he learns of her secret loan and forgery.

Early reviews of the play focused on Ibsen's handling of the institution of marriage. The reviewer for the Danish newspaper *Faedralandet* argued that the play portrayed marriage as an arrangement that corrupted both husband and wife.[3] Others argued that *A Doll's House* should not be taken seriously as a statement of women's rights since the transformation of Nora, toward the end of the play, was incomprehensible.[4] Nora's "incomprehensible" act occurred when she walked out on her husband and her children at the end of the play. The German actress Hedwig Raabe refused to perform the play as written. "I would never leave *my* children," she argued.[5]

In Germany, Ibsen's plays were not protected by copyright law; there was little he could do to stop a theater company from writing its own ending for the play. Bowing to public pressure, Ibsen agreed to revise the ending, making it more palatable to Raabe and to a German audience. He came up with the following:

> HELMER. GO THEN! (*Seizes her arm.*) But first you shall see your children for the last time!
> NORA. Let me go! I will not see them! I cannot!
> HELMER (*draws her over to the door, left*). You shall see them. (*Opens the door and says softly.*) Look, there they are asleep, peaceful and carefree. Tomorrow when they wake up and call for their mother, they will be—motherless.
> NORA (*trembling*). Motherless …!
> HELMER. AS YOU ONCE WERE.
> NORA. Motherless! (*Struggles with herself, lets her travelling bag fall, and says.*) Oh, this is a sin against myself, but I cannot leave them. (*Half sinks down by the door.*)
> HELMER (*joyfully, but softly*). Nora!
> (*The curtain falls.*)

A Doll's House opened in Flensburg, with this ending (which Ibsen called a "barbaric outrage") in February 1880. Several other productions of the play later opened, also with this new ending, in Dresden, Hanover, and Berlin.

In England, Ibsen's original ending was also unpalatable. Henry

Arthur Jones and Henry Herman were given the job of sanitizing Ibsen's play, under the new title *Breaking a Butterfly*. Jones and Herman's adaptation opened at the Princess Theatre in London on March 3, 1884. "Toward the middle of the action Ibsen was thrown to the fishes," wrote H.L. Mencken of this adaptation, "and Nora was saved from suicide, rebellion, flight, and immorality by making a faithful old clerk steal her fateful promissory note from Krogstad's desk."[6]

A private staged reading in London in 1883, this time unadulterated, featured the playwright George Bernard Shaw in the role of Krogstad. It starred Karl Marx's youngest daughter Eleanor as Nora and was presented in the drawing room of her house in Bloomsbury.[7] Both as an actor and as a playwright, Shaw admired Ibsen's freedom of expression, his use of subtext and exposition, all that was well made in the Norwegian realist's plays. He would soon become one of Ibsen's most ardent disciples. In 1891, he penned an influential and flattering essay on Ibsen's work under the title "The Quintessence of Ibsenism." The first public production, in England, of Ibsen's unabridged play opened in 1889, with Janet Achurch as Nora.

Ibsen was launched as an international sensation with his play *A Doll's House*, but he did not rest on his laurels after that. In the thirty years that followed, he wrote several classics of the early realist period. These include *Ghosts* (1881), *An Enemy of the People* (1884), *The Wild Duck* (1884), and *Hedda Gabler* (1890). His last play, composed late in his career and influenced by the symbolist movement, was *When We Dead Awaken* (1899). But the play for which he is most well-known continues to be *A Doll's House*. It has been produced in theaters around the world, both in its original form and in radical re-workings such as Stef Smith's *Nora: A Doll's House* at the Citizen's Theatre in Glasgow in 2019, wherein Nora is presented in three different decades in the 20th and 21st centuries. While Laura Kieler's name may not be much-remembered outside of Norway nowadays, Nora Helmer is still the subject of much discussion among theater historians and audience members around the world.

CHAPTER 15

A Mighty Personage

Ubu Roi, *Théâtre de l'Œuvre, Paris, December 10, 1896*

On December 10, 1896, a mighty personage slouched across the stage. Fat, infantile, greedy, violent, self-absorbed, given over to gluttony and other forms of gratification, Ubu was the forerunner of much that was to come. He can be seen today as the progenitor of the futurist, Dadaist, and surrealist movements and as a forefather of the theater of the absurd. After he'd waddled to the footlights of the Théâtre de l'Œuvre that evening, his first word sent the audience into paroxysms of joy and anger. "Merdre," he shouted, which is nowadays translated not as "shit" but as the somehow more vulgar "shitr." Such was the pandemonium in the crowd that it took fifteen minutes before another of the character's lines could be spoken.

Ubu is, of course, the title character of Alfred Jarry's seminal play *Ubu Roi.* The play's provenance is itself interesting. It all began as a schoolboy prank. The 15-year-old Jarry, with his friends Henri and Charles Morin, created a puppet show about their physics teacher Félix-Frédéric Hébert at their school in Rennes. In the puppet show, Hébert become Hébe, with a predilection for avarice, boastfulness, and power-mongering. The youthful Jarry and the Morins mounted various puppet shows, with Hébe as their subject, that were cheerfully attended by their classmates. Hébe became more than a physics teacher; he was a professor of pataphysics, the science of imaginary solutions, and a master of "phynances."

As years passed, the Morins lost interest in the work, but Jarry continued to adapt the script for public performance. In Jarry's subsequent drafts, *Ubu Roi* became not merely a sendup of a high school teacher but a study of the small-mindedness of the French bourgeoisie. When the play was finally given a production at Aurélien Lugné-Poë's Théâtre de l'Œuvre in Paris, Charles Morin attempted to claim some credit for the production, but his brother Henri had given Jarry license to do whatever he wanted with the play.[1]

92

The Théâtre de l'Œuvre production was accompanied by a program handmade by the 24-year-old Jarry in schoolboy fashion. Before the play began, the author himself stepped out on to the stage—walking like a robot in a baggy suit, his hair plastered down—and offered a brief introduction to the piece. "You are free to see in Monsieur Ubu however many illusions you care to," he announced, "or else as a simple puppet—a schoolboy's caricature of one of his teachers who personified for him all the ugliness in the world."[2]

Jarry had envisioned a production, patterned after la guignol, in which the characters would be costumed as marionettes. The director Lugné-Poë had found Jarry to be implacable in his vision for the production, which included an acting style characterized by marionette-like movement, non-naturalistic staccato speech rhythms, and the use of masks. Furthermore, Jarry had been stubborn in his insistence on the use of placards (carried across the stage to announce scene changes) and what one critic described as a "hodge-podge style of scenic painting."[3]

Firmin Gémier, the brave actor playing Ubu, could be seen as a precursor to the unlucky actor who incurs the wrath of the title character and is forced off the stage at the beginning of *Cyrano de Bergerac*. After his initial line had led to a shouting match between factions in the audience, Gémier calmed the waters by improvising a solo dance. He was then allowed to proceed until the word "merdre" was used a second time. Fist fights broke out in the audience. Many spectators left the theater in disgust. One of Jarry's supporters shouted at them, "You wouldn't have understood Shakespeare or Wagner either!"[4] A riot ensued.

What exactly had caused such a pronounced and emotional difference of opinion in the audience? Jarry's detractors were exasperated by the play's school-boyish infantilism, its use of profanity, and its depiction of the bourgeoisie as crude and self-serving. They saw in the play a nihilism that was intensely political, that threatened to undermine a democratic way of life. Jarry's supporters were capable of admiring a play that freed itself from the pseudo-scientific tenets of realistic and naturalistic theater, the theater of Ibsen, Strindberg, and Zola which had become popular. Realism had been founded partially on the back of Charles Darwin's theories of evolution (there were also other influences in realism's development, including the burgeoning new technologies of photography and film), and more particularly on the idea that human evolution is based on heredity and environment. In the view of the symbolists, some of whom were in the audience that night, such slavish attention to Darwin's theories led to an impoverished theater where imagination and attention to the spiritual and the non-analytical had no place.

Three opinions stand out. The symbolist poet Mallarmé wrote Jarry a congratulatory note after the opening. "With the skill of a sure and sober dramatic sculptor, and with a rare and durable clay upon your fingers, you have set a prodigious figure on his feet," Mallarmé wrote. "He enters into a repertoire of high taste and haunts me."[5] W.B. Yeats, who was also in the audience on December 10, admired the play's freedom from the restraints of realism but found himself saddened by the brutish spectacle. In his memoir *The Trembling of the Veil*, Yeats wrote:

> Feeling bound to support the most spirited party, we have shouted for the play, but that night at the Hotel Corneille I am very sad, for comedy, objectivity, has displayed its growing power once more. I say, "After Stephane Mallarmé, after Paul Verlaine, after Gustav Moreau, after Puvis de Chavannes, after our own verse, after all the subtle colour and nervous rhythm, after the faint mixed tints of Conder, what more is possible? After us the Savage God."[6]

While Yeats had mixed feelings about the play, the director of the production Lugné-Poë thought it an unqualified disaster. Not only had the play been shouted off the stage, but it had also cost him a lot of money. The measly 1,300 francs he had made from the box office did not begin to cover the costs of producing the play.

While it limped through a second performance, *Ubu Roi* did not see a third night at the Théâtre de l'Œuvre or anywhere else in Jarry's lifetime. Because of the riot it had caused, the play was banned in Paris. Jarry went on to write two sequels, entitled *Ubu Cuckholded* and *Ubu in Chains*, but neither was given a production before Jarry died at an early age.

Jarry spent the rest of his brief life imitating the grotesque character he had created. He spoke with the staccato rhythms of Ubu, often using the character's inflated figures of speech. He referred to the wind as "that which blows" and to his beloved bicycle as "that which rolls." He began carrying a loaded revolver with him on his peregrinations, taking frequent target practice, frightening a neighbor lady who was afraid that her children might accidentally be shot. "If that should ever happen, madame," he said to the woman, "we should ourselves be happy to get new ones with you."[7] He referred to himself using the royal "we," and he moved into a flat with a ceiling so low that his guests had to crouch while visiting him while he, diminutive as he was, could just barely stand erect. Jarry took to abusing absinthe and ether, factors that hastened his death by tuberculosis at the age of 34. His last request, on his deathbed, was that someone should bring him a toothpick.

Despite its brief and turbulent initial run, Jarry's play that started as a schoolboy's prank remains as an important precursor of developments that took place in the 20th century, especially developments in absurd theater. Its reliance on violent humor and its presentation of an absurd existence make the play an influential harbinger of the absurdist movement.

Alfred Jarry on his beloved bicycle (Wikimedia Commons).

In his book *Theatre of the Absurd*, Martin Esslin writes of *Ubu Roi*: "a play that had only two performances in its first run and evoked a torrent of abuse, appears in the light of subsequent developments as a landmark and a forerunner."[8]

CHAPTER 16

A Purse to the Jaw

The Little Foxes, *National Theatre,*
New York, February 13, 1939

One night in 1939, Lillian Hellman shared a taxi with Tallulah Bankhead and two theater critics. They were on their way home from a Broadway performance of *The Little Foxes* at the National Theatre, in which Bankhead was starring, but the playwright and the famous actress were not getting along. According to one of the critics, Joseph Wood Krutch, Bankhead turned to Hellman in the back seat and hissed, "That's the last time I act in one of your god-damned plays."[1] Hellman's response was a violent one. She slammed her purse into Bankhead's jaw. Taken aback by the purse-swinging incident and by Hellman's behavior, Krutch decided "that no self-respecting Gila monster would have behaved in that manner."[2]

The Little Foxes opened on Broadway on February 13, 1939. Bankhead, who was by that time a well-known movie star, played the lead role of Regina Hubbard Giddens. Also in the cast were Frank Conroy as Horace Giddens, Dan Duryea as Leo Hubbard, and Carl Benton as Oscar Hubbard. *Variety* magazine later cited Bankhead as the Best Actress of the 1938–39 Broadway season for her work in the role. The production ran for 410 performances before embarking on a two-season tour of the United States. Hellman's play is now considered a classic of the 20th century.

Based in part on a real-life crisis in Hellman's extended family, *The Little Foxes* is about the plight of Regina, a Southern woman who fights against patriarchy in her struggle for wealth and freedom. Faced with a system in which only sons are considered legal heirs, Regina schemes against her avaricious brothers to gain some part of the family inheritance. She eventually pressures her brother Leo into stealing railroad bonds and, later, blackmails her brother by threatening to reveal the theft unless she is given majority ownership in a family cotton mill. As a result of this blackmail, Regina is left wealthy but completely alone. Even her own daughter refuses to have anything to do with her. The title of the play, originally suggested by Hellman's friend Dorothy Parker, comes from the Songs of Solomon. "Take us the foxes, the little foxes, that spoil the vines," the King James version reads, "for our vines have tender grapes."[3]

To be clear, the squabble between playwright and actress was not about artistic differences. Bankhead loved playing Regina and would later say that it was "the best role I ever had in the theatre."[4] The feud began as a controversy over an international incident—the Soviet Union's invasion of Finland in 1939. An avowed anti-communist, Bankhead wanted to donate a portion of the proceeds of one performance to create a Finnish relief fund. Hellman, who was involved in the Communist Party of America at the time, blocked the proposal, as did her producer and director Herman Shumlin. Bankhead went directly to the press. "I've adopted Spanish Loyalist orphans and sent money to China," she said, "causes for which both Mr. Shumlin and Miss Hellman were strenuous proponents."[5] Bankhead wondered aloud why the playwright and producer were suddenly so "insular." For her part, Hellman disliked the pro–Nazi sentiments that she claimed were surfacing in Finland. "I don't believe in that fine, lovable little Republic of Finland that everyone gets so weepy about," she wrote back. "I've been there and it seems like a little pro–Nazi Republic to me."[6]

Bankhead was fearless in her private and public lives. She'd been born into a political family in the state of Alabama. Her father, a life-long Democrat, was speaker of the United States House of Representatives from 1936 to 1940. Bankhead's acting career had begun at the age of 15, when she entered a contest in *Picture Play* and won a trip to New York and a small part in a silent movie. When she arrived in New York, Bankhead stayed at the Algonquin Hotel, hobnobbing her way into the Algonquin Round Table (a loose association of writers, wits, and actors who met weekly in the hotel bar) and fraternizing with the likes of Eva Le Gallienne and Ethel Barrymore. After landing other roles in silent movies, Bankhead moved to London, where she appeared in a dozen plays over the next eight years. Her most notable West End successes were in *The Dancers* and *They Knew What They Wanted*, the latter winning a Pulitzer Prize in 1925.

When she returned to the United States in 1931, she starred in several Hollywood movies, earning top billing over Cary Grant, Charles Laughton, and Gary Cooper in *Devil and the Deep*. A 1932 interview in *Motion Picture* magazine earned Bankhead the ire of the Hayes Committee, which had been put in place to regulate the morality of the movie industry. In the interview, Bankhead ranted about her need for a lover. "I haven't had an affair for six months," she said. "Six months! Too long....."[7]

Bankhead was quickly promoted to the Hayes Committee's "Doom Book," which contained a list of actors and actresses considered "unsuitable for the public." She went back to the theater. Bankhead appeared in

Shakespeare's *Antony and Cleopatra* at the Mansfield Theater in New York in 1937 and was famously reviewed by John Mason Brown in *The New York Evening Post*. Brown began his review with a great one-liner: "Tallulah Bankhead barged down the Nile last night as Cleopatra—and sank."[8]

Like her father, Bankhead was a lifelong Democrat. She was a good friend of Harry Truman, supporting his campaign for re-election in 1948. She sat with President Truman during his inauguration in January 1949, and together they watched the inauguration parade. When the South Carolina float went by, carrying governor and segregationist Strom Thurmond, Bankhead booed. Although she was a Southern Democrat, she opposed racism and segregation and championed the civil rights movement.

Lillian Hellman's life and career were no less steeped in controversy. Born in New Orleans in 1905, she began her literary career in 1930, earning fifty dollars a week as a reader for Metro-Goldwyn-Mayer in Hollywood. She met Dashiell Hammett, the famous mystery writer, in a Hollywood restaurant and embarked on an affair with him that would last, on and off, until his death in 1961. At Hammett's bidding, she began work on a play based on a book entitled *Bad Companions*. The play, about two schoolteachers whose career and lives are ruined when a student accuses them of lesbianism, was entitled *The Children's Hour*. It opened on Broadway in 1934 and ran for 691 performances.

In 1935, Hellman joined the League of American Writers, a group composed largely of Communist Party members and sympathizers. Her next Broadway success was with *The Little Foxes*. Through the 1940s and 50s, Hellman's Communist leanings proved detrimental to her career. In November 1947, several leaders in the motion picture industry decided to deny employment to writers who refused to testify before the House Un-American Activities Committee. Hellman quickly wrote a rebuttal of the new policy. "It was a week of turning the head in shame," she wrote; "of the horror of seeing politicians make the honorable institution of Congress into a honky tonk show; of listening to craven men lie and tattle...."[9] When questioned later by the committee, Hellman took the Fifth Amendment rather than name friends and colleagues as subversives. Despite all of that, she continued writing plays. Her last major success on Broadway was *Toys in the Attic*, which opened in 1960 and ran for 464 performances.

The altercation in the back seat of the New York cab was not the first moment of unhappiness between the playwright and the actress. Wary of Bankhead's scarlet reputation, Hellman had originally wanted Ina Clare or Judith Anderson to play the part of Regina. Shumlin had overruled her, sensing rightly that Bankhead's star power as well as her reputation for immorality would dovetail nicely with the playing of the character.

There were also rumors that Shumlin and Bankhead were having an affair during rehearsals for the play, and those rumors probably did not sit well with Hellman.[10]

A temperamental actress and a diva, Bankhead threatened to walk away from the play on numerous occasions, and Drema Paige was hired secretly to understudy the role in case Bankhead decided to quit the production.[11] Bankhead's biographer Lee Israel called the relationship between the playwright and the actress Damoclean: "Hellman knew that Tallulah Bankhead, in spite of her self-preservation, was not very smart or sophisticated politically. And Tallulah knew that Hellman, for all her brilliance, was not a pretty woman. And each knew what the other knew."[12] Hellman's friend Dorothy Parker later commented that "Lilly does things the hard way. Why didn't she have sense enough to get Harpo Marx instead of Tallulah."[13]

After their jaw-slamming set-to, Hellman's relationship with Bankhead was, at best, strained. Turning down Bankhead's request for a pro–Finland fundraiser, Hellman and her producer suggested that money might be raised, instead, for Spanish loyalists fleeing France at the end of the Spanish Civil War. Bankhead, and the rest of the acting company, refused to take part in such a scheme. As a result of the feud, the playwright and the actress became bitter enemies, refusing to speak to one another for the next twenty-five years. Later in life, Hellman was prepared to admit that Bankhead had been successful in the role of Regina, but she often tempered her praise with examples of the actress' petulance or of her lack of attention given to aspects of the character.[14]

Despite the feud, *The Little Foxes* was an extraordinary success. One reviewer suggested that Bankhead's work in the leading role constituted "one of the most electrifying performances in American theatre history."[15] The success of the Broadway run led to a Hollywood film version for which Hellman wrote the screenplay. Several of the original Broadway cast landed parts in the movie, but not Tallulah Bankhead. She was, by all accounts, incensed when she learned that Bette Davis had been hired to play Regina in the motion picture.[16] It was a lesson that many actors have learned the hard way: don't cross the playwright if you want to get the part. What must have been even more difficult for Bankhead to accept was that Davis had seen Bankhead in the role on Broadway and that she had patterned her characterization closely on Bankhead's performance.

The movie's director William Wyler feuded with Davis about her derivative characterization, and his cutting remarks prompted her to absent herself from the set for 16 days. Davis was finally persuaded to return to the movie set after Wyler asked Hellman to write her a letter that would help "exorcise Bankhead's ghost from her performance." In her letter, Hellman buttered up the reticent Davis. "I am bewildered that you are having so much trouble with Regina," she wrote. "You will be better as Regina than Bankhead could ever have been: better by looks, by instinct, by understanding."[17] For some modern reviewers, like Andre Soares, Hellman was right in her support of Davis. Soares calls Davis "a model of self-control" in her cinematic performance as Regina. "I never got to see Tallulah Bankhead's stage Regina," he writes, "but I doubt it that Bankhead, no matter how good, could have been more effective than Davis."[18]

Theater Out of Doors

Some of the most spectacular events in theater history have occurred in the out-of-doors. Prior to the 16th century, almost all theater was produced al fresco during daylight hours, partly owing to the limited resources of theater companies and partly owing to the limited lighting capabilities of those companies. The Greeks and Romans of classical antiquity produced their plays in vast outdoor arenas, often built into a hillside where audience members could be seated with unobstructed views of the stage. The religious plays of the Middle Ages were often performed on a platform built atop a wheeled cart that could be transported into the open end of large courtyards. Shakespeare's theater in London had an open roof which enabled his company to fire off a wad-loaded cannon on occasion through the wooden O. When European settlers first arrived in what is now Canada at about the same time that Shakespeare and his men were performing at the Globe, their theater was by necessity out-of-doors. They had no buildings big enough to accommodate the grand performances that were sometimes envisioned.

When Sophocles' trilogy, including *Oedipus Tyrannus*, opened at the City Dionysia in Athens in March 427 BC, no one knew that the play would become a standard bearer for tragedies in the centuries that followed. While scholars of today generally regard *Oedipus Tyrannus* as the best tragedy of its age, the trilogy to which it belonged was not deemed particularly noteworthy in 427 BC. In fact, the trilogy received second prize at the City Dionysia in that year. The first prize went to a young poet named Philocles, whose works survive only in a few insubstantial fragments.

On December 28, 1598, the Lord Chamberlain's Men moved their theater, beam by beam, from its original site in Shoreditch to the other side of the Thames. In so doing, they freed themselves from a Puritan landlord and created the conditions whereby their company could flourish. The theater, rebuilt outside the city walls in Southwark, was re-named The Globe. It became the home of William Shakespeare and the Burbages, and it produced a barrage of plays that are now considered classics. It also made the company sharers rich men; it enabled Shakespeare, for example, to retire to an opulent house in Stratford-upon-Avon by the time he was fifty years old.

While Shakespeare was writing for the Globe, a lawyer named Marc Lescarbot penned a dramatic entertainment to celebrate the homecoming of community founders Samuel de Champlain and Jean de Biencourt de Poutrincourt. The two founders had been exploring the coastline of North America, looking for salubrious places in which to settle, and they returned to Port Royale to a heroes' welcome. "The Theatre of Neptune" was performed on boats and on the shoreline of what is now Nova Scotia. It was a celebration of European colonialism, infamous now for its unpalatable portrayal of the local Mi'kmaq and for its hegemonic portrayal of the European settlers.

CHAPTER 17

Second Prize

Oedipus Tyrannus, *The City Dionysia,*
Athens, March 427 BC

In late March 427 BC, the tragedy that eventually defined the entire genre of classical tragedies was performed at the City Dionysia in Athens. Sophocles' masterpiece *Oedipus Tyrannus* was part of his trilogy of Theban tragedies. The other two plays in the trilogy are not extant. While many scholars have regarded *Oedipus Tyrannus* as the best tragedy of its age, the trilogy of which the play is a part won second prize at the City Dionysia.[1] First prize went to a young poet named Philocles, the nephew of Sophocles' longtime competitor Aeschylus.

The City Dionysia was a major event in the cultural life of Athens. According to legend, the festival was first established after the citizens of the border town Eleutherae gifted a statue of Dionysus to the city. When Athenians rejected the statue and the cult of Dionysus, the god afflicted the men of the city with a plague that affected their genitalia in unhappy ways. Only after Athenians accepted Dionysus as a god did he lift the plague.[2]

Dionysus was thereafter revered as the god of the grape harvest, of fruitfulness and vegetation. Worshipping him was intended to ensure that spring followed winter, that the grapes would grow and the land would be bountiful. In time, because celebrations of the god were often drunken orgies, Dionysus also became associated with sexual ecstasy, irrational behavior, and insanity. When, in 1872, Friedrich Nietzsche wrote his famous book *The Birth of Tragedy from the Spirit of Music*, he argued that the best tragedies of ancient Greece were created out of a tension between Dionysian disorder and Apollonian logic.

The Athenian festival lasted for about a week. One of the first duties of the archon, an elected magistrate who oversaw various aspects of city government in the young democracy, was to organize the City Dionysia. In 427, the archon in charge was Diotimus. His job was to choose two reeves

103

and ten curators to help with organization. On the first day of the festival, citizens would march to the southern slope of the Acropolis, carrying a wooden statue of Dionysus. Among their other props were various phalluses made of wood or bronze. They also pulled a cart on which a much larger phallus was stationed. Bulls were herded to the theater at the Acropolis as part of the initial procession.

Also appointed by the archon, the choregoi were afforded a place of prominence in the procession. The choregoi were wealthy citizens who were appointed to help finance the preparation of dramatic productions as part of the Dionysia. (Then, as now, public funding for the arts was viewed as essential.) The choregoi paid for costumes, rehearsals, the scenery, and the training of the chorus for each chosen playwright. Sometimes expenditures were in the region of three thousand drachmas per playwright, which was ten times more than a skilled worker might earn in a year. For their financial contributions, the choregoi were celebrated during the procession. If their sponsored trilogy was eventually victorious in the play competition—as Sophocles' trilogy was not—they also shared the prize with the playwright. After a win, they might expect a monument to be erected in the city in their honor.[3]

After the initial procession, which was called the pompe, there were dithyrambic competitions involving song and dance. The bulls were sacrificed in honor of the god, and citizens were treated to a feast. A second procession, called the komos, occurred immediately after the feast. The komos almost invariably disintegrated into drunken revelry through the streets of Athens. The next five days were set aside for theatrical performances. At least three of those days were devoted to tragic trilogies like the one Sophocles had written. On other days, comedies were performed. At the end of the festival, prizes were awarded.[4]

For almost fifty years, Sophocles was the darling of the City Dionysia. He'd burst on to the scene in 468 BC, when he was almost thirty, with a trilogy that defeated Aeschylus who was the reigning dramatic master of the age. According to Plutarch, Aeschylus was so incensed by his loss that he emigrated to Sicily a short time later.[5] Sophocles competed in about thirty dramatic competitions after his first win. He was victorious in at least 24 of them, not a bad record considering that the formidable Aeschylus had won only 13 competitions while marvelous Euripides only won four.

Sophocles is credited with several innovations which led to a more nuanced theater in his lifetime. One of his earliest innovations was the addition of a third on-stage actor in his tragedies, a change which simultaneously reduced the role of the chorus and created the possibility of triangular conversations. This triangular structure can be observed in Oedipus

Tyrannus, when the Messenger explains to Oedipus and his wife/mother Jocasta how the child Oedipus had been rescued from a death by exposure on Mount Cithaeron. Spurred on by Sophocles' work, the older Aeschylus began to write three-character plays in his later years. Sophocles also expended greater energy on characterization than his predecessors, exploring in Oedipus a character ruled by pride but also by deep-seated psychological urges.

When he died at the age of 91 in 405 BC, Sophocles had lived a full and productive life. He had seen both the Persian and Peloponnesian Wars. He had served in the Athenian campaign against Samos. He had written more than 120 plays, of

Sophocles; cast of a bust in the Pushkin Museum (Wikimedia Commons).

which only seven have survived in complete form. His death inspired several apocryphal stories. One account suggests that he died, choking on grapes, at a festival in Athens. Another intimates that he expired from the strain of attempting to recite a long sentence from his play *Antigone*. Yet another maintains that he died of happiness, having won the City Dionysia with his play *Philoctetes* in 409 BC.[6] A few months after Sophocles' death, an anonymous poet included this eulogy in a comedy entitled *The Muses*: "Blessed is Sophocles, who had a long life, was a man both happy and talented, and the writer of many good tragedies; and he ended his life without suffering any misfortune."[7]

While *Oedipus Tyrannus* was not singled out for the highest praise in 427 BC, the play and the playwright were celebrated in subsequent centuries. In Aristophanes' play *The Frogs*, written shortly after Sophocles had died, Dionysus descends to the underworld for the purpose of devising a competition to bring back one of the great tragic writers and thereby to revitalize theater and state. Sophocles at first refuses to compete for a return to the world of the living because of his easy-going nature, but he agrees to assume the throne of Aeschylus in Hades after Aeschylus bests Euripides in the competition and wins his passage to the world of the living.

Writing his famous *Poetics* in 335 BC, Aristotle saw fit to use *Oedi-pus Tyrannus* as an example of the best tragic writing and the most complete expression of his own theory of what a tragedy should be. Sophocles' play had everything Aristotle admired in tragedy: a strong plot, deep characters, an inspired philosophical stance, great use of language, a rhythmical structure, and a dramatic sense of spectacle. Modern critics tend to agree with Aristotle. Edith Hall calls *Oedipus Tyrannus* a "definitive tragedy," noting the play's "magisterial subtlety of characterization."[8] Cedric Whitman suggests that *Oedipus Tyrannus* "passes almost universally for the greatest extant Greek play."[9]

Perhaps an even greater indication of the power and endurance of Sophocles' play can be found in psychological literature. Sigmund Freud famously named a psychological complex after the play's title character. In Freud's theory, the Oedipus Complex refers to a male child's unconscious desire to sleep with his mother and kill his father. Freud argued that Sophocles' play was a modification of a longstanding myth. In *The Interpretation of Dreams*, Freud describes Oedipus and our relationship to him. "His destiny moves us because it might have been ours—because the Oracle laid the same curse upon us at our birth as upon him," Freud writes. "It is the fate of all of us, perhaps, to direct our first sexual impulse towards our mother and our first hatred and our first murderous wish against our father."[10]

Not a bad record for a play that won second prize at the City Dionysia in 427 BC.

CHAPTER 18

Moving the Globe

The Globe Theatre, London, December 28, 1598

On December 28, 1598, Puritan landowner Giles Allen was celebrating Christmas at his country home in Essex. Allen was a wealthy man but not a lover of theater. Twenty-two years earlier, he had leased a plot of land in Shoreditch to an entrepreneur named James Burbage. On that site, Burbage had built a large theater and had gained success, purveying theatrical entertainments to the citizens of London. The land lease had expired in 1597, but Allen appeared ready to grant the Burbages another lease of 21 years, with a proviso that the building would only be used as a playhouse for another five years.

But two things happened in 1597: James Burbage died, leaving the theater in the hands of two of his sons; and all the theaters in London were closed on moral grounds that summer, after a seditious production of *The Isle of Dogs*, performed by the Earl of Pembroke's Men at the Swan Theatre. When the theaters re-opened in 1598, Allen decided, probably on religious grounds, that he no longer wanted a playhouse on his property. He refused to entertain the idea of a new lease with James Burbage's sons, thereby forcing them to rent the nearby Curtain Theatre for a time. Allen tucked into his Christmas meal as the year came to a close, thinking that he was now sole owner of the land and the building that stood upon it. He was sorely mistaken.

When James Burbage signed the land lease, on April 13, 1576, he agreed to pay Allen roughly £14 per year for the duration of the 21-year lease. Burbage's vision put him at the forefront of a movement to create permanent theater spaces, the first permanent theater spaces in London since Roman times. Born in 1531, Burbage had apprenticed as a joiner (a woodworker) before acquiring the acting bug. He'd married Ellen Brayne, the daughter of a London tailor, in 1559.[1] Ellen Brayne's brother John would eventually become co-owner of The Theatre, as it was grandly titled, and Burbage's brother Robert probably had a hand in building it. Constructed mostly of wood, but with a ring of stone tiles at the circumference of its open roof, The Theatre was a successful venture, both artistically and financially. On sunny afternoons, hundreds of patrons streamed out of the city gates, past the Bethlehem Insane Asylum and through open fields, to attend shows there. Soon other theaters—the Curtain, Newington Butts, the Rose, and the Swan—were built to compete for seemingly insatiable London audiences.

A great deal had changed in the London theater community between 1576 and 1598. When James Burbage passed away in 1597, he left his eldest son Cuthbert in charge of The Theatre's management. Also by 1598, James Burbage's younger son Richard had become an actor of note, rivalling Edward Alleyn as one of London's greatest tragedians. Burbage's sons had surrounded themselves with some of London's finest acting and writing talents, including the comedian Will Kempe and the playwright William Shakespeare. The company was on the edge of greatness when the Shoreditch lease expired. Patronized by the Lord Chamberlain, the Burbages had sold shares in their enterprise, wisely keeping 50 percent of the shares to themselves. In 1594, Shakespeare became a sharer, owning 12.5 percent of the theater and its profits. Under this co-operative system, shareholders divided the gate after paying off any show-by-show hires. They also took apprentices, young boys who were taught the skills of acting and musicianship, and to read and write, and who were given walk-on parts and sometimes women's roles in the all-male productions.

On December 28, 1598, while Giles Allen celebrated the Christmas holidays in faraway Essex, Richard and Cuthbert Burbage and other members of their company systematically dismantled The Theatre, beam by beam. They had tried for over a year to renegotiate their lease on the Shoreditch land, but Allen was adamant that he no longer wanted a theater company at work on his property. According to legend, the Burbages dismantled the building and hauled it away in the space of one night. This is unlikely, because The Theatre was a large building, three stories tall; it probably took the Burbages and their men several days to complete the project. Luckily for the theater company, Allen could not get back to London in time to stop them (although some of his friends and servants did put up a resistance). Having hired their friend and carpenter Peter Street to oversee the demolition, the Burbages afterwards hauled the lumber to Street's warehouse on the waterfront in Bridewell. It must have been cold and hurried work. The stone tiles at the circumference of the roof were probably dropped and broken. The company waited until the following spring to transport the timbers across the Thames to a marshy area near Maiden Lane in Southwark.

Outside city walls and restrictive city laws, Southwark was as disreputable and dangerous in the 1590s as Shoreditch had been in previous years. Patrons had to walk across the London Bridge to attend theaters there, in a locale replete with gamblers, thieves, and prostitutes. Marshalsea prison was located in Southwark. Londoners could attend bull- and bear-baiting exhibitions there or one of the several theaters in the low land. By the time the Lord Chamberlain's Men began to build the Globe, out of timbers reclaimed from The Theatre, there were already several other theaters nearby. These included Newington Butts (built in 1577), the Rose (built in 1587) and the Swan (built in 1594). Even as the Globe was being built, pleasure seekers were marching across London Bridge by the hundreds to attend exhibitions and theatrical performances each afternoon. They were just as eager to get back across the bridge to safer confines within the city walls before night fell.

The Globe, though built with The Theatre's timbers, was perhaps larger than The Theatre had been.[2] Evidence suggests that the Globe accommodated up to three thousand spectators, including groundlings who were crammed into the courtyard in front of the stage and more fashionable attendees who probably leaned against railings around the covered circumference of the building. There were other modifications, as well. The Globe featured a thatched roof around the circumference of its "wooden O" (a fact of historical significance) whereas The Theatre had a stone tile roof. Because the Globe was erected on a flood plain, a bank of raised earth, reinforced by timber, had to be created to raise the structure above the flood line. Probably completed in the summer of 1599, the Globe opened in September of that year, possibly with a production of *Henry V* or *Julius Caesar*.

A court case followed hard upon, as they say. Allen brought a lawsuit against the Burbages and Peter Street. He alleged that, on December 28, 1598, Richard Burbage gathered together a gang of 11 other men and unlawfully tore down The Theatre. The 12 men, he said,

> armed themselves with divers and manye vnlawfull and offensive weapons, as namelye, swordes daggers billes axes and such like And soe armed did then repayre vnto the said Theater And then and there armed as aforesayd in verye ryotous outragious and forcyble mannere and contrarye to the lawes of your highnes Realme attempted to pull downe the sayd Theater.[3]

According to Allen, the Burbages prevailed in dismantling The Theatre against the remonstrances of Allen's servants and friends. There followed a complicated series of suits and countersuits. The Burbages claimed that, while Allen owned the land in Shoreditch, the theater building belonged to them. Allen made noises about James Burbage not having lived up to his end of the lease agreement. He accused the Burbages of threatening prospective witnesses with physical violence and of causing others to commit perjury. When he eventually lost his lawsuit, Allen complained that Cuthbert Burbage had employed a series of dishonesties to win a favorable decision.

Over the next fifteen years, the theater scene in London witnessed a renaissance. Shakespeare wrote his best plays for the Globe, while he was a sharer in the Lord Chamberlain's Men. Other playwrights rose up in his wake. Ben Jonson was writing for the stage during this period. John Webster, John Marston, Francis Beaumont, and John Fletcher were composing their blood-and-guts revenge plays. Even if Shakespeare had never been born, the late Elizabethan and early Jacobean periods would probably be remembered for the greatness of their writers and actors.

The Globe would eventually fall upon hard times. On June 29, 1613, the theater burned to the ground, after a theatrical cannon misfired during a performance of Shakespeare's *Henry VIII*. A wad of flame lodged in the dry thatch at the circumference of the roof (where the stone tiles had been), spreading to the wooden beams at the top of the building. The theater was quickly evacuated. Sir Henry Wotton described the incident in a letter to his nephew Sir Edward Bacon, written on July 2:

> Now, King Henry making a masque at the Cardinal Wolsey's house, and certain chambers being shot off at his entry, some of the paper, or other stuff, wherewith one of them was stopped, did light on the thatch, where being thought at first but an idle smoke, and their eyes more attentive to the show, it kindled inwardly, and ran round like a train, consuming within less than an hour the whole house to the very grounds.

No injuries were reported except for one man whose burning britches had to be extinguished with a bottle of ale.[4] The Globe was rebuilt the following year, but the fire had hastened Shakespeare's retirement. Faced with the prospects of either putting up capital for a new building or simply walking away from it, Shakespeare elected to return to his hometown in Stratford-upon-Avon. He purchased an opulent house in the bucolic village and lived out the rest of his life in the company of his wife and daughter. He was not yet fifty years old when he retired, a sign that his career as a playwright had gone very well indeed. The Globe Theatre survived for about thirty years after Shakespeare's retirement. The Puritans closed the Globe in 1642, along with every other theater in London, seeking to eradicate the moral laxity that theater, in their view, encouraged. They tore the Globe down in 1643 to make room for tenement housing. Six years later, at the hands of Oliver Cromwell, the King of England lost his head. Theater would not be seen in London for the next ten years.

In 1988, a team of Museum of London archeologists descended upon Southwark with a view to excavating various historical sites in advance of commercial development. In February 1989, they discovered the remains of the Rose Theatre. On October 12 of the same year, another team of archeologists announced that they had discovered a part of the foundations of the Globe, buried deep in the earth. Although the discovery was limited to three wall foundations (about 40 feet by 30 feet) and one stair turret, these findings reinvigorated attempts to discern the exact dimensions of the original Globe.[5] Until that time, conjecture about the Globe's size and appearance was primarily based on a sketch made by one Wenceslas Hollar in preparation for his 1647 engraving entitled "Long View of London." Based on the dig that followed the initial discovery of the foundations, theater historians and archeologists were able to conclude that the original Globe was a 20-sided polygon, approximately 80 feet in diameter.

Long before the discovery of the Globe's archeological remains, the American actor-director Sam Wanamaker had advocated for a new, rebuilt Globe Theatre on the banks of the Thames. Wanamaker created the Globe Theatre Trust in 1970. He spent the next 23 years raising funds and working with architects and historians to design the new building. Armed with archeological evidence from the Museum of London dig, Wanamaker spearheaded a drive to secure a site, not on the foundations of the Old Globe but in the vicinity. Construction had started on the new building by the time Wanamaker died in December 1993.

The new theater recreated the original as faithfully as possible. Elizabethan construction methods were employed. Carpenters fixed the rough-hewn beams together with wooden pegs instead of screws or nails. Artisans were called in to thatch the roof in accordance with Elizabethan standards. The building, finished in 1996, boasted a thrust stage patterned after the original, a large pit, and three tiers of seating. Mark Rylance was appointed artistic director of the theater in 1996. He opened the theater by playing the lead in *Henry V* that same year.

Having once stood in the pit on a blazing hot summer's day, I can attest to the fortitude of those early groundlings who watched spellbound, without a chair to sit in, at the Globe four hundred years ago. *Othello* was playing on the occasion of my visit there. Jet airplanes roared overhead as the new Globe is directly below one of the flight paths into Heathrow Airport. The sun beat down upon us. I leaned against a railing in front of the seating area. Other patrons leaned against me in an effort to stay on their feet through the three-hour performance. During one of Iago's soliloquys, a pigeon flew down from the thatch and alighted on the stage. The actor playing Iago astutely delivered the remainder of his soliloquy directly to the bird. The pigeon seemed spellbound, refusing to fly away or avert its gaze. This was actor-audience interaction at its finest. I can only imagine that the ghosts of Shakespeare and Richard Burbage would have been pleased.

CHAPTER 19

Good Cheer

The Theatre of Neptune, *Port Royal, New France, November 14, 1606*

On November 14, 1606, French settlers performed "The Theatre of Neptune" at Port Royal in New France. Written to celebrate the return of the port's founders (who had been exploring the coast for a more habitable place to live), the brief nautical extravaganza was based on the time-tested trope of the triumphal entrance. The ancient Romans had composed similar extravaganzas to celebrate the return of famous military heroes. Like the Romans, the French were in the business of hegemony, of colonizing new territories for military and economic advantage, and by that time they had developed their own traditions of masques and nautical rituals. As theater historian Leonard Doucette writes, "The Theatre of Neptune" is part of the Jesuit reception tradition of dramatic dialogues but also a tradition "that is representative of a broader segment of French society: the public masques and triumphal entries, the nautical extravaganzas and allegorical galas so integral to French (and English) courtly life since the Renaissance."[1]

"The Theatre of Neptune" is sometimes billed as the earliest piece of theater conceived and performed in North America. Such a designation does a disservice to the many Indigenous cultures that had proliferated through the Americas before the arrival of Europeans. These Indigenous cultures had their own traditions that might be referred to as theatrical. They danced and drummed to celebrate a successful hunt or heroism in battle. There was also a strong tradition of storytelling among the Indigenous tribes of North America. Most of these theatrical celebrations were eventually viewed as barbaric by European colonists, and many were banned by the beginning of the 20th century.

Marc Lescarbot, the man who wrote and produced "The Theatre of Neptune," was an author, poet, and lawyer. A native of Picardy, he'd studied law in Paris. His education had been classical; he studied ancient and

HISTOIRE
DE LA NOVVELLE
FRANCE

Contenant les navigations, découvertes, & habitations faites par les François és Indes Occidentales & Nouvelle-France souz l'avœu & authorité de noz Rois Tres-Chrétiens, & les diverses fortunes d'iceux en l'execution de ces choses, depuis cent ans jusques à hui.

En quoy est comprise l'Histoire Morale, Naturele, & Geographique de ladite province: Avec les Tables & Figures d'icelle.

Par MARC LESCARBOT *Advocat en Parlement, Témoin oculaire d'vne partie des choses ici recitées.*

Multa renascentur quæ iam cecidere, cadéntque.

A PARIS

Chez IEAN MILOT, tenant sa boutique sur les degrez de la grand' sale du Palais.

M. DC. IX.

AVEC PRIVILEGE DV ROY,

Cover page of Lescarbot's *Histoire de la Nouvelle France* (Project Gutenberg).

modern literature and became fluent in Latin, Greek, and Hebrew.[2] When one of his clients, Jean de Biencourt de Poutrincourt, invited Lescarbot to participate in an expedition to New France, he jumped at the opportunity. The expedition party embarked on May 13, 1606, and arrived at Port Royal in July. Lescarbot spent a year in Acadia, where he encountered Mi'kmaq and Malecite Indigenous tribes. He returned to France in the summer of 1607 and published a poem entitled "Le defaite des sauvages armouchi-quois." He would later write his masterpiece *Histoire de la Nouvelle-France* (1609), an oft-quoted book about Canada's early history.

The colonists at Port Royal had seen a harsh winter in the months before Lescarbot and his party arrived. Scurvy, or land-sickness as it was known, was a common complaint among the colonists. At the time, the disease was associated with idleness and the lack of physical exercise. The explorer Samuel de Champlain, who had been living in the colony from its earliest days, suggested that the way to combat idleness during long, hard winters in New France was to establish a tradition of feasting days, speeches, and theatrical exhibitions. He created a society called The Order of Good Cheer, which still exists in French-speaking Canada. Lescarbot was put in charge of the inaugural event of the Order, while Champlain and Poutrincourt explored the coastline south of Port Royal. As Doucette writes, the mood in the colony was anxious and confused. During the winter of 1604–05, two years earlier, 35 of their compatriot Frenchmen across the bay in Sainte-Croix had died of scurvy. Poutrincourt's ship was late coming home, and the little garrison at Port Royal would have been in trouble "if their leaders, along with their pilot, locksmith, surgeon, apothecary, and carpenter had not returned with their ship, supplies, and expertise."[3] Lescarbot, who had only been in North America for a few months, was left in charge of the colony.

Lescarbot had a lively mind. He devised an entertainment to welcome home Poutrincourt and Champlain as glorious explorers. He composed an epic poem in which a series of Roman gods and four Sauvages greet the returning adventurers with glowing monologues. Lescarbot enlisted almost the entire French colony in the enactment of the play, which was to be performed on the waters of the Annapolis Basin, within sight of the settlement. The company rehearsed steadily through the autumn of 1606. They were ready to perform when Poutrincourt and Champlain returned to the settlement in mid–November.

The extravaganza began with Neptune's oration to the returning explorers. As Doucette conjectures, it is possible that Lescarbot himself played Neptune. The character, trident in hand, sat in a small boat that was decorated to resemble a chariot. The boat was drawn by six Tritons who guided it to Poutrincourt's landing craft. Neptune began by referring to Poutrincourt as "mighty Sagamo," which is Mi'kmaq for "leader," and Mi'kmaq words were sprinkled elsewhere in the play. Neptune's initial speech offered a description of his own powers and beneficence, without which Poutrincourt and his men would never have survived their journey. He addresses Poutrincourt directly: "Thyself indeed despite thy deeds of daring/ Had'st never sighted land, my sea-lanes faring,/ Nor won the joy of landing on this coast."[4]

The trumpets sounded, and another boat, containing four Indigenous characters, bobbed into view. While Lescarbot had a sympathetic interest in the Mi'kmaq and their way of life, it is difficult to ignore the imperialist themes in his play. Most likely played by French colonists, the Mi'kmaq characters are placed in a position of subservience to the colonizing Europeans. They thank the colonizers for arriving with their advanced weaponry, and they offer gifts—a Mi'kmaq custom that is subverted in Lescarbot's play—to demonstrate inferiority. The Third Sauvage claims to be smitten by love and lust; he hurriedly offers a gift of ornaments made by his lover so that he may return to her as soon as possible. As Doucette writes, the Mi'kmaq and their aged leader Membertou, who were present on the shoreline as audience members, "must have smiled incredulously if they understood anything of what the third 'Indian' says." There is also an intimation, in the gift-giving, that the French are better hunters than the Mi'kmaq. The Fourth Sauvage is unable to offer a gift to the French leaders because his hunt had been unsuccessful.[5]

The language of colonization often revolves around the colonizer's superiority as ordained by Nature or by God. Colonizers have a right to the hitherto "undiscovered" land because they are superior beings, from a superior culture. The notion that the French are somehow better hunters than the Mi'kmaq is in keeping with the colonizing impulse. Perhaps even more significant is the appeal to the Roman gods in Lescarbot's play, an appeal that traces European civilization back to the Romans. The gods' approval stretches back to pre–Christianity; it suggests that the French colonizers are destined to rule by virtue of Providence. There is also a quality of false bravado in Lescarbot's inflated language and hero-worship. The French colony was likely overwhelmed by their own presence in a terrifying and hostile land that didn't look at all like France, and they were imposing their own aesthetic to make the unfamiliar seem knowable.

Likely the first entertainment presented by the Order of Good Cheer, Lescarbot's spectacle did not stop at the end of the play. After the performance, the celebrants retired to the main room of the Habitation for an evening of feasting, speeches, and alcohol. A sumptuous meal was prepared, with local fish and game on the menu. Although there were about seventy men living in Port Royal in 1606 (fifty of whom had participated in the spectacle, according to Lescarbot), only 15 gentlemen of birth were named as founders of the Order. Nova Scotia historian Beamish Murdoch later recounted the first iterations of the Order:

> There were fifteen guests, each of whom in his turn, became steward and caterer of the day. At the dinner, the steward, with napkin on shoulder, staff of office in hand, and the collar of the order round his neck, led the van. The other guests in procession followed, each bearing a dish. After grace in the evening, he resigned the insignia to his successor, and they drank to each other in a cup of wine. It was the steward's duty, to look to supplies, and he would go hunt and fish a day or two before his turn came, and add some dainty to the ordinary fare. During the winter they had fowl and game in abundance, supplied by the Indians and by their own exertions. Those feasts were often attended by Indians of all ages and both sexes, sometimes twenty or thirty being present. The sagamore, or chief, Membertou, the greatest sagamore of the land, and other chiefs, when there, were treated as guests and equals.[6]

Lescarbot's description of the feasting provides evidence of the hierarchization of the colony, with gentlemen of good birth (and occasionally Mi'kmaq chiefs) seated at the head table.

Four hundred years after the first presentation of Lescarbot's spectacle, Montreal's Optative Theatrical Laboratories (OTL) presented a theatrical deconstruction and response, entitled *Sinking Neptune*, during a fringe theater festival in that city. As Kailin Wright maintains, "OTL's play responds to Lescarbot's imperialism, voices Mi'kmaq people's experiences of colonization, and critiques histories of Canadian drama that begin with Lescarbot's colonial performance and the arrival of the Europeans." The poster for the play featured Neptune, in an ornate canoe, declaiming, "This play is about cultural genocide." In its presentation, OTL enacted Lescarbot's play in its entirety but framed it with a press event that critiqued colonial attitudes in the play. Throughout the enactment, Lescarbot's narrative was interrupted by quotations from Indigenous writers and artists and by a character based on and named after Canadian theater historian Alan Filewod.[7]

Lescarbot's masque was clearly a narrative about colonizing North America. The play relegated Mi'kmaq characters to a role of subservience to the French imperialists. One could play fast-and-loose with the idea of firsts—First Peoples, first explorers, first settlers, first among a social hierarchy—but clearly Europeans were not the first people to set foot in North America. That said, "The Theatre of Neptune" was the first *European* drama produced on North American shores.

A Tale of Two Countries

The latter half of the 19th century has become known as a time of theatrical stagnation in England. On the British stage, inconsequential melodramas, revivals, and imported Continental fare became the order of the day. While Henry Irving's company at the Lyceum flourished with classical plays and melodrama, no significant playwrights were at work in England between 1871, when the realist T.W. Robertson died, and the early 1890s when Arthur Wing Pinero, George Bernard Shaw, and Henry Arthur Jones achieved success. Critics like William Archer were quick to note the divide between British and Continental theater. In 1886, Archer voiced his unhappiness with the current state of British theater in his book *About the Theatre*, at the same time giving hope for the future. He asked if British theater, with its emphasis on comedy and melodrama, deserves the attention it was currently getting. "The reader must determine for himself what that answer shall be," he said.

> If he regrets the decline of opera-bouffe; if he laments the decease of cup-and-saucer comedy; if he thinks frank farce and popular melodrama utterly hopeless and despicable forms of art; if he holds Messrs. Jones, Grundy, and Pinero inferior both as craftsmen and as artists to Messrs. Robertson, Byron, and Burnand—then he will doubtless conclude that the theatre does not deserve the increased attention it commands. If, on the other hand, he agrees with me in believing that the changes and developments I have indicated are on the whole for the better, he will let the dead past bury its dead....[1]

The British stage, in 1886, was characterized by some fine actors—Henry Irving being one—but not many up-and-coming playwrights.

A theater aficionado, Charles Dickens saw his own novels adapted, with or without his permission, in London's major and minor theaters. He had many theatrical friends, including William Charles Macready and Wilkie Collins, and when he transformed a room in his house into a small theater, he preferred to act in plays rather than write them. For that reason, Wilkie Collins was contracted to write *The Frozen Deep* while Dickens distinguished himself in the role of Richard Wardour. *The Frozen Deep*, a story about the hoped-for rescue of Sir John Franklin's men who'd perished in the North-West Passage, eventually became one of Queen Victoria's favorite plays.

Henry Irving's company has often been celebrated for its renditions of Shakespeare's plays, but he was equally well-known for his work in melodramas, a genre that became popular in the early 1800s and remained so well into the 20th century. Melodramas are known for their steady heroes and heroines and for their mustachio-twirling villains, but more recent studies have emphasized the psychoanalytical aspects of the genre.[2] Irving premiered the role of Mathias in *The Bells* on November 25, 1871, and reprised the role steadily through his career. Irving's rise to stardom was relatively quick; he was manager of the Lyceum Theatre by 1878. His productions were elaborate and detailed—often noted for their brilliant stage effects—and he made especially good use of the new electrical lighting system that was available to him after that date. But he was most widely known for his acting. Even Edward Gordon Craig, who did not like actors as a rule, was appreciative of Irving's skill, arguing that Irving's Mathias demonstrated "the finest point the craft of acting could reach." The night before he died at the early age of 67, Irving was on stage in the role of Mathias.

Meanwhile, movements were afoot in Germany to regenerate the art form. Richard Wagner began a nationalistic surge that soon became popular in the rest of Europe—a theatrical celebration of a country's history and mythology. In operas like *Die Meistersinger* and *Der Ring des Nibelungen*, he celebrated the Teutonic past, replacing Italianate operatic traditions with traditions more suitable to the German stage. In his theoretical writings, which include *Opera and Drama* (1852) and *The Purpose of Opera* (1871), he expressed a dislike for the developing trend toward realism and argued for the idea of a Gesamtkuntswerk (unified artwork) in which all elements of a theatrical production are fused into a meaningful whole. Hugely successful, Wagner managed to have a theater built to his own specifications and for his own purposes. The Bayreuth Festspielhaus was completed in 1876, in time to mount the last installment of Wagner's *Ring Cycle*.

In a small duchy, miles from the Festspielhaus, the Duke of Saxe-Meiningen began working on his own theatrical ideas. Building on the work of other German theatrical reformers like Gotthold Lessing, Friedrich Schiller, and Johann Wolfgang von Goethe, whose ideas about production and dramaturgy were groundbreaking, Georg II wanted to create an acting ensemble free of the egos of star actors. Like Wagner, he wanted a theater of unified vision and, in the process of building his company, he established himself as the first theatrical director in the modern sense, controlling all aspects of production. When it opened in Berlin in 1874, his production of *Julius Caesar* took the capital by storm. The result was instant recognition for the Meiningen Players (or the Meininger, as they were affectionately known) but also instant acrimony with some of the major theaters in Berlin.

CHAPTER 20

In the Palm of One's Hand

The Frozen Deep, *Tavistock House*, *January 5, 1857*

Charles Dickens had an interesting relationship with the theater of his time. He loved drama and performed his own work aloud on many occasions. In later life, Dickens transformed his home, Tavistock House, into a small theater where he and his influential friends could rehearse and perform plays that interested them. As the editor of *Household Words*, Dickens would often attend patent and minor theaters in London, where he would sometimes witness adaptations of his own work for the stage. Because there was little in the way of copyright protection for writers in the 1830s, 40s and 50s, hack playwrights were free to read the first few installments of *Oliver Twist* or *David Copperfield* (which were published serially in magazines) and to provide their own endings. These pirated revisions of his work were a source of exasperation, and sometimes amusement, for Dickens.

When Dickens decided to produce Wilkie Collins' play *The Frozen Deep*, he did so out of a sense of patriotism. The play was very loosely based on Sir John Franklin's failed navigation of the North-West Passage, which was the subject of much inquiry in Dickens' lifetime. The North-West Passage was the hoped-for sea-route to the Orient through Arctic waters in the Canadian North. Franklin had led an expedition to the Passage in 1845, departing from England with two ships, the *Erebus* and the *Terror*. Both ships became ice-bound in the Victoria Strait. Within a year, Franklin and nearly two dozen of his men had died. The surviving crew members, led by Franklin's deputy Frances Crozier, abandoned the ships and set out for the Canadian mainland, where they eventually disappeared.

Franklin's wife persuaded the Admiralty to launch several searches for the missing expedition. All were inconclusive. In 1854, Dr. John Rae reported that there had been sightings of Franklin's men as they trekked through the Arctic wastes. More shocking to the British public, and to

Lady Franklin, were Dr. Rae's assertions that there had been evidence of cannibalism among the starving sailors. Lady Franklin countered these assertions by reaffirming that her husband and his men were Christian, able "to triumph over any adversity through faith, scientific objectivity, and superior spirit."[1]

Dickens also discredited the Inuit eyewitness accounts, on which Rae had based his findings, choosing to malign the Indigenous population rather than impugn Franklin's men. "We believe every savage in his heart covetous, treacherous, and cruel," he wrote, "and we have yet to learn what knowledge the white man—lost, houseless, shipless, apparently forgotten by his race, plainly famine-stricken, weak, frozen, and dying—has of the gentleness of Esquimaux nature."[2] The racism inherent in Dickens' statement was prevalent in England at the time. Dr. Rae was categorized as a foreigner, as well, as a Scot who did not share the patriotic aims of the British military.

Dickens had visited Canada in 1842; he knew something about the country. The idea of creating a play about the Franklin expedition originated with Dickens, but he was too busy writing *Little Dorrit* in 1855–56 to devote much time to the project. He gave the idea to Wilkie Collins, a novelist and friend, but insisted on supervising many details in the composition and production of the play. Early in the process, Dickens was in touch with his scene painters about creating sets for each act. At the beginning of October 1855, Collins sent Dickens a draft of the first two acts of *The Frozen Deep*. Dickens revised the draft in detail and then returned it to Collins. As Peter Ackroyd writes, "He described these changes to Collins as 'some cuts' but in fact they were much more extensive than that, since his purpose was to emphasize the role and the character of the man he himself was to play, Richard Wardour, the 'hero' who helplessly loves a woman but who in the end sacrifices himself to save the life of a rival."[3] Dickens wanted a more heroic portrayal of the explorers' behavior than had been provided by John Rae.

In *The Frozen Deep*, the sailors end up on the coast of Newfoundland, where most of them are rescued and returned home. Only two sailors, Frank Aldersley and Richard Wardour, are left behind. We learn that the two men were both in love with the same woman, back in England, but that the woman Clara Burnham had favored Aldersley and rejected Wardour. By the end of the play, Clara Burnham has arrived in Newfoundland with her friends and is sheltering in a cave. Wardour rushes in, a maniac, starving, and in extremis. He is accused of murdering Aldersley but fights his way out of the cave and returns, soon after, with a famished, weak, but living Aldersley in his arms. Wardour's strength fails at the end of the play, and he dies at Clara's feet.

There were three notable opening nights of *The Frozen Deep*. The first occurred on January 5, 1857, when what might be called a dress rehearsal was performed at Tavistock House. The second was a benefit performance which played before a royal audience on July 4 of the same year. The third was a performance at the 1000-seat Free Trade Hall in Manchester.

For the Tavistock House production, Dickens had enlisted his family and friends to act. His son Charley played Lieutenant Steventon and his daughters Mary and Kate played two of the female roles. Wilkie Collins enacted the role of Aldersley. Dickens was obsessed with the part of Wardour. His suggested alterations had transformed the character from a villain (as he had been portrayed in early drafts) to a hero. In preparation for the opening, he wandered through the countryside, reciting the part aloud. His son Charley later recalled Dickens' frenzied portrayal of Wardour in rehearsals:

> In his demented condition in the last act he had to rush off the stage, and I and three or four others had to try and stop him. He gave us fair notice, early in the rehearsals, that he meant fighting in earnest in that particular scene, and we very soon found out that the warning was not an idle one. He went at it after a while with such a will that we really did have to fight, like prize fighters, and as for me, being the leader of the attacking party and bearing the first brunt of the fray, I was tossed in all directions and had been black and blue two or three times before the first night of the performance arrived.[4]

Charles Dickens (Wikimedia Commons).

Dickens managed to sustain that physical exuberance and high emotion in performances at Tavistock House and elsewhere.

The first performances at Tavistock House took place in a converted school room in the house, with the windows removed and a stage added. Dickens called it "the tiniest theatre in the world"; it held about 90 spectators. The opening night audience consisted of servants and tradespeople. Four more performances, in early January, played to Dickens' influential friends, including judges and members of parliament. Several reviewers attended the Tavistock production and admired Dickens' performance. John Oxenford wrote that Dickens' appeal "to the imagination of the audience, which conveyed the sense of Wardour's complex and powerful inner life, suggests the support of some strong irrational force."[5]

It was clear, after five performances, that Dickens was not finished with the play. When his friend Douglas Jerrold, best known for his nautical melodrama *Black-Eyed Susan*, died unexpectedly on June 7, 1857, Dickens decided to revive *The Frozen Deep* in benefit performances for Jerrold's wife and children. While Tavistock House was too small for a fundraiser of this sort, the Royal Gallery of Illustration on Regent Street was somewhat more apt. Originally built as a private art gallery, the Royal Gallery had been remodeled to house dioramas and musical entertainments. The stage was not large, and the gallery (where the audience sat) was long and narrow.[6] On July 4, 1857, Dickens and his company performed *The Frozen Deep* at the Royal Gallery, to an audience that included the Queen, Prince Albert, and their children, as well as literary lions like William Thackeray and Hans Christian Andersen.

The performance was a resounding success. The Queen was particularly affected by the play. She asked for Dickens to be presented to her immediately after the July 4 performance, but Dickens refused to come out of his dressing room. "I could not appear before Her Majesty tired and hot," he said later, "with the paint still upon my face...."[7] The Queen forgave Dickens this small indiscretion. In her diary, afterwards, she wrote glowingly of the play and of Dickens' performance. Buoyed by his success, Dickens added three more performances at the Royal Gallery that July.

When it became apparent that not enough money had been raised to sustain Mrs. Jerrold and her children, Dickens arranged to give further performances of the play in the much larger Free Trade Hall in Manchester. Because the Free Trade Hall was expansive, Dickens grew concerned that the amateurs in the cast, including his own daughters, would not be capable of projecting their voices to the back row of the auditorium. He replaced them with professional actors, among them Ellen Ternan and her mother and sister.

The Ternans were a prominent theatrical family in the northern provinces. Ellen Ternan's father Thomas had at one time simultaneously managed both the Newcastle Theatre and the Doncaster Theatre. Ellen Ternan had made her stage debut in Sheffield when she was three years old, billed with her two sisters as the "infant phenomena." It is possible that Dickens had seen her perform at the Haymarket Theatre in London the year before they met. Ellen Ternan was 18 years old when she acted in *The Frozen Deep*, the same age as Dickens' daughter Kate. She was described in *The Era* as "a debutante with a pretty face and well-developed figure."[8] She and her mother Frances and her sister Maria first met Dickens during three days of intense rehearsals in London, before leaving by train for Manchester.

Even among professional actors, Dickens stood out in the Manchester production. Wilkie Collins later recalled that Dickens' performance "literally electrified the audience." After the run, Dickens congratulated himself on the emotional response he received. "It was a good thing to have a couple of thousand people all rigid and frozen together, in the palm of one's hand," he wrote, "...and to see the hardened Carpenters at the sides crying and trembling at it night after night."[9] Even Maria Ternan, who played Clara Burnham on those evenings, recalled shedding tears at Dickens' performance.

While Dickens' work on *The Frozen Deep* reframed the Franklin tragedy as one of unmitigated heroism, it also changed Dickens' life irrevocably, for he fell in love with young Ellen Ternan during the Manchester run of the play. "I have never known a moment's peace or content, since the last night of *The Frozen Deep*," he would later write to Wilkie Collins. "I do suppose that there never was a man so seized and rended by one spirit."[10]

A year after the closing of the play, Dickens did the unthinkable, flying in the face of Victorian morality. He left his wife and quite probably made Ellen Ternan his mistress. While divorcing his wife was out of the question, Dickens would later keep Ellen Ternan and her mother in a house in Condette, near Bologne, France, that he rented in the years between 1860 and 1864. As Peter Ackroyd writes, there has been much speculation about Dickens' life with Ellen Ternan during this period: "that they were unhappy lovers, that Ellen had had a child and was bringing it up secretly in Condette, that she had had a miscarriage or abortion, that the child had died."[11]

Ackroyd could find no conclusive evidence of a full-blown sexual affair or of a child who had been born out of the union. It is clear, however, that Ternan would accompany Dickens on his many junkets to other countries, only refraining from joining Dickens on a reading tour in America in 1867 for fear that the press might uncover their relationship. By that time, as Ackroyd writes, Dickens "could not bear the contemplation of such a long absence" from Ternan, and she "could not travel with so public a man in any compromising capacity."[12]

Ternan was with Dickens at the deadly Staplehurst rail crash—they were likely on their way to London from Condette—in the only first-class carriage that managed to stay on the tracks. Despite all obstacles, their relationship lasted 12 years. When Dickens died on June 8, 1870, he left Ellen Ternan with a thousand pounds, enough money for her to retire comfortably while she was still in her thirties. Six years after Dickens' death, Ellen Ternan married George Wharton Robertson, who was 12 years younger than she. Together they ran a boys' school in the seaside town of Margate on the south-east coast of England. Ternan died in 1914.

CHAPTER 21

First Knight

The Bells, *Lyceum Theatre, London, November 25, 1871*

On November 25, 1871, the actor Henry Irving was on his way home to Fulham after scoring a resounding success on the first night of *The Bells* at London's Lyceum Theatre. His spirits were high as he sat beside his wife of almost three years, Florence nee O'Callaghan Irving, and they traversed the foggy city. They had just attended the opening night party, where Irving had basked in the praise of his fellow actors. Florence had not enjoyed the party. "Eager to get home," writes Irving's biographer and grandson Laurence Irving, "she expressed nothing but a querulous anxiety that her husband might be boring the company."[1]

Three years earlier, Florence's family had been opposed to the idea of an engagement between their well-born daughter and a lowly actor. Her father, a former Master-at-Arms to William IV and then a Surgeon-General in India, "had come to a quick choleric boil and had forbidden all communication between the lovers."[2] It was almost as though his disapproval had pushed "a modest flirtation over the border into a grand passion."[3] The ill-matched couple had married on July 15, 1869. Like her imperious father, Florence had little respect for the acting profession and, on the evening of Irving's opening, she was probably tired. She was pregnant with their second child. She had not enjoyed the play or Irving's performance in it as the guilt-ridden Mathias.

Before he appeared in *The Bells*, Irving had had successes on the London stage but was still considered a minor actor. In 1867, Ellen Terry had acted with him in an adaptation of *The Taming of the Shrew* at the Queen's Theatre. She later remarked, of that time, "I never consciously thought he would become a great actor."[4] But the victorious opening night of *The Bells* had secured for Irving a place among the best actors working in England at the time, and he knew it. On the carriage ride home after the opening night, he placed his hand on his wife's arm and said, "Well, my dear, we too shall soon have our own carriage and pair!"

Florence was unable to share in her husband's exuberance. "Are you going on making a fool of yourself like this all your life?" she asked him. Irving did not reply. He stopped the carriage and climbed down to the cobblestones near Hyde Park Corner, walking off into the night. He did not return to the family home that evening or any evening after. Refusing to have anything to do with his wife or (for a protracted period) with his children, Irving made the theater his paramour.

The Bells, as it turned out, ran for 151 nights and made Irving a bona fide star of the London stage. He performed in the play on many occasions throughout his life. The set designer and theorist Edward Gordon Craig, who had little respect for actors in his later life, saw the play more than thirty times and declared that Irving's performance as Mathias demonstrated "the finest point the craft of acting could reach."[5] Irving performed the part of Mathias the night before he died of a stroke, on October 13, 1905, at the age of 67.

Written by Leopold David Lewis, the play was based on a French melodrama entitled *Le Juif Polonais* (1867) by Émile Erckmann and Alexandre Chatrian. It is set in an Alsatian village inn, the property of a burgomaster named Mathias, on Christmas Eve 1833. Mathias and his wife Catherine are particularly joyous, as the play begins, because their daughter Annette is about to be married to the handsome, brave, and honest Christian, quartermaster of the gendarmes. But an insidious guilt is eating away at Mathias for, on a Christmas Eve fifteen years earlier, he had murdered and robbed a Jewish seed merchant, disposing of his body in a lime kiln.

The big scene, the one that left the audience spellbound, occurs in the third act. Returning to his bedroom from the Christmas celebrations, Mathias readies himself for sleep. As he exits into a side room, the lighting changes and a dream sequence begins to play behind a scrim on the upstage wall. An entire court of law appears, and Mathias is escorted into the dock. He is charged with murder and, after a mesmerist hypnotizes him, Mathias reenacts the horrific crime. At the end of the courtroom scene, which is clearly a scene that has played itself over and again in Mathias' troubled mind, he is sentenced to be hanged. When the lights change and the courtroom disappears, Mathias rushes back into his bedroom, grasping at a nonexistent hangman's noose around his neck. As his alarmed family enters to help him, Mathias suffers a heart attack and dies. This twist ending, coupled with Irving's marvelous acting, helped to make the production a huge success.

On its opening night at the Lyceum, the play was presented to a sparse audience that was not impressed with its first two acts. The critic George R. Sims sat with the playwright that evening and noted that plenty of seats in the stalls were vacant. "The play left the first-nighters a little dazed," he wrote. "Old fashioned playgoers did not know what to make of it."[6] After the fantastic dream sequence in Act Three, according to Sims, the Lyceum spectators were at first dumbfounded and then moved to rapturous applause. "But when the final curtain fell," he wrote, "the audience, after a gasp or two, realized they had witnessed the most masterly form of tragic acting that the British stage had seen for many a long day, and there was a storm of cheers." For his part, Irving milked the applause by playing the character's remorse right into the curtain call. Sims described the scene. "Then, still pale, still haggard, still haunted, as it were, by the terror he had so perfectly counterfeited, the actor came forward with the sort of smile that did not destroy the character of the Burgomaster or dispel the illusion of the stage." Ever the showman, Irving rode that wave of applause into the history books. He'd probably learned a thing or two about making a curtain call during his apprenticeship in the provinces.

Nothing in Irving's early years suggested that he would become a world-famous actor. He was born John Henry Brodribb at Keinton Mandeville in Somerset, the son of a commercial traveler. During his few years of formal education, he competed in an elocution contest but came in second to a child named William Curnow (who later became editor of the *Sydney Morning Herald*).[7] Irving was apprenticing in a law firm when, at the age of 13, he saw Samuel Phelps, who by then was actor-manager at the Sadler's Wells Theatre, perform Hamlet on stage and was inspired to become an actor. Phelps had become especially well-known for restoring Shakespearean production to the original texts in the first folio and dispensing with the adaptations of Colley Cibber, Nahum Tate, and others.

After seeing Phelps perform, Irving took acting lessons, got letters of introduction, and ended up working, under the pseudonym Henry Irving, at a theater in Sunderland. When Irving was booed off the boards after a bout of stage fright, early in his career, the established

Henry Irving (Wikimedia Commons).

actor Samuel Johnson offered moral support. For the next ten years, Irving worked in various stock companies in Northern England and Scotland. By 1866, he was acting and sometimes directing in London, at Ruth Herbert's St. James Theatre. It was not until he performed Mathias in *The Bells*, and began his long association with the Lyceum, that Irving distinguished himself from the pack of leading men then working in London.

Irving took full responsibility for the management of the Lyceum Theatre in 1878, entering into a stage partnership with Ellen Terry at the same time. As his reputation as an actor grew, so did his reputation as a director. His productions were known for meticulous attention to detail. When gas lighting gave way to electricity in the 1890s, Irving was among the first to experiment with color-tinted and directional lighting effects. He was also among the first to dim the lights in the auditorium as the stage curtain was drawn, which had not been a standard practice in the era of gas and limelight. Irving became lifelong friends with his stage manager and biographer Bram Stoker, who wrote glowingly of Irving's expertise with lights: "The part most noteworthy, and which came from Henry Irving's incomparable brain and imagination, was the production of effect."[8] It is likely that Irving was the model for Stoker's Count Dracula in the celebrated novel, so closely did the character resemble Irving and so greatly did Stoker admire the actor-manager.[9]

By all accounts, Irving was intensely loyal to friends and former colleagues who had helped him early in his career as an actor. As his fame grew at the Lyceum, he regularly hired the actors with whom he had worked in the provinces, including Samuel Johnson. His relationship with Ellen Terry, which was likely romantic as well as professional, also survived the entire period of his long career. She was Ophelia to his Hamlet and Portia to his celebrated Shylock. When her illegitimate son Teddy (whose father was the architect-designer Edward William Godwin) was in his early twenties, Irving hired the young man to play Hamlet at the Lyceum. Terry herself left the Lyceum company voluntarily in the late 1890s when it became apparent that, as she grew older, there were fewer and fewer roles for her to play. Irving was even loyal, in a fashion, to fellow actor Richard Archer Prince who had murdered William Terriss at the stage door of the Adelphi Theatre and who had issued death threats against Irving from his room at the Broadmoor Criminal Lunatic Asylum. Irving did not press charges and refused to submit a letter to the Home Office demanding Prince's continued incarceration, although he was advised to do so.

Acting had been a disreputable profession in England before Irving's time, although earlier actors like David Garrick and Sarah Siddons had done much to elevate the profession at the end of the 18th century. The profession was equated with poor moral hygiene, with lying and hypocrisy. In northern England, landowners were warned to take their clothing off the clotheslines when travelling troupes of actors came to town. In some boroughs, actors could not be buried in consecrated ground until the end of the 18th century. Actresses were especially maligned. How could they be expected to satisfy Victorian codes of purity and morality when it was well known that they shared dressing rooms with the men in their company? Furthermore, there were no accredited acting schools in the first half of the 19th century that would give credibility to the unhappy profession. In Irving's day, actors commonly learned their profession by apprenticing to a mentor and moving up through the ranks as they proved themselves. The era of RADA and acting programs at universities was in the future.

Henry Irving was instrumental in changing all that. Accolades were heaped upon the celebrated actor in later life. He received honorary degrees from the universities of Dublin (1892), Cambridge (1898), and Edinburgh (1899). He frequently toured the United States and Canada with his acting company, treating North America to the best in British theater. More importantly, Irving received the first theatrical knighthood in 1895.[10] It might be argued that the man who walked off into that crisp evening in 1871 had helped to transform the actor's lot from a debased existence to a respectable one. Max Beerbohm labeled Irving "the Knight from Nowhere," simultaneously insulting the actor and his hometown in Somerset.

Irving's family prospered, as well. He eventually reconciled with his children and helped their careers as best he could. His elder son, Henry Brodribb Irving, became an actor of note. His younger son, Laurence Irving, was a dramatist.[11] When Henry Irving was knighted, his long-estranged wife Florence insisted upon being called Lady Irving. Her husband had never divorced her, after all, and he had never remarried.

CHAPTER 22

The Meininger

Julius Caesar, *Friedrich Wilhelm Municipal Theatre, Berlin, May 1, 1874*

On May 1, 1874, the Meiningen Ensemble presented Shakespeare's *Julius Caesar* at the Friedrich Wilhelm Municipal Theatre in Berlin. It was the company's first major foray out of its own tiny duchy, and the choice of play was controversial. Shakespeare's work had fallen out of favor amidst the rising tide of nationalism in Germany. Richard Wagner's wife Cosima had written in her diary, only six weeks earlier, that "a veritable school has risen against Shakespeare."[1] The Meiningen Ensemble had made a questionable choice of play, and they eventually landed at the center of another kind of controversy, a foray into which the Crown Prince Friedrich Wilhelm III soon waded.

Georg II, Duke of Saxe-Meiningen, was no stranger to controversy. In opposition to his own father, Bernard II, he had sided with Prussia during the Seven Weeks' War. When Austria was defeated in 1866, Bernard II was forced to abdicate, and Georg took control of the duchy. Unceremoniously removed from power, Bernard spent the rest of his life as a private citizen while his only son ruled the Duchy. Later, during the Austro-Prussian War, Georg performed well as a soldier, leading two regiments from Meiningen and fighting in nearly every battle. Through his loyalty and prowess, he became a trusted friend of the Emperor Wilhelm I and would remain so until the Emperor's death in 1888.

Then there was the matter of Georg's marriages. He married Princess Charlotte of Prussia in 1850, and the couple had four children. Charlotte died in childbirth in 1855. He next married his second cousin Princess Feodora in 1858, but the marriage was unhappy. Feodora died in 1872 of scarlet fever. In 1873, when Georg entered into a morganatic marriage with the actress Ellen Franz, another storm of protest ensued. Georg's longtime friend and mentor Kaiser Wilhelm was angered by the marriage. The ex–Duke Bernard also opposed the union. Court officials resigned. The army refused to salute Georg's new wife, who was given the title "Baroness von Heldburg." Through all of this, Georg II and Ellen Franz demonstrated remarkable poise in the face of outrage and complaint. Ellen was well-loved by the commoners in the Duchy, and she remained at Georg's side until his death in 1914.[2]

The Duke of Saxe-Meiningen loved the theater, and he was good at producing plays. He commenced his theatrical career when he came to the helm of the duchy in 1866. He hired Ludwig Chronegk to play comic roles in the same year, soon elevating him to the position of company manager. In 1867, he hired Ellen Franz to play Juliet. While he accepted advice from both Chronegk and Franz (who often sat beside him in the theater during rehearsals), Georg took charge of almost every aspect of production, from the supervision of set and costume design to the specifics of actors' vocalizations and blocking. Building on the directorial reforms of Goethe, who had produced Schiller's plays with a steady hand in the heady days of Weimar Classicism, Georg wanted to create a true ensemble, with no star actors doing star turns. Like John Philip Kemble and Charles Kean, whose antiquarianism had brought a sense of historical accuracy to Shakespearean productions, Georg's overall aim was to create historical exactitude in the mise-en-scène through detailed research of set, costumes, and manners. His crowd scenes were especially lifelike at a time when most theaters hired supernumeraries at the stage door and gave them little direction. He would often gather people into small spaces to make the crowds look larger than they were, and he would divide the actors into status-based groupings. Although he did not create his productions in a theoretical vacuum, Georg's theatrical work was marked with a unity of vision that was largely unparalleled in his own country or anywhere else in Europe. With the success of his company, Georg II became widely known as the first theatrical director, in the modern sense, as the one person who oversees and controls set construction, lighting, sound, costumes, and acting.

The 1874 production of *Julius Caesar* offers evidence of Georg's attention to detail. He originally commissioned the painter Ernst Handel to create the sets, but he was unhappy with Handel's antiquated colorization. He then hired Richard Wagner's set designer Max Bruckner to repaint the sets and to make other corrections. Georg had specific ideas about how all five battle scenes in the last act might be played in a single setting. As Ann Marie Koller writes in her book *The Theater Duke,*

> He thought of the downstage area as the Plain of Philippi with a rocky height rising on stage right. In the middle of the stage was a gully over which arched a high bridge. Behind the gully, the terrain covered with the gravestones of long-dead Philippians ascended toward the towers and battlements of the besieged city lying on the heights. While Octavius and Antony with their armies

marched from stage right into the valley, Brutus and Cassius with their legions began a slow descent from the heights. The armies moved, fighting, to stage right.[3]

The typical busyness of Georg's settings is apparent in this description. As the battle ended and the curtain was about to fall, the audience was treated to "the chilling picture of the victorious commanders standing high on the bridge, lighted only by torches, looking down on their defeated enemy lying in the shadows."[4]

Also typical of the duke's approach was his casting of the actors. The three principal roles of Caesar, Cassius, and Brutus were played by actors who were relatively unknown. Joseph Nesper played Caesar, although he was much younger than most of the elderly character actors who were typically cast in the role during that period. Leopold Teller played Cassius, and Wilhelm Hellmuth-Bram was cast as Brutus. Only Mark Antony was played by a well-known actor—Ludwig Barnay, who had been recruited only a month or two before the show opened.

A reviewer for *Allgemeine Zeitung* admired the ensemble's singleness of purpose. "There is no movement, no placement, no step, no accent of the mood," the reviewer wrote, "that is not suited to the spiritual content of the scene...." He singled out the crowd scenes "which shattered the audience by their reality and pleased it at the same time by the beauty of the pictorial groups."[5] The largely unknown actors of the ensemble had accomplished what more prestigious companies could not: a unified vision of the play.

The theater was not filled to capacity on the second night of the run, but soon word-of-mouth and critical opinion spread. The critics were divided into two camps: those who admired the production, and those who felt that Georg's emphasis on set decoration degenerated the art form. Critic Hans Hopfen was most outspoken and vitriolic in his review of the production. He noted the director's obvious talent but criticized his filling of the stage with the "fripperies" of set design. "What then is the purpose of tragedy?" he asked. "To arouse pity and terror. When there is so much on the stage, then my pity is for the actors, and my terror for the degeneration of the art."[6] Berlin was alive with controversy over the production, and soon the Meiningen Ensemble was playing to sold out houses. As Ernst von Possart later wrote, "[E]ven political events receded into the background. For weeks the mighty city breathed the thoroughly artistic atmosphere originating in the grandiose Forum scenes and the exciting crowd scenes, which up to that time no one had even imagined."[7]

Even Crown Prince Friedrich Wilhelm was swept up in the glory of the production. A day after seeing the Meiningers' work, he penned a sharply worded letter to the General Intendant at the Koniglisches

Schauspielhaus. Since the Schauspielhaus had better financial resources than the Meiningers, he argued, "it should be able to provide better scenery and costumes than that provincial theater."[8] The Intendant, Count Botho von Hulsen, replied that the Meiningen company did not know the ABCs of costuming. Friedrich Wilhelm's letter, and his criticisms of von Hulsen, eventually started a turf war. Blaming the duke for this sudden attack on his theater's artistry, von Hulsen resolved to fight the Meiningers on his own turf when they next appeared in Berlin. A year later, when Georg announced that he would bring a production of Kleist's *Die Hermansschlacht* to the capital, von Hulsen rushed his own production of the play on to the boards of the Schauspielhaus before the Meininger could arrive.

By that time, however, the Meininger had made its mark as one of the most accomplished and prestigious theater companies in the world. Ludwig Barnay, the actor who played Antony, remarked that Lord Byron's famous statement could have been applied to him after the first performance of *Julius Caesar*: "I awoke one morning to find myself famous."[9] Barnay and the entire company became famous for its ensemble approach and its attention to detail, and their reputation grew in subsequent years. Georg mounted ever more elaborate yearly tours, playing largely in Germany, Austria, and Hungary between 1874 and 1878. The company toured to Prague in 1879 and to Amsterdam in 1880. They had a residency at Drury Lane in London in 1882, and they toured to Brussels in 1888. Nemirovich-Danchenko saw them when they toured to Russia in 1885, and Stanislavsky was in the audience when they returned to Moscow in 1890.

Although Georg II was most well-known for his work on Shakespeare's tragedies, he was also interested in producing the work of his contemporaries. His early interest in Ibsen led to an 1876 production of *The Pretenders* which did not garner entirely positive reviews but which Ibsen himself admired. Ibsen saw the production while it was on tour in Berlin. "At the beginning of the month I went to Berlin to be present at the first performance of *The Pretenders*, which was splendidly staged by the Court Theatrical Company of the Duke of Meiningen," he wrote to his friend and fellow dramatist Ludwig Josephson. "The play was received with great applause and I was called before the curtain several times."[10] As Ann Marie Koller writes, "The play provided the Meininger an opportunity to display the specialties for which they had become famous: artistic grouping and moving of crowd, realistic battle scenes, effective off-stage sounds, all rehearsed to perfection and employed with taste and imagination."[11]

Georg's work also influenced other luminaries of the realist and naturalist movements. André Antoine, an innovator in the naturalist movement, was influenced by Georg's productions. Antoine saw the Meiningen

Ensemble when they toured to Brussels in 1888 with *The Winter's Tale* and *Wilhelm Tell*, the year after he founded Théâtre Libre. He later adopted some of Georg's directing techniques, particularly those techniques associated with the creation of crowd scenes on stage. "They showed us things absolutely new and very constructive," Antoine wrote to critic Francisque Sarcey. "Their crowds are not like ours, composed of elements picked haphazard, working-men hired for dress rehearsals, badly clothed and accustomed to wearing strange and uncomfortable costumes...."[12] Like Antoine, Konstantin Stanislavsky fell under the spell of Georg's work. After viewing the Meininger in Moscow in 1890, he commented "that, for the first time, Moscow had seen historically real productions, well-directed mob scenes, fine outer form, and amazing discipline."[13] Particularly thrilled with the way in which the Meiningen Players got to the thematic heart of each play they produced, Stanislavsky adopted some of Ludwig Chronegk's rehearsal methods but was also critical of Chronegk's "despotic" style. "Only with time, as I began to understand the wrongness of the principle of the director's despotism," Stanislavsky later wrote, "I valued the good that the Meiningen Players brought us, that is, their director's method for showing the spiritual contents of the drama."[14] Georg's work on classical and contemporary dramas made him not only an important purveyor of unity and historical specificity in the work of Shakespeare but also an influential presence in the development of the realist and naturalist movements.

CHAPTER 23

Genius or Madman?

The Ring of Nibelung, *Bayreuth Festspielhaus, Germany, August 13, 1876*

On August 13, 1876, when the Bayreuth Festspielhaus officially opened for the premiere of Richard Wagner's four-opera cycle *The Ring of Nibelung*, both the theater and the operas had been years in the making. The event was attended by a who's who of domestic and foreign leaders as well as many of the leading composers of the day. Kaiser Wilhelm I was there, as was King Ludwig II, Emperor Dom Pedro II of Brazil, the King of Wurttemburg, the Grand Duke of Saxony-Weimar, Grand Duke Vladimir of Russia, and an assortment of princes, princesses, counts, and countesses. Anton Bruckner, Edvard Grieg, Peter Tchaikovsky, and Franz Liszt were also in attendance. Karl Marx, who had denounced Bayreuth as a "Fool's Festival of the State Musician, Wagner," was notably absent.[1] Even though Marx did not deign to attend, one thing was clear: few cultural events, inside Germany or out of it, had ever aroused as much enthusiasm among operagoers.

The sheer pomposity of the undertaking had attracted a great deal of attention in previous years. Some critics had derided the proposed festival and its 15-hour *Ring* cycle as an act of vanity, verging on insanity. Theodor Puschmann, a Munich psychiatrist, had published a treatise in 1872 in which he made the claim that Wagner was clinically insane. In *Richard Wagner: eine psychiatrische studie,* he argued that Wagner's conditions included "chronic megalomania, paranoia, ambiguous ideas, and moral derangement."[2] Others, including Wagner's patron King Ludwig II of Bavaria, regarded him as an unparalleled genius. King Ludwig had stood by Wagner through many of the years leading up to the opening, expressing amazement at Wagner's talents and, more importantly, donating money. In the years since the opening, others have celebrated Wagner's genius. His biographer Ernst Newman wrote, a half century later, that Wagner was "a far better conductor than any of his conductors, a far better actor than any of his actors, a far better singer than any of his singers in everything but tone."[3]

It took Wagner 16 years to complete the Ring cycle, so ambitious was the project. The cycle consisted of four operas: *Das Rheingold* (*The Rhine Gold*); *Die Walkure* (*The Valkyries*), *Siegfried*, and *Götterdämmerung* (*Twilight of the Gods*). Begun in 1848 and not completed until 1874, the cycle's plot is long and complicated. It revolves around a magic ring that grants its owner the power to rule the world. The dwarf Alberich steals the ring from the Rhine maidens, and the ruler of the gods, Wotan, in turn steals the ring from Alberich. Wotan is later forced to surrender the ring to the giants Fafner and Fasolt, to pay them for building Valhalla. Siegfried, Wotan's mortal grandson, eventually kills Fafner and wins the ring, but he is betrayed by Alberich's son. The Valkyrie Brunnhilde, who is also Siegfried's lover and Wotan's daughter, gains possession of the ring. After returning the ring to the Rhine maidens, she commits suicide. The gods are defeated, and Valhalla is destroyed.

The musical orchestration is equally as complex as the story. Wagner wanted an opera free of arias and choruses, wherein the music interpreted the emotional elements of the storyline. He solved the problem of dealing with a large cast of characters by writing leitmotifs to introduce many of them. In performance, a larger than normal orchestra is required to play a variety of instruments, some of them out of the ordinary. Anvils, tam tams, Wagner tubas, and steer horns are played during the cycle. The music is beautiful and powerful.

Wagner needed a concert hall in which to perform his masterpiece, and he envisioned something far from the bustle of a major city and far from the ostentation of other opera houses. By the time Wagner began writing his Ring cycle, German opera houses had become a setting where the rich and aristocratic came to see and be seen. Patrons rented boxes near the stage so they could swan about in their expensive clothing. Listening to the music was a low priority for the rich and famous. Wagner had also grown tired of impresarios who mounted productions merely to gain a financial windfall, with little concern for music or musicians. Frederic Spotts expresses the problem succinctly in his book *Bayreuth: A History of the Wagner Festival*:

> In Wagner's view the core problem was money. That, not art, was what animated impresarios. To them opera was a business and the objective was profit, not musical excellence. But audiences were also at fault. They regarded opera as an evening's light entertainment and a means of flaunting their social status.[4]

Wagner viewed music as a means of redeeming society, and he wanted it to be taken seriously. He insisted that his ideal opera house, if it were to be built, would be located in a remote area, somewhere out of reach of the grating sounds and odors of industrialization. In a letter to Franz Liszt, he wrote that his Ring cycle needed to be performed in a quiet place, away from "the smoke and disgusting industrial smell of our urban civilization."[5] Initially, Wagner had his heart set on a meadow near Zurich, but his patron King Ludwig had other ideas. Ludwig hired the architect Gottfried Semper to design an edifice that might be situated in Munich. When Wagner resisted the idea, the two finally settled on a site in the small provincial town of Bayreuth, where a theater roughly based on Semper's design was eventually built.

Money became an issue. Against the better judgment of his courtiers, King Ludwig became a major financial contributor to the project. Wagner was also forced to find financial backing elsewhere, securing a donation of 900 thaler from Sultan Abdulaziz of the Ottoman Empire. He also embarked on ceaseless concert tours to help pay for the project. These tours, and the grind associated with them, would eventually have a detrimental effect on Wagner's health.

Although Wagner had been speaking and writing about building his own theater since the 1840s, he did not have the pleasure of laying the foundation stone until May 22, 1872. It was a rainy day and also Wagner's 59th birthday. The band played Wagner's "March of Homage" to King Ludwig, and then the stone was lowered into place. Wagner tapped the stone three times with a hammer, intoning, "Be blessed, my stone, endure for long and be steadfast."[6] The theater was finally completed in 1876. In keeping with Wagner's desire for a "classless" space, the auditorium had thirty rows of stepped seating, rising toward the back of the house. There was a small box at the rear of the theater, intended originally for Wagner and his friends, and a balcony above it, seating about 300 people. The orchestra pit was partially hidden under the stage, and on the stage was a double proscenium arch, meant to represent a "mystic chasm" between the reality of the audience and the ideal world of the play.[7]

The initial round of rehearsals began on July 1, 1875, with individual singers and piano accompaniment. Wagner used these rehearsals to coach individual cast members. Two of his tenors, Albert Niemann and Georg Unger, became problematic during these early rehearsals, because both of them wanted to play Siegfried. Niemann began to sulk when he was cast instead as Siegmund, and Unger had to take full-time voice lessons to meet the vocal demands attached to the character of Siegfried. On August 2, the orchestra arrived and played for the first time. Wagner had decided to use the best musicians from various opera houses rather than hiring an established orchestra. The rehearsals proceeded for 12 days after that, with Wagner seated on the stage at a small table, following the score and sometimes singing along with the cast members.

Rehearsals resumed, with a second round, the following spring, even before the construction of the Festspielhaus was completed. As Frederic Spotts writes, several scenes were particularly challenging to stage. The first was the opening scene of *Das Rheingold*, in which the Rhine Maidens are intended to be swimming. For this effect, Carl Brandt designed a contraption that suspended the maidens in mid-air while stagehands swung them about at the end of ropes to which they were tethered. The three singers who played the Rhine Maidens at first refused to use the perilous machinery, but they were eventually persuaded that the contraption was safe. The Ride of the Valkyries presented similar problems. The effect was eventually created by drawing images on glass slides and projecting them on to the stage by means of a magic lantern. And the dragon in *Siegfried* had been manufactured in London. It arrived in sections, as Spotts writes, "tail first and head last—its neck was lost in transit, apparently misdirected to Beirut—and the unfortunate monster aroused more pity than fright!"[8]

King Ludwig was invited to attend a preview of *Das Rheingold*. Although he was initially loath to attend with a full audience, Ludwig was thrilled with the new theater and with the first opera of Wagner's cycle. He wrote Wagner a complimentary letter after seeing the preview and then returned at opening to watch the rest of the cycle. "You are a god-man," he wrote to Wagner afterwards, "the true artist by God's grace who has brought the sacred fire from heaven to earth to cleanse, sanctify and redeem it!"[9]

The opening night did not go as planned or even as well as the preview had gone. Scene changes were botched. The prop ring was misplaced. Brandt could be heard, even out in the auditorium, yelling at the stagehands. Wagner was disconsolate. He sat in his office after the show and moped, even as the audience was calling for him during the final bows. While Wagner was unhappy, there were differing opinions among the spectators. After seeing the entire cycle, Grieg argued that the operas were all "divinely composed and to pick out any one passage at random is to pick out a pearl."[10]

Others were not so complimentary about Wagner's proposed new genre of music drama. "It is no opera at all," the reviewer for *The Times* opined. "It is a play, the speeches in which are declaimed rather than sung, to orchestral accompaniment...." Eduard Hanslick wrote in *Neue Freie Press* that Wagner's *Ring* would "not be the music of the future."[11] As Oscar Brockett maintains, Wagner's limitations were evident at the Bayreuth opening. Despite his anti-realistic theorizing, it became apparent in production that Wagner was aiming for illusionism. Visually, writes Brockett, the productions at Bayreuth "differed little from those seen elsewhere."[12]

After the opening of his masterwork in his grand new theater, Wagner fell into a prolonged depression. For all his years of work, he felt that he had created little more than a pedestrian piece of theater. The production had lost money, and Wagner quickly abandoned his plan to restrict the *Ring* cycle to performances in Bayreuth only; he released the cycle for general performances, and then absconded with his family to Italy. A few years later, he would write to King Ludwig, stating that he "had given birth only to a very ordinary child of the theatre; he had constructed nothing more than an empty vessel."[13]

Wagner passed away on February 13, 1883, less than seven years after the Bayreuth Festival opened. He was convinced, in his final years, that no one would succeed him and that the festival would die. A hundred and fifty years later, though, both the Festspielhaus and the Ring cycle are still going strong, although locals sometimes deride the building "as having the charm of an Oktoberfest beer tent and the elegance of a railway station."[14] And while Wagner did not live up to all of his theoretical anti-realist statements, his work did have a profound effect on the anti-realists who followed, including such luminaries in stage design as Adolphe Appia. Although Appia never met Wagner and never worked at Bayreuth, he was drawn to the man and his style of theater. In 1895, Appia wrote *The Staging of Wagnerian Drama*, and his best-known scenic designs were of Wagner's operas. As George R. Kernodle writes, Appia viewed his work "as completing the work of Wagner," especially as Wagner had never really found a staging that would suit the idealized realm of Teutonic myth.[15]

Political Theater

Sometimes in the theater, politics and storytelling collide. The results can be electrifying, shifting the spectators' perspective on a current issue in new and exciting ways. The results can also be acrimonious, angering political figures of the day, and creating problems for playwrights, producers, and actors. The following section deals with three evenings in the theater that challenged the political status quo.

Bertolt Brecht's play *The Threepenny Opera*, when it opened in Berlin in 1928, was a departure from the realistic and expressionistic fare that was common in theaters of the day. Brecht was a disciple of Erwin Piscator in his quest for a "political, confrontational, documentary" theater. Brecht wished to alienate the audience from the onstage spectacle and the actor from the role he or she was playing, to make spectators think rather than feel. Furthermore, he was a Marxist who would go on to write controversial plays like *The Resistible Rise of Arturo Ui* and *The Caucasian Chalk Circle*. Like his composer Kurt Weill, Brecht fled Nazi Germany in the 1930s. He settled in the United States for some time but was brought before the House Un-American Activities Committee (HUAC) for questioning. Leaving the United States on October 31, 1947, the day after his HUAC appearance, Brecht returned to Europe, eventually landing in Soviet-controlled East Berlin, where he would spend the remainder of his life. He died there in 1956.

Peter Weiss, who began his playwriting career just as Brecht's was winding down, was a disciple of Antonin Artaud. In his books *The Theatre of Cruelty* and *Theatre and Its Double*, Artaud espoused a gritty form of theater that "can be used to subvert thought and logic and to shock the spectator into seeing the baseness of his world." In *Marat/Sade*, Weiss exploited violence and nudity to achieve these ends. At the finish of Peter Brooks' celebrated production of the play, cast members mimicked the audience by clapping rhythmically during the curtain call. That one act silenced the crowd and demonstrated the cast's derision of its bourgeois audience.

When Tomoyoshi Murayama opened an experimental production based on the Korean tale of Ch'unhyang in 1938, he was probably unaware that his work would lead to colonial discord. The production was greeted with great enthusiasm in its initial Japanese tour. Audiences were enthralled by the charming story and by the inclusion of what one critic calls "colonial kitsch." When the production toured Korea, however, critics mocked and derided it. They didn't like the costumes or the mannerisms of the actors, and they certainly did not like the fact that the play's iconic male hero was played by a woman.

CHAPTER 24

Threepenny

The Threepenny Opera, *Theatre am Schiffbauerdamm, Berlin, August 31, 1928*

The Threepenny Opera opened at the Theatre am Schiffbauerdamm in Berlin on August 31, 1928. It had been Bertolt Brecht's idea to adapt John Gay's folk opera as a modern critique on capitalism. He and his collaborator Kurt Weill had spent a summer in the south of France, working on the play (according to Weill's wife, the actress Lotte Lenya) "like crazy, writing, changing, tossing, writing anew, taking a break only to walk down to the sea for a few minutes."[1] In the end, Brecht came up with a script that was considered, by at least one reviewer, a "mish mash" of styles and genres, and Weill produced a musical score that seemed at odds with the action of the play, somewhere between jazz and popular music.[2] In its first iteration, the play was not entirely popular. Even on opening night, according to another of Brecht's collaborators Elizabeth Hauptmann, "the audience was peeved." According to Philip Glahn, "Brecht's idea of having the viewer observe the re-arrangement of the set between acts was in particular met with scepticism and irritation."[3] The critics were no less antagonistic. Glahn quotes the critic for *Neuen Preußsiche Kreuz-Zeitung*, who wrote, "The whole thing is best described as literary necrophilia, the only remarkable thing the insignificance of the object it was committed on."[4]

Based on John Gay's *The Beggar's Opera*, Brecht and Weill's play relates the story of a charismatic criminal named Macheath, sometimes called Mack the Knife, as he indulges in criminal activity, charms women, and evades the police and capital punishment. Gay had written his 1728 opera as a satire, in part, on fashionable London's obsession with Italian opera. While setting their play in 19th-century London, Brecht and Weill managed to throw in various references to the Berlin underworld of the 1920s.

Ten days before *The Threepenny Opera* premiered, Weill wrote his publisher about the quality of the play's music. "I think I've written a good

143

Original poster for *The Threepenny Opera* (Wikimedia Commons).

piece," he said, "and that several numbers in it, at least musically, have the best prospects for becoming popular very quickly."[5] Weill's score for the play would eventually prove to be one of his most successful compositions. In 1959, Bobby Darin took Weill's opening song for the play, jazzed it up, and created one of the biggest pop hits of all time with his rendition of

"Mack the Knife." The lyrics of the song might be read as an allegory of the inner workings of a capitalist society where the Wolves of Wall Street keep their knives sharpened but concealed. Glahn quotes the first four lines of Weill's song as proof of this: "Oh, the shark has pretty teeth, dear/ And he shows them pearly white/ Just a jack knife has Macheath, dear/ But he keeps it out of sight."[6]

Born in 1898, Eugen Berthold Friedrich Brecht was studying medicine at Munich University when an interest in theater led him to become a newspaper critic instead of a doctor. He wrote his first full-length play *Baal* in 1918 and his second play *Drums in the Night* in 1919. In the 1920s, he became a disciple of Karl Marx, seeking to inject Marxist theory into his own work. In 1924, he moved to Berlin, working as an assistant to Max Reinhardt at the Deutsches Theatre. In 1927, he joined Erwin Piscator's dramaturgical committee, which was tasked with finding new plays in its quest to build an "epic, political, confrontational, documentary theatre." Piscator was interested in man as a social animal. "For us, man portrayed on the stage is significant as a social function," Piscator wrote. "It is not his relationship to himself, nor his relationship to God, but his relationship to society which is central."[7] Brecht adopted Piscator's theories whole-heartedly, later re-enunciating them in his own essay "The Modern Theatre Is an Epic Theatre." In Brecht's iteration, epic theater would ask the question, "Why pretend that we are not pretending?"

Brecht's theories of an epic theater were based on the innovations of others. From the Expressionists, he inherited a writing style—their brief, seemingly disconnected scenes, abstract settings, and characters based on type. From Piscator, he learned how to deal with social phenomena on the stage. Eventually, Brecht developed the notion of a dialectical theater, a theater that coolly examined social problems and sought solutions to those problems. He was fond of comparing his audience to spectators at a boxing match, smoking cigarettes and analyzing each of the boxers' strategies. He located major differences between traditional (or Aristotelian) theater and epic theater. Whereas Aristotelian theater is based on direct action, epic theater is based on narrative and storytelling. In Aristotelian theater, the audience becomes emotionally engaged in the play. In epic theater, the audience remains aloof, engaged intellectually but not emotionally. Aristotelian theater offers suspense about the outcome whereas epic theater offers suspense about the process. Aristotelian theater unfolds in a linear fashion—beginning and middle and end—while epic theater unfolds in a series of episodic curves. The playwright seeks to absent himself in Aristotelian theater. In epic theater, the playwright is always present; he is the storyteller.[8]

"Alienation" becomes a key word in Brecht's articulation of epic theater. He writes of two types of alienation. The first type is referred to as

"*Entfremdung*," a word employed by Marx to describe man's internal alienation in a capitalist society. According to Marx, working men and women are forced to make an internal division; they are paid to provide their employers with their time and energy for eight or ten hours per day while the rest of their time is devoted to private goals and aspirations. *Entfremdung* becomes a theme in several of Brecht's plays.

The second type of alienation Brecht referred to as *Verfremdung* or the *Verfremdungs-effekt*. The word describes Brecht's efforts to alienate the audience from the onstage spectacle. He reinforced the audience's awareness that it was witnessing a theatrical spectacle by keeping the house lights on, by having the actors address the audience directly, by the use of lighting and signs and non-realistic sets, and so forth. Whereas music was utilized in Aristotelian plays to heighten emotion, Brecht often used music for the opposite effect—to make spectators stop feeling so they could think more clearly. *Verfremdung* extended to the acting, as well. Brecht was fond of comparing acting in one of his plays to witnessing and reporting a car accident out in the street. As the victim is being carted off in an ambulance, the actor is asked to relate the story of the accident, as clearly and efficiently as possible, as if to a police officer who is taking notes.

Brecht's Marxist thinking, and Weill's association with him, did not make the two men popular with Adolf Hitler. Fearing recrimination, incarceration, or worse, Brecht left Germany in 1933, moving first to Denmark, then to Sweden, then to Finland. In 1941, he and his wife Helene Weigel settled in the United States. Brecht became involved with several other German ex-pats in the Hollywood film community during the war years, co-writing the screenplay for Fritz Lang's *Hangmen Also Die!* While in the United States, he wrote some of his most famous plays, including *The Good Person of Sechuan*, *The Resistible Rise of Arturo Ui*, and *The Caucasian Chalk Circle*. Weill also fled Nazi Germany in 1933, fearing repercussions because of his Jewish heritage. He continued to be active as a composer, receiving the inaugural Tony Award for his musical score of Elmer Rice's play *Street Scene*. Weill moved to New York City in 1935, remaining in the United States until his death from a heart attack in 1950.

While Brecht's Marxist ideals did not make him popular in Hitler's Germany, they also did not make him popular in the United States, before or after the Second World War. His *Threepenny Opera* premiered on Broadway in 1933, received mixed reviews, and closed after 13 performances. When *Galileo* opened on Broadway in 1947, with Charles Laughton in the title role, the play ran for seven nights. *The Resistible Rise of Arturo Ui* was not given a Broadway production until 1963. It ran for only five nights. As J. Chris Westgate writes, "Not surprisingly, Broadway demonstrated confusion about and hostility toward epic theater during the 1930s and 1940s...."[9] Luckily, Brecht's plays have found a home in university drama departments across the United States and Canada since the early 1950s, and they continue to be produced in university settings in North America and elsewhere.

During the "red scare" years, Brecht was blacklisted by movie studio bosses in Hollywood. Called before the House Un-American Activities Committee (HUAC) on October 30, 1947, Brecht testified that he had never been a card-carrying member of the Communist Party. He made jokes, before the committee, about his lack of command with the English language. He was thanked for his cooperation. On October 31, the day after his HUAC appearance, Brecht left the United States and returned to Europe. He eventually landed in East Berlin, where he began work on the establishment of a new theater company called the Berliner Ensemble. Performing in the Theatre am Schiffbauerdamm, the Ensemble would soon become world famous for its experimental work in political theater. Brecht died of a heart attack on August 14, 1956, a year after receiving the Stalin Peace Prize. He was buried across from Hegel in Berlin's Dorotheen-städtischer Friedhof cemetery, under a gravestone that bore no epitaph. As Philip Glahn writes, Brecht had composed many epitaphs for himself during his lifetime, probably the best being "He made suggestions/We accepted them."[10]

Although it sometimes confused and irritated audiences and critics, *The Threepenny Opera* was Brecht and Weill's first major theatrical success, running for more than 400 performances in its original production. It was also one of the most important theatrical events that took place in Germany during the Weimar period. While not the fullest realization of Brecht's theories on epic theater, the play offered Brecht the opportunity to critique capitalism. "In an allegorical fashion," writes Philip Glahn, "Brecht displays how the struggle of the market and its Darwinian laws of survival are carefully hidden behind seemingly abstract bank transferrals, boardroom meetings and stock-market numbers...." In a London cobbled together from Brecht's reading of detective novels, Glahn continues, "The prostitutes and cripples are shown as victims of interrelated circumstances—industrialization, warfare, and modern forms of traffic as well as reparations and Weimar prosperity."[11] Paradoxically, while the success of the play made Brecht a star and gave him the financial prosperity to pursue other opportunities, he was "uneasy about its effects and continued working feverishly to develop what is now known as Epic Theatre."[12]

CHAPTER 25

Coughing and Sighs

The Song of the Chaste Wife, *Shinkyō Theater*
Company, Japan and Korea, March 1938

In March 1938, well-known Japanese playwright and theater director Tomoyoshi Murayama opened an experimental new production of a play based on the traditional Korean story *Ch'unhyang*, sometimes referred to in English as *The Song of the Chaste Wife*. Performed by his Shinkyō theater company, the production toured major centers in Japan, receiving rave reviews. When Murayama took the production to Korea, the reception was vastly different. In Seoul, for example, the production was openly derided, and Murayama was scorned as a cultural illiterate.

Japan was an imperial power in 1938; it had colonized Korea, Taiwan, Manchuria, and South Sakhalin. At the apex of its power, the Empire of Japan encompassed more than 20 percent of the world's population. Like most colonizers, Japan was eager to present itself as a benevolent master, bringing new ideas and technology to its more backward possessions. It reveled in the traditional cultures of its colonies and imported elements of those cultures back to Japan for public consumption. One can see the same colonizing strategy in almost every case of colonizing hegemony; many of the exhibits at the British Museum, for example, are artifacts from Britain's current or former colonies. The 1938 production of *Ch'unhyang* was viewed by its Japanese audiences as a charming example of Korean traditional theater, updated and made better by Japanese know-how.

Every Korean knows the story of Ch'unhyang. Nayoung Aimee Kwon sums it up admirably in her essay "Conflicting Nostalgia: Performing *The Tale of Ch'unhyang* in the Japanese Empire." *The Tale of Ch'unhyang* is the story of a young man from a wealthy family who falls in love with a girl of indeterminate social class. Her name is Ch'unhyang. Her father is an aristocrat, but her mother is of a lower class. The two lovers embark on a brief but passionate affair before they are separated by their families. Through a series of complications and trials, their love is tested, but Ch'unhyang

148

overcomes these tests "through steadfast adherence to her 'chastity,' or loyalty to her husband." The story ends happily with a dramatic reunion of the lovers.[1] Originally part of a song narrative tradition, the story is also known as *Ch'unhyang ka* (*The Song of Ch'unhyang*) in Korea.

If there was a theater director in Japan who might successfully produce a Japanese version of the story, it was Murayama. His theater experience was vast and far-reaching. He'd studied at Tokyo University and then at Humboldt University in Berlin, Germany. An avowed leftist, he was initially drawn to the proletarian theater movement of the 1920s. He'd alarmed Japanese authorities with his Marxist production of *Borokundanki* in 1929. The play was based on an historical incident during which Chinese communist labor union leaders had incited their workers to riot. Arrested as a threat to public peace in 1930, Murayama was released later that same year. He was an outspoken critic of Japanese militarism and an advocate for the down-trodden everywhere.[2] Murayama also had strong sympathies for the people of Korea and for Korean art. He'd undertaken two brief tours of Korea to acquaint himself with the people and customs of the land, although recent commentators have questioned just how much he'd learned during those tours.

Murayama had gone some distance towards arriving at a production of *Ch'unhyang* that had authenticity and a sense of "Koreanness." He'd hired a Korean ex-pat, the writer Chang Hyŏkchu, to translate the story into Japanese. Chang was himself a controversial figure back home in Korea. He had been born there in 1905 and had studied Japanese while in school. During Chang's formative years, the Japanese were involved in a program of erasing cultural difference in Korea. Korean-language journals and newspapers were censored and banned, and Korean citizens were encouraged to take Japanese names. Chang had bought into this program whole-heartedly; he moved to Japan when he became an adult and established himself as part of the *bundan* (literary establishment) there, achieving success as a writer both in Japanese and in Korean.

Once he had received Chang's translation of the play, Murayama set about altering the script to suit his own needs and tastes. He revised sections and added a scene, near the end, that was grafted from another version of the play, written by the playwright Yu Ch'ijin. He cut down the six acts of Chang's version of the play to five acts. In production, he introduced elements of Kabuki and modern theater techniques into the play, mixing in Korean traditions and color, as he understood them. Assessing his own work after the fact, Murayama wrote, "it was met with an extremely favorable critical response by many."[3] Because he had only a fleeting knowledge of Korean habits and customs, Murayama's introduction of local "traditions and color" into the play seemed quite shallow to Korean audiences.

While the performance was almost entirely in Japanese, Murayama used coughing and sighs as the recognizable marking of "Koreanness," as well as a few Korean words like "*ne*" ("yes") and "*aigo!*" (loosely translated as "oh my!").

Perhaps the most controversial alteration that Murayama made to the story was to have a cross-dressing female play the part of the aristocratic male hero. While at the outset this kind of gender-blind casting might be viewed as an avant-garde touch that was ahead of its time, it also made a racial statement about an iconic Korean hero. In justifying his casting, Murayama suggested that no Japanese actor in his troupe had the ability to assume the Korean grace and suppleness of the character. As Kwon later wrote, "What first appears to be a revolutionary experiment in queering gender constructions is tinged with racialist views that hark back to the imperial ideology of the time." By insisting that the suppleness and grace of a Korean male hero could only be replicated by a Japanese actress, Murayama persisted in stereotyping Korean males as "effeminized."[4] Kwon suggests that Korean audiences perceived Murayama's casting of the character as an act of colonization. It is not difficult to surmise, from Kwon's summation, why a Korean audience might have reacted to the production quite differently from Japanese audiences.

Performances in Korea were paired with roundtable discussions of the production, many of them carefully staged, as Kwon suggests, to "promote the appearance of harmonious exchange."[5] One particular round table discussion, and the one Kwon characterizes as an accurate reflection of Korean thinking about the play, took place in Seoul. A statement made at the beginning characterized the general tone of the discussion. "It is said the reception in Japan was quite good," one of the respondents offered, "but that does not mean the performance was indeed a success because what can the Japanese know or understand about *Ch'unhyang* in the first place?"[6] The round table then proceeded to poke fun at the production, at the costumes and hairstyles and mannerisms of the actors. There was much joking and laughter which Kwon interprets as irreverence toward the colonizing impulse. The object of the round table's jokes was Murayama, she suggests, and his obliviousness to Korean habits and customs. According to Kwon, the Korean critics treated Murayama's grand trans-national spectacle "as mere slapstick comedy."[7] While they were in no position to confront their Japanese overlords, the critics were able to undermine the imperial ideology through an irreverent attack on a Japanese attempt to appropriate their culture.

After 1945, when the Second World War ended and Japanese colonies were dispersed, Korea was at last freed of Japanese imperialism. When he came to be viewed as a traitor in his home country, Chang Hyŏkchu responded by becoming a naturalized Japanese citizen and taking his wife's surname. He wrote exclusively in Japanese from that time forward, publishing several books under the penname Noguchi Kakuchū, including *Forlorn Journey, Foreign Husband*, and *Poem in a Storm*. Chang died in Japan in 1997. The director of the production, Murayama, was twice imprisoned in Japan during the war years, eventually moving to Korea and then to Manchuko. Returning to Japan at the end of the war, he founded a new theater company and then restructured the company as the Tokyo Art Troup. Murayama died in 1977. The 1938 production of *Ch'unhyang* was largely submerged or forgotten in the years that followed, only to resurface when academics like Nayoung Aimee Kwon began to research the production seventy years later.

CHAPTER 26

Acid Test

*Marat/Sade, Aldwych Theatre,
London, August 20, 1964.*

Peter Brook directed three ground-breaking productions in one decade, all of them under the auspices of the Royal Shakespeare Company. The first of these was his 1962 production of *King Lear*, with Paul Scofield in the title role. The last was a bold interpretation of *A Midsummer Night's Dream*, which Brook directed in 1970. In between these two dates, Brook directed perhaps his most daring work, a production for the RSC that wasn't Shakespeare. In 1964, he collaborated with playwright Peter Weiss on a production of *The Persecution and Assassination of Marat as Performed by the Inmates of the Asylum of Charenton Under the Direction of the Marquis de Sade.*

Marat/Sade (the play's abbreviated title) was first produced in German at the Schiller Theatre in West Berlin on April 29, 1964, under the direction of Konrad Swinarski. Brook attended several of Swinarski's rehearsals and discussed the possibility of an English-language version of the play with Weiss. In August 1964, Brook directed the English-language version at the RSC's alternative home, the Aldwych Theatre in London. It was Brook's production that brought worldwide attention to the play and its author.

Peter Weiss had an interesting life and career, before and after writing *Marat/Sade*. Born in Germany to a Jewish father and a Christian mother, Weiss was 15 years old when his family emigrated to London in 1935. Through most of his early working life, Weiss was a painter in the surrealist tradition. He taught painting at the People's University in Stockholm and illustrated *The Book of One Thousand and One Nights* in its Swedish edition. He directed several short experimental films and one full-length feature entitled *Hagrigen (The Disappeared)*. Weiss began writing plays in the 1950s, but none of his early works was as successful as *Marat/Sade*. In the 1960s, Weiss' politics became increasingly left-wing and radical. He publicly supported Fidel Castro's communist government in Cuba and spoke vehemently against U.S. involvement in Vietnam. After suffering a heart attack in 1970, Weiss spent the next decade writing his three-part novel, *The Aesthetics of Resistance*, about European resistance against Nazi Germany.[1]

Peter Weiss (Dietbert Keßler; Wikimedia Commons).

Weiss' play about Marat and the Marquis de Sade was considered a radical departure from conventional theater when it first appeared on the London stage. Almost entirely a play-within-a-play, *Marat/Sade* is set in the historical Charenton Asylum, where inmates have been encouraged to perform a play, written by the Marquis de Sade, about the murder of Jean-Paul Marat. Most of the actors play inmates of the asylum. The hospital's director, Coulmier, supervises the performance and presents it to a bourgeois audience. As Robert Cohen suggests, the play has a historical basis; Sade was indeed an inmate in the Charenton Asylum in 1808, and his description of Robert-François Damiens' execution is based on authentic sources.

Although the play is set on July 13, 1808, several other dates and epochs enter into the picture. The murder of Marat took place 15 years earlier, in 1793. Weiss wrote the play in 1963, just as the long restorative period of the Federal Republic of Germany was coming to an end. Modern audiences receive the play in the present, resulting in a purposeful disorientation about time and place. "This complex and disorienting structure tends to subvert attempts at assigning *Marat/Sade* a stable meaning," writes Cohen, "and gives it the characteristics of a postmodern drama of playful arbitrariness and undecidability."[2]

Evident throughout Weiss' play is the influence of Bertolt Brecht. The alienating device of the play-within-a-play was one Brecht used on occasion. Similarly, the use of music in the play to interrupt the action with political commentary was a Brechtian tool for alienating the audience from the onstage action. While *Marat/Sade* is never as openly didactic as, for example, Brecht's *A Caucasian Chalk Circle*, at the center of Weiss' play is a dialectical discussion about Marxism and the hegemony of capitalism.

On one side of the debate is Sade, the cynical, aristocratic Marquis, who has sympathy "for the goals of the revolution, while his hatred of the old/ new elite is undiminished." On the other side is Coulmier, who "feels it necessary to come to the defense of Napoleonic society."[3]

In the middle of this dialectic is Marat who functions, as Cohen writes, as Sade's "other" in the debate. In the first act of the play, Marat tells Sade, "[Y]ou may have fought for us last September/ but you still talk like a nobleman." Marat does not share Sade's indifference. "I don't watch unmoved," he says. "I intervene."[4] As Cohen writes, Weiss himself vacillated between the positions of Sade and Marat in his political life but, "as a consequence of his own political evolution," increasingly favored Marat's more active stance toward revolution.[5]

More important, though, was Brook's use of Antonin Artaud's dramatic theory in his direction of the play. While Weiss later acknowledged the Artaudian nature of his play, he claims to have written it without consciously thinking of Artaud's theories:

> But I didn't think of Artaud when I wrote *Marat/Sade*, which grew out of its own material and had to be played in a certain way in the atmosphere which the material created. However, Peter Brook *was* thinking of Artaud before he produced *Marat/Sade*, and he used Artaudian techniques. This is a director's method, and for a writer it's secondary. When I speak about the audience reaction I want, I mean that if there are very strong events on stage, they shouldn't be acted in either a sadistic or a masochistic way, because either one makes it impossible to analyze the situation.[6]

Artaud, who had died in 1948, was an advocate of the Theatre of Cruelty. In his manifestos, *The Theatre of Cruelty* and *Theatre and Its Double*, Artaud espoused a theater that would become "a communion between actor and audience in a magic exorcism; gestures, sounds, unusual scenery, and lighting combine to form a language, superior to words, that can be used to subvert thought and logic and to shock the spectator into seeing the baseness of his world."[7] Artaud asserted that his theater could be identified "with a kind of severe moral purity which is not afraid to pay life the price it must be paid."[8] Brook's adherence to Artaud's doctrine can be seen in the shocking nudity of *Marat/Sade*, in the extreme violence of the inmates, and in the play's castigation of its bourgeois audience.

At the end of Brook's production, cast members clapped rhythmically in unison at the same time as the audience applauded, which had the effect of killing the applause and demonstrating the cast's derision for its bourgeois spectators. "Everything about this play is designed to crack the spectator on the jaw," Brook later wrote, "then douse him with ice-cold water, then force him to assess intelligently what has happened to him, then give him a kick in the balls, then bring him back to his senses again."[9]

Brook's production of *Marat/Sade* was a part of the *Theatre of Cruelty* season at the Royal Shakespeare Company, for which 12 young actors were hired to rehearse with Brook and Charles Marowitz, the American director who later founded the Open Space Theatre in London, for a period of 12 weeks and then to perform for the public in a five-week run beginning January 12, 1964. Actors began by devouring *The Theatre and Its Double.* There was much discussion about forms of madness and how these would manifest themselves in an era during which sedative drugs were not commonly used. The actors found inspiration in various Goya etchings and would use those etchings as a starting point for improvisations. As Amanda Di Ponio writes, the goal of the *Theatre of Cruelty* season was to initiate the actors in the theories of Artaud. She provides a list of the improvisational exercises, overseen by Brook and Marowitz, that were eventually turned into public performances:

1. Spurt of blood cries
2. Artaud scene
3. Spurt of blood
4. Typewriter
5. By Jove
6. Heathcliffe
7. Spine
8. Exercise
9. Public Bath
10. The Screens sc. 17
11. Letter from the Lord Chamberlain
12. Guillotine
13. Mime Scene
14. Hamlet

Artaud had called for a theatre that explored other, more penetrating means of communication than spoken language. "Training began by experimenting with sounds, working with an array of various objects to discover new resonances," writes Di Ponio. "Thereafter, movement was added, and both worked together to release non-naturalistic emotions through sound, first by working with objects-turned-instruments, and then through the development of the actor's own voice."[10] In the course of workshops and rehearsals, according to one of the actors, Robert Langdon Lloyd, they "experimented with other forms of communication besides words."[11] He recalls an exercise where two actors would each be given a box of matches and asked to communicate by rattling the boxes. "The extraordinary thing," he said, "was that there was complete agreement, rare, when we all witnessed that a true back and forth communication had taken place."[12] By the time *Marat-Sade* was in rehearsal, other actors than the original 12 were cast in major roles in the play.

The Aldwych production featured Patrick Magee as the Marquis de Sade, Ian Richardson as Jean-Paul Marat, and Glenda Jackson as Charlotte Corday. Langdon Lloyd played Jacques Roux. Brook encouraged his actors to immerse themselves in the behavior of the insane asylum as it was before 1808, asking them "to cultivate an act of possession."[13] On the first day of rehearsals, Brook announced to his assembled cast something to the effect of "what we are attempting here is impossible."[14] Michael Coveney wrote, later, about the shock value of Brook's production:

> The shock of seeing a stage full of catatonics, schizophrenics, paranoiacs and manic depressives was overwhelming: none, except Marat, could "remember" the script, so they needed constant prompting. Marat declaimed his speeches as if he were already dead. The music was clangorous and jagged, with cymbals, bells and an organ. The actors performed the songs in a Brechtian cabaret style, disrupting the play and banging on the set, pouring buckets of blood down the drains during the mass guillotining sequence.[15]

London audiences had seen nothing like it before. Some spectators walked out of the theater. Others were spellbound. As Coveney wrote, "It changed the lives of most people who saw it, including future innovative artists such as Mike Leigh and David Hare." One spectator died in the auditorium during a performance.[16]

The critics were divided in their opinions of Weiss' play and Brook's production, during its appearance on Broadway the following year. The critic for *The New Yorker*, Millie Painter-Downes, called the production "a dazzling theatrical experience." A *Newsweek* critic found the play pretentious: "Beneath all the business, all the violence and startling gestures, is a vacuum. Weiss, for all his pretentions, is a conventional socialist and an extremely limited philosopher." A reviewer for *Time* magazine labelled the play "inspired sensationalism."[17]

Peter Brook was not interested in what he called "the deadly theatre," in which mothballed plays are performed in accordance with what is traditional. "In the theatre, boredom, the slyest of devils, can appear at any moment," Brook wrote in *There Are No Secrets*. "The slightest things and he jumps on you, he's waiting and he's voracious."[18] Brook wanted a theater that made audiences think and feel. In his introduction to the published version of *Marat/Sade*, Brook wrote,

> I know of one acid test in the theatre. It is literally an acid test. When a performance is over, what remains? Fun can be forgotten, but powerful emotion also disappears and good arguments lose their thread. When emotion and argument are harnessed to a wish from the audience to see more clearly into itself— then something in the mind burns. The event scorches onto the memory an

outline, a taste, a trace, a smell—a picture. It is the play's central image that remains, its silhouette, and if the elements are rightly blended this silhouette will be its meaning, this shape will be the essence of what it has to say.[19]

Brook did not want comfortable laughter or sensationalized emotion in his work; he wanted to create theatrical images that scorched themselves on to the memory of his audience.

In 1970, after the success of his three groundbreaking productions, Peter Brook left England to work in Paris. With Micheline Rozan, he co-founded the International Centre for Theatre Research. The company, which eventually performed at the Théâtre des Bouffes du Nord in Paris, employed actors from many nations. At the Bouffes du Nord, Brook collaborated with French playwright Jean-Claude Carriere on productions of *Timon d'Athens* and *La Tempête*. Probably most famous was their production of *Mahabharata* in 1985, based on the Indian epic poem.

By the time he left England, Brook had made an indelible mark on British theater in general and on the Royal Shakespeare Company specifically. Known primarily for traditional productions of Shakespeare's plays until the 1960s when Peter Hall took over the reins of the company—and not for experimentation—the RSC became associated with groundbreaking productions of Shakespeare and modern playwrights, partly through Brook's influence. His work led the way for other directors to tackle risky projects. Without Peter Brook, we may not have witnessed later pieces of experimentation like Trevor Nunn's psychological examination of *Macbeth* in 1976 or his celebrated production of *Nicholas Nickleby*, co-directed with John Caird in 1980. For all Brook's other successes, however, *Marat/Sade* remains as the gold standard of theatrical experimentation in the experimental 1960s.

Reactions to War

Theatrical movements in the first half of the 20th century can be characterized by their attitudes toward one or both world wars. To some theatrical practitioners, the idea of a military battle, particularly as armies evolved to find increasingly impersonal ways of killing, was utter madness. To others, war was a calling that ensured the evolution of mankind in a world where only the fittest survive. To others still, war was evidence of the absurdity of human existence. Why were we born? So that we might die.

The futurists were ardent in their celebration of militarism, especially in the machine age. Their paradigm of manhood was the broad-shouldered, square-jawed youth, his eyes firmly set on the days to come. In mechanized war, the society with the best and the most powerful machines—tanks, ships, and airplanes—would prove itself the fittest. Not for the futurists were libraries and museums. Instead of classical drama, they preferred brief, fast-moving entertainments like those seen in music halls and cabarets. When the quarrelsome Filippo Tommaso Marinetti came along, he wrote plays and fought duels with regularity. He also fought in both world wars.

Max Ernst and the Dadaists took the opposite stance toward war. They detested military activity and thought of it as irrational. Since insanity seemed to be the true state of the world, they sought to portray insanity in their art. While the headquarters of the Dadaist movement had been in Zurich in the last years of the Great War, the most famous Dadaist exhibition took place in the courtyard of a Cologne pub in April 1920. Audiences were channeled through the men's washroom into an open courtyard where a young woman, dressed in white as though she was at her first communion, recited lewd poetry. The audience was also encouraged to destroy one of Ernst's own sculptures, using a hatchet that had been set nearby for that purpose. The Cologne police shut down the exhibition on a charge of obscenity.

The realists were not known for taking a stance for or against militarism, but certainly Tennessee Williams' famous play *The Glass Menagerie* speaks of war. First performed in 1944, the play is set against a backdrop of foreign battles like Guernica and a world "lit by lightning." War is never far from the embattled Wingfield family. When Tom Wingfield finally returns to the deserted family home after running away, he is costumed as a merchant sailor. The merchant marine in which Tom served played a vital role during the Second World War, ferrying supplies and goods in and out of U.S. waters.

Samuel Beckett served in the French underground during the Second World War, as did existential philosophers Jean-Paul Sartre and Albert Camus. Whereas Sartre and Camus developed a philosophy of alienated mankind during and after the war, Beckett sought to put the absurd world on stage. In 1953, he premiered his play *Waiting for Godot*, about two tramps waiting for somebody who never arrives, at Théâtre de Babylone in Paris. A London production followed in 1955, but perhaps the most famous production ran for one night only at San Quentin Prison on November 19, 1957. As one prisoner put it, the San Quentin production, performed before hardened criminals who knew what it was to be ostracized, was "pretty special."

CHAPTER 27

Marinetti

The Feasting King, *Théâtre de l'Œuvre, Paris, April 3, 1909*

On April 3, 1909, Filippo Tommaso Marinetti's futurist play *The Feasting King* opened at Théâtre de l'Œuvre in Paris. The production was directed by Aurélien-Francois Lugné-Poë, who had earlier directed Alfred Jarry's ill-fated production of *Ubu Roi*. The opening night audience greeted Marinetti's play with loud derisive booing and whistling. Critics were almost entirely negative in their reaction to the play, which closed after three performances. Not to be outdone, Marinetti asserted that one of the tenets of the new futurist movement was the desire of the artist to be heckled. He nevertheless fought a duel with one of his most strident critics, whom Marinetti felt had overstepped the bounds of civility.

The Feasting King was a departure from Marinetti's earlier poetic writing, and the play owes a debt to the symbolist movement of the late 19th century. The plot hinges on cookery: who gets fed and who gets eaten. Set in a vaguely medieval period, *The Feasting King* focuses on the King of the "Royaume des Bourdes," whose royal chef Ripaille has committed suicide after the late delivery of a fish to the King's table. Before his death, the royal chef did not see fit to reveal his secret recipe for the pills which had made it possible to feed an entire populace. The Kitchen Boys volunteer to prepare a banquet in the chef's absence, but their real plan is to take over the royal kitchen. A character labelled The Idiot encourages the populace to look beyond their hunger and to embrace the Ideal, but he is beaten for speaking up.

Waiting too long for his banquet, the King dies of hunger. The Kitchen Boys finally bring out the food and, later, the pickled body of the King. The populace squabbles over the tastiest morsels and turn on the Kitchen Boys, who have hidden much of the food away. The final act opens with the populace and their leader, Estomacreux, bloated and unhappy after their obscene meal. Estomacreux vomits, and the King emerges from

his belly, crowned with teeth. He tries to restore order, but the dead populace rises from the swamps into which their bodies have been thrown to
launch a new assault against the King. The populace's reappearance her-
alds a new age of creation, destruction, and regeneration.[1]

Born in Alexandria, Egypt, in 1876, Marinetti had an international
upbringing. His father, a lawyer, had come to Egypt at the invitation of
Kehdive Isma'il Pasha (also known as Ismail the Magnificent) to serve as a
legal adviser for foreign companies involved in a modernization program.
The young Marinetti was educated in Egypt, France, and Italy. He was an
avid reader of poetry, at the age of 17 starting a school literary magazine
entitled *Papyrus*. When Marinetti publicized Émile Zola's novels in the
school, his Jesuit teachers expelled him. Zola's novels, with their graphic
depictions of sex, violence, and social misery, were considered shocking
and transgressive in his own day.

Marinetti obtained his baccalaureate at the Sorbonne in 1894 and
graduated in law at the University of Pavia in 1899. He decided, early on,
to abandon his law career and to become a writer. Despite his devout
espousal of Italian nationalism, much of Marinetti's early work was written in French. Marinetti did not marry until late in life. He met the writer
and painter Benedetta Cappa in 1918. They married in 1923 in order to
avoid legal problems that might otherwise have arisen during a lecture
tour to Brazil. The union produced three daughters and several works of
art, including a mixed media assemblage entitled *Tattilisimo (Tactilism)*.[2]

Founder of the futurist movement, Marinetti had sought a break
from the past, a break from the agricultural traditions of his industri-
ally backward Italian homeland. He disliked museums, schools, libraries,
and art galleries. He spoke of the "new man," his jaw firmly set against
the future, of the racing car and "heroic technology."[3] He glorified speed,
industrialization, and the cool efficiency of machines. He'd been involved
in a car accident on the outskirts of Milan in 1908, veering into a ditch
to avoid two cyclists—an event which only strengthened his resolve to
promote the value of machines. For Marinetti and the futurists, war was
man's highest calling. Even after he was wounded in an artillery battle on
the Isonzo front, during World War I, he was undeterred in his celebration
of militarism, patriotism, and beautiful ideas worth dying for. After a long
recuperation, Marinetti returned to active service in the Italian army, participating in the victory at Vittorio Veneto in 1918. His sound-poem "Zang
Tumb Tumb" is an account of the Battle of Adrianople.

A warrior and a thinker, Marinetti was also an artist. He is today best
known as the author of the "Futurist Manifesto," first published on the
front page of *Le Figaro* on February 20, 1909. A reaction to the complacency of Italian literature in the 19th century, the manifesto declared that

art "can be nothing but violence, cruelty, and injustice."
Marinetti wanted revolution;
he wanted to jolt a compla-
cent bourgeoisie away from
its nostalgia about the past.
A key word in the futurist
movement was "dynamism";
Marinetti and his associ-
ates wanted change and
transformation. Some of the
machismo of the new futurist movement is hinted at in
article ten of the manifesto.
"We want to demolish museums and libraries," Mari-
netti wrote, "fight morality,
feminism and all opportun-
ist and utilitarian coward-
ice." Furthermore, futurism

Filippo Tommaso Marinetti (Wikimedia Commons).

was a young man's game. When the movement was founded in 1909, most
of its proponents were not yet 30 years old. Marinetti made it clear that
he expected other young men to take over the movement by the time he
was 40. The 1909 manifesto was long on theory and short on the specifics
of what futurist art might look like. It nevertheless became the subject of
much debate across Europe.

As David Ohana writes, the futurist movement preceded the fascist movement in Italy by ten years, but both movements became inextricably connected in the 1920s and '30s. According to Wyndham Lewis,
Marinetti's ultra-nationalism "guided Mussolini towards fascism."[4] As
a 34-year-old demobilized soldier, Mussolini had attended one of Marinetti's theatrical evenings in 1917 and had been impressed by the futurists' provocative manipulation of the crowd.[5] Later, Marinetti began to
equate Mussolini with the "new man" that futurists so admired. "His massive head is like a rock," wrote Marinetti, "and his ultra-dynamic eyes dart
forth with the speed of a racing-car."[6] According to David Ohana, the
futurist movement consisted of a utopian vision of the future while the
fascist movement was rooted in history:

> Futurism created a political mythology whose material was drawn from
> the world of the future and the human imagination, and its concepts there-
> fore were undoubtedly difficult for the masses to accept or for institutions
> to absorb, while the fascist establishment constructed a political mythology

whose concepts were drawn from the history of imperial Rome, a fact that facilitated its acceptance by the masses. In other words, the collective mentality was faced with a choice between the concepts of an artistic élite and futuristic images like the racing car on the one hand, and, on the other, the desire to reconstruct an imperial Rome, to embrace the European Christian past, the art of the Renaissance and the heritage of the Risorgimento—in short, the history of Italy.[7]

The two movements—one imaginatively leaping toward the future, the other firmly rooted in a nationalistic vision of the past—made strange bedfellows for a time.

Marinetti sought to realize his first manifesto by providing examples of his own art, but those examples did not win public approval. *The Feasting King* was a case in point. The reception of his first novel *Mafarka il futurista*, in 1910, was marred by an obscenity charge. During the subsequent trial, Marinetti was declared innocent. In that same year, he discovered that there were some youthful allies to his cause in the Italian arts community. The artists Umberto Boccione, Luigi Russolo, and Carlo Carra had adopted his philosophy. Russolo would later become famous for his treatise "The Art of Noises," in which he extolled the virtues of bruitisme, arguing that everyday noises are reflections of the cataclysmic soul of life. Russolo himself gave several concerts in which car horns, factory whistles, and school bells were orchestrated to become musical symphonies. Buoyed by his new allies, Marinetti began organizing futuristic evenings in which a variety of artists presented works and declared their manifestos while spectators threw vegetables at them. Later, writers like Bruno Corra and Emilio Settimelli joined the ranks of the much-derided futurists.

A typical futurist event was usually preceded by the arrival of Marinetti and his associates at a local railway station, where a crowd of supporters waited to accompany them en masse to their hotel. There was often a police presence, as disturbances were expected, and the local hall was filled with adversaries who "could not wait for the beginning of the event in order to scream and throw tomatoes."[8] The poet and painter Francesco Cangiullo described the goings-on inside the Vardi Theatre in Florence in 1914:

> The showers of potatoes, oranges, and fennel became infernal. In such situations Marinetti would come out with topical quips: this time, it was; "I feel like a glorious Italian battleship in the Dardanelles, but the strong Turks aim badly." Then a potato caught him full square in the eye, and Carra yelled. "Throw an idea instead of potatoes, you fools." The theatre calmed down a bit, but when Marinetti, reciting Palazzeschi's "Clock," reached the lines: "Oh, how beautiful to die with a red flower opening at one's temples," a member of

the audience offered him a revolver; "Carry on. Kill yourself!" To which Marinetti replied, "If I need a ball of lead, you deserve a ball of shit!"

Other futurist evenings were equally as provocative. David Ohana describes "The Funeral of the Dead," a theatrical piece that was part of an international exhibition at the Safrieri Gallery in Rome on April 13, 1914. The poet Giacomo Balla was a central figure, with painter Fortunato Depero and others in supporting roles:

> Balla strode at the head of the funeral procession which moved slowly among the spectators towards the platform on which the dead man was to be laid, and Depero and Radient strode after them with their heads concealed in black paper with openings only for the eyes and nose. On their shoulders they bore the corpse of a conservative critic, whose head, made by Cangiulo, lay on a powdered book. While a funeral march was played on the piano, Balla rang a cowbell from time to time and sang nonsensical words in a tremulous voice. Marinetti gave a speech in honour of the dead man supporting the futurists' declarations. In order to mask "the stench of the corpse," he lit a cigarette and asked the vigorously active audience to do the same.[9]

The futurists did not shy away from controversial subjects or visceral enactments.

Two later manifestos helped to clarify the futurists' position on matters theatrical. In "The Variety Theatre" (1913), Marinetti adopted a more positive tone. He proclaimed the variety theater—music halls, nightclubs, and circuses—superior to traditional theatrical forms. He liked the variety theater's speed, its brief entertainments, and its interaction between actor and audience, but he wanted to go further than that in his attempt to awaken the audience from its complacency. Often, his suggestions for audience manipulation went beyond the absurd. He wrote about smearing glue on the chairs of spectators so that they could not leave, about the use of powder to cause sneezing, about creating disturbances by selling more than one ticket for the same seat. He also wanted to destroy the fashionable "picture frame" stage that was popular in the period; he advocated eliminating the fourth wall, by having actors move about among audience members.[10]

In 1915, Marinetti brought his ideas into sharper focus in "The Futurist Synthetic Theatre." Synthetic drama, which would be the form futurist theater would take while it lasted, was brief and disparate. "To compress into a few minutes, into a few words and gestures, innumerable situations, sensibilities, ideas, sensations, facts, symbols," Marinetti suggested, was the art of the futurist.[11]

Derided by the critics, the combative Marinetti involved himself in several duels during his artistic career. Perhaps the most famous of these occurred in the Parc des Princes, on the outskirts of Paris, on April 16,

1909. The critic Charles Henri Hirsch had panned Marinetti's *The Feasting King* and had accused the playwright of having an affair with the poet
Jane Catulle Mendes. Marinetti issued a challenge and Hirsch accepted.
The duel, with fencing foils, was reported in the *New Zealand Evening Post*
on June 2, 1909:

> In the first encounter M. Marinetti was pricked in the right wrist, but the blade
> did not penetrate deeply. The next nine bouts were of an exciting and desper-
> ate character, each combatant making furious attempts to place the other hors
> de combat. The swords flashed dazzlingly in the sunshine, and the two men, as
> they gained or gave ground, looked for all the world like fighting cocks.[12]

Hirsch's sword snapped in the tenth round of fighting, and he had to be
provided with another weapon. He sustained a deep wound in the right
forearm in the eleventh round, and the fight was stopped after Hirsch's
arm became too stiff to continue. Marinetti must have relished the publicity he received after dueling Hirsch. He did not hesitate to challenge
others. In 1911, after a presentation at the Lyceum Club in London, he challenged an Irish journalist to a duel for offering a perceived slight against
the Italian army. In Rome, on April 30, 1924, Marinetti was himself injured
in a duel with Italian journalist Carlo Ciminelli.

   We can observe the high point of the futurist movement in the publication and performance of 76 short plays written by Marinetti and others, entitled *The Sintesi*, in 1915–16. Produced in several Italian cities, in
groups of ten or twelve plays, *The Sintesi* varied widely in terms of subject matter and theme. Some of the brief plays were distillations of well-
known dramas, of the works of Shakespeare and Alfieri. Most of the plays
in *The Sintesi* ignored the past altogether, concentrating instead of moods
and situations. Francesco Cargillo's "Detonation" is typical of the brevity
of the pieces. The curtain rises on a deserted road at night. After a period
of silence, we hear a gunshot, and then the curtain falls. Marinetti's brief
play "Feet" offers the spectator seven scenes in which the curtain rises only
far enough to reveal the actors' feet. The scenes are representations of dis-
tilled moods—anxiety, violence, work, love—but are otherwise disconnected. Some of the plays sought to involve the audience in an antagonistic
manner. Corra and Settimelli's "Gray + Red + Violet + Orange" features
an onstage actor who singles out one of the spectators, accusing that person of murder.

   By the end of the First World War, evidence of the horrors of armed
conflict made the futurists' agenda unpalatable in most of the world. After
the conflict to end all conflicts—after so much death and carnage—the
glorification of militaristic aggression seemed perverse. In Italy, though,
futurism remained an artistic force until the 1930s. Marinetti and others
continued to search for new ways in which futurism could assert itself. In

1918, the painter and air force pilot Fedele Azari organized a performance of aerial theater over the camp at Busto Arsizio. Azari described the artistry and the "rush" of such a performance:

> We futurist aviators love to roar up perpendicularly and dive vertically into the void, to turn in the intoxication of yawing with our bodies glued to the small seats by the centrifugal force, and to abandon ourselves to the whirl of spirals that press around the spiral staircase embedded in the void; to turn over two, three, ten times in increasingly happy loops, and to lean over in whirling barrel rolls; to swirl, skidding, to rock ourselves into long falls like dead leaves, or to stun ourselves with a breathless series of spins; in short, to roll, to rock, to flip over on the invisible trapezes of the atmosphere, to form with our airplanes a great aerial pinwheel.[13]

Marinetti himself published a "Manifesto of Futuristic Cooking" in 1930, attacking traditional Italian foods like pasta, which he blamed for laziness and a lack of virility among men. He predicted that pills would one day replace traditional foods as a source of human energy.

In March 1919, Marinetti was elected to the central committee of the Fascist movement in Italy, but in that same year rifts between the futurist and fascist movement began to appear. As Ohana writes, the fascist establishment began to compromise with political necessities and "became too conservative for Marinetti."[14] Mussolini wanted to form an alliance with the Vatican, a move that Marinetti opposed at a meeting of the second national congress of fascists in 1920. Although he publicly disagreed with Mussolini, Marinetti nevertheless maintained his membership in the fascist party. In 1929, he was elected president of the Fascist Writers' Union, and in that same year, he wrote a glorifying portrait of Mussolini, asserting that the future leader had not fallen prey to an unbending ideology. "As an ideologist," Marinetti declared, "he would be held back by ideas that are often sluggish or by books that are always dead. Instead he is free, free as the wind."[15]

When Mussolini rose to power in the 1930s, Marinetti tried to ingratiate himself with the new fascist regime. He wanted futurism to be declared the official state art of Italy. Unfortunately for Marinetti, Mussolini was by that time largely uninterested in art. When the fascist agenda eventually led to the Second World War, Marinetti dutifully volunteered for active service. At the age of 65, he fought on the Eastern Front for a few weeks in 1942, until ill health prevented him from further service. Marinetti died of a heart attack two short years later, on December 2, 1944, while working on a collection of poems praising the wartime achievements of an Italian commando unit.[16]

While the futurist movement had lost its primary spokesman, many aspects of the movement have survived without Marinetti. The modern air show can trace its lineage back to Azari's aerial display in 1919. There are still concerts of synthetic, machine-based, or industrial music performed at festivals under the name of bruitisme, a form that was popular with the Dadaists and the futurists. And some of Marinetti's sound poems are still published and performed for modern audiences.

CHAPTER 28

Dada

Dada Early Spring,
Cologne, April 1920

In April 1920, Max Ernst and his friends organized a Dadaist performance in the courtyard of a pub. They had been excluded from a museum exhibition elsewhere in Cologne, and their courtyard exhibition was an act of rebellion against the artistic establishment. Entitling their exhibition "Dada Early Spring," they channeled their audience through a men's bathroom, past the urinals and into a garden where a young woman, dressed in virginal white robes, recited lewd poetry. Among the other artistic exhibits was a skull in a pool of blood. Elsewhere in the courtyard, spectators were encouraged to destroy a sculpture Ernst had created. He'd attached a hatchet to the sculpture for that very purpose. The local police shut down the exhibition, probably because of the young woman and the lewd poetry more than anything else, with trumped-up obscenity charges for an apparent display of public nudity. The charges were dropped when it became apparent that the offending display was in fact Albrecht Durer's 1504 engraving of Adam and Eve.

Max Ernst (Dutch National Archives; Wikimedia Commons).

Max Ernst was born in 1891 in the town of Brühl, near Cologne, into a large middle-class family. His father was an amateur painter and a teacher of deaf students. By the age of 18, Ernst was studying philosophy, art history, psychiatry, and literature at the University of Bonn. His interest in psychiatry led him to visit local asylums, and he eventually grew interested in the artwork of the mentally ill. While at university, Ernst also began painting, aligning himself with a group of artists known as Die Rheinischen Expressionisten. In 1912 and 1913, his work—strongly influenced by the Cubists and the Expressionists—was exhibited in several group exhibitions at galleries in Cologne. In 1914, Ernst was drafted into the German army, serving both on the Eastern and Western Fronts. Several German expressionist painters died in action during the war, and the effect of the war upon Ernst was both devastating and transformative. Demobilized in 1918, Ernst married an art history student named Luise Strauss—one of several brief marriages that Ernst entered into during his long life. In 1919, he and social activist Johannes Baargeld and several others founded the Cologne Dada group, publishing several short-lived magazines and organizing Dada exhibitions.[1]

The Dadaist movement was a reaction to the horrors of the First World War. Since insanity seemed to be the true state of the world, Dadaists sought to reflect that state in their art, replacing logic and reason with calculated madness, substituting discord and chaos for balance and harmony. The movement had been launched in Switzerland in 1916 when artists like Hugo Ball and Tristan Tzara gathered at the Cabaret Voltaire in Zurich. The term "Dada" had been chosen at random from the dictionary. It is French baby talk for "horse." Early spokesmen argued that any name would have served the purpose of describing the movement.

While Dada might, at first blush, look like a childish art form, the movement also sought truth in its own peculiar way. The movement's watchwords were spontaneity, discontinuity, and complete freedom. Having rejected futurism's glorification of war as the supreme activity of the human race—an activity which ensured technological progress and the survival of the fittest—Dada borrowed much else from the futurists' arsenal. Musically, bruitisme was favored, the creation of symphonies from everyday noise. Using bruitisme's techniques, the awakening of a major city could be depicted with a clattering of pot lids, rattles, and typewriters. Artistically, both the futurists and the Dadaists brought collage to the fore. What better way to depict post–World War I life than in the fragmented photos and words of magazines and newspapers? Dada poets wrote poems consisting entirely of nonsense syllables. Hugo Ball's "Gadji beri bimba," for example, featured these lines: "gadji beri bimba glandridi laula lonni cadori/ gadjama gramma berida bimbala glandri galassassa laulitalomini."[2]

ausstellung

DADA-VORFRÜHLING

Gemälde
Skulpturen
Zeichnungen
Fluidoskeptrik
Vulgärdilettantismus

die urne des dadaisten max ernst erfreut sich außerordentlicher beliebtheit wiewohl ich mir selber die größte mühe ——— ——— gebe

——— baargeld ———

(ich habe kein kissen für meine urne)

Program, *Dada Early Spring* (International Dada Archive, Special Collections & Archives, The University of Iowa Libraries).

If those words sound familiar to a modern audience, it is most likely because the Talking Heads adapted them into a rock song in 1979.

The Dadaist movement was short-lived. It died, largely through lack of interest, in 1924, after Tzara's friend André Breton broke ranks and published the "Manifesto of Surrealism." The surrealist movement was much more concerned with the mysteries of subconscious thought than the Dadaists had been. Artists like Salvador Dalí sought to produce dream landscapes by juxtaposing the familiar and the strange. Many surrealists worked in the realm of the motion picture, still with the idea of exploring the workings of the subconscious. Great movie directors like Jean Cocteau and Luis Buñuel emphasized in their work some of the characteristics handed down to them by Dadaists—spontaneity, chance, and the juxtaposition of disparate cinematic elements. Buñuel's work on his short film *Un Chien Andalou* (1929), with its graphic presentation of an eyeball being sliced open, is often hailed as a groundbreaking piece of surrealist filmmaking, and Cocteau's great movie *Orpheus* (1950), which features Orpheus' descent into Hades through a pane of mercury, is a classic of French surrealist cinema.

While Dada's heyday was soon over, Max Ernst continued to lead a bohemian lifestyle, punctuated by periods of consternation and unhappiness. In 1921, Ernst met the poet Paul Eluard, who purchased several of Ernst's paintings and collages. Ernst soon moved in with Eluard and his wife Gala in Paris, leaving behind his first wife and a son and participating in a ménage à trois with the Eluards that lasted several years. His artistic work blossomed during this period. He invented the surrealist technique known as *frottage*, in which pencil rubbings of various objects are used as a source of images. He collaborated with Joan Miró on designs for the ballets of Sergei Diaghilev. In 1927, Ernst married the painter Marie-Berthe Aurenche after a whirlwind courtship. Together they appeared in the Buñuel film *L'Age d'Or* in 1930. Ernst applied for a divorce from Aurenche in 1936.

Three years earlier, the Nazis had put Ernst on a list of proscribed artists because of his controversial adherence to Dadaist and surrealist methods. Two of his paintings were among those the Nazis labelled "the art of decay" and included in the Degenerate Art Exhibition in Munich in 1937. At the outbreak of the Second World War in 1939, Ernst was interned by the French government as an undesirable foreigner near Aix-en-Provence but released after a few weeks. He was arrested by the Gestapo soon after the German occupation of France, but managed to escape and travel to America, aided by his benefactor, the American heiress and art collector Peggy Guggenheim. Ernst married Guggenheim in 1941, but the marriage did not last. He married Dorothea Tanning in Beverly Hills in 1946 and lived with her in Sedona, Arizona, until 1953. Inspired by the starkness of the Arizona desert, Ernst wrote a book entitled *Beyond Painting* (which gave him a degree of financial stability) and sculpted his masterpiece "Capricorn." He moved back to France with Tanning in 1953 and died on April 1, 1976, in Paris, at the age of 84.

When I began teaching theater history at the University of Saskatchewan, I thought it would be engaging to have my students make presentations on the various theatrical movements of the early 1900s. In those years, I was allotted a classroom in the campus' Physics Building. I remember three students who were assigned the task of delivering a twenty-minute presentation on Dada. They began by reciting nonsense poetry to the class. Their presentation soon devolved into a pseudo-angry confrontation with their classmates. At that point, the presenters threw open the door of the classroom and went running down the hallway, shouting "It! It! It!" at the top of their lungs. Other professors were delivering lectures in other classrooms in the building at the time, most of them to do with astrophysics or quantum theory. My students returned to our particular classroom sometime later, sat down sedately, and informed me that their presentation was complete. Five minutes remained before the end of class-time. We were discussing the presentation and its merits when an elderly, bespectacled physics professor opened the door. He poked his head in and asked, in an agitated voice, "Is everyone quite sane here?"

I couldn't argue with the physics professor or with my students. I apologized profusely for our loud outburst. The physics professor gave me a derisive look and marched away, slamming the door behind him. The shutting of that door pretty much summed up the elderly professor's feelings about theater and about me. Later, as I reflected upon the experience, I had little choice but to give my presenting students straight A's on their assignment. They had, after all, provoked the same response that Max Ernst and his Dadaist friends had sought to provoke in Cologne on that April evening in 1920.

CHAPTER 29

Ill Omens

The Glass Menagerie, *Civic Theatre,* Chicago, December 26, 1944

Thomas Lanier Williams might have been forgiven for thinking that his big opening night was going to be a fiasco. A 55-year-old actor was co-producing, co-directing, and playing the role of the twenty-year old male lead. A washed-up silent movie star, prone to bouts of alcoholism, was cast as the controlling mother. She couldn't get the Southern accent right, and she was chronically unhappy with her costumes. A half hour before the curtain, she was dyeing the bathrobe she was to be wearing that night a different color than what the costume designer wanted. The stage carpenter had quit a few days earlier. Opening night of *The Glass Menagerie* was going to be a washout.

The Glass Menagerie opened at the Civic Theatre in Chicago on a snowy December 26, 1944. It was common, at the time, to try out new plays in centers like Chicago before a Broadway run. The production was co-directed by Eddie Dowling and Margo Jones. Alongside Dowling and Laurette Taylor, Julie Haydon acted in the role of Laura Wingfield, and Anthony Ross played Jim O'Connor.

The play had arrived on the Chicago stage after a labyrinthine journey. It had all started when Williams wrote a short story entitled "Portrait of a Girl in Glass," an autobiographical piece based on the author's relationship with his mother and sister.[1] The young son of the triangulated family narrates the short story. It revolves around the appearance of a gentleman caller who breaks the heart of the narrator's sister Laura. We are given a great deal of detail about the inner workings of Laura's mind in the short story—she listens to her absent father's old jazz records on the victrola, she repeatedly reads a children's book about a one-armed lumberjack named Freckles, and she plays with her menagerie of crystal glass animals. The short story, unlike the play, has no mention of Laura's physical handicap, a limp that makes her otherness visible to the audience.

The character is based on Williams' real-life sister Rose, whose aberrant behavior and diagnosis of schizophrenia led Williams' parents to have her lobotomized in 1943. Williams was haunted for the rest of his life by his own inability to help his sister.

Also in 1943, Williams' fledgling literary career landed him in New York City. To support his writing habit, he got a job working as an usher in a cinema. He loved the movies, having once won a ten-dollar prize for writing the best review of *Stella Dallas* in a Loews Theatre contest. His apprenticeship in New York was brief. Later in the same year, his agent secured a contract, at $250 a week, for Williams to write screenplays at MGM in Hollywood.

Williams was put to work on various screenplay ideas. He wrote a preliminary treatment for a movie about Billy the Kid. He worked on a screenplay based on "Portrait of a Girl in Glass." The screenplay was entitled *The Gentleman Caller*. There is some evidence to suggest that Williams had envisioned Ethel Barrymore and Judy Garland as mother and daughter, if the screenplay were ever to be produced. Williams was laid off three months into his Hollywood sojourn, after he had refused to work on a screenplay for a child actress. Although his days as a screenwriter were short-lived, the influence of the cinema in what eventually became *The Glass Menagerie* can be heard and seen throughout the play. An almost ceaseless soundtrack of background music accompanies the play, for example, and the action begins with the equivalent of a cinematic flashback.

While the play owes some debt to its background in the movies, it owes more to its genesis as a short story. The play, like the short story, offers us a simple plot that can be summed up in a single sentence: a gentleman caller arrives and destroys the dearly held illusions of a mother and a daughter. A character-study really, and not of the well-made play variety, *The Glass Menagerie* is all about Amanda in the first act and all about the gentleman caller in its second act. It is not the type of theatrical fare that Chicago audiences were used to seeing.

Then there was the matter of Eddie Dowling, who had agreed to produce the play as long as he could have the role of Tom. Dowling had been born Joseph Nelson Gaucher in 1889, the son of a French-Canadian father and an Irish American mother. He was an entertainer at an early age, singing for pennies on sidewalks in Woonsocket, Rhode Island. Dowling quit school in grade three and went to work as a cabin boy on a ship at the age of 11. He joined the boys' choir at St. Paul's Cathedral in London and then came back to America, where he landed a role on Broadway in *The Velvet Lady* in 1919. Dowling met his wife Rae, a dancer, while he was working for the Ziegfeld Follies. He had political aspirations, as well. A friend of

Franklin D. Roosevelt, he sought a nomination to the United States senate in 1934 but was unsuccessful. His work on the role of Tom was his greatest success as a dramatic actor.

It's not entirely clear why Dowling took a chance on hiring Laurette Taylor to play Amanda. Born in 1883, Taylor was only six years older than Dowling, but she'd lived a more storied life. She'd made her Broadway debut in 1908 in *The Great John Ganton* and had appeared in *The Girl in Waiting* in 1910. It was her role in *The Girl in Waiting*, when she was 27, that made her a star. According to Brooks Atkinson, Taylor had developed an acting style that was unique. "By the time she was in her late teens," Atkinson wrote, "she had created a highly individual technique of acting that was spontaneous and eloquent; it consisted of variations in tempo, tentative movements that were not quite completed, quizzical glances, absorption in what other actors were saying...."[2] Taylor would go on to make an even bigger hit in the 1919 production of *Peg o' My Heart*, written by her husband J. Hartley Manners. She would later star in the motion picture adaptation of the play, directed by King Vidor.

Taylor's life began to unravel when her husband died in 1928. She began drinking heavily and haranguing fellow actors during rehearsal. These habits sidetracked her career through much of the 1930s. She disappeared from public life for five years. In 1938, she began her comeback, appearing in a leading role in a revival of Sutton Vane's *Outward Bound*, directed by Otto Preminger, at the Playhouse Theatre on Broadway. At the play's end, on opening night, she was reportedly given 22 curtain calls. The play ran for approximately six months, from December 22, 1938, until July 22, 1939. After *Outward Bound*, Taylor again disappeared from public life for a time, only to resurface as Amanda in *The Glass Menagerie* in 1944.

Even before *The Glass Menagerie* opened, both the producer and the playwright were predicting unhappiness. "They all told me what a silly ass I was to put up all this money," Dowling said, two weeks before opening. "I don't want to go to Chicago."[3] While Dowling was fretting, Williams became increasingly disillusioned with Taylor's evolving performance, which he called "corny." After one of the Chicago rehearsals, Williams wrote in his diary, "Well, it looks bad, baby."[4] Dowling pushed Williams for rewrites, but Williams refused, saying that he couldn't find the tranquility to write in Chicago.

When the play opened on that snowy December evening in 1944, the audience seemed unreceptive. "It was a strange night," Eddie Dowling later said. "There was no applause for anybody, no applause on entrances, nothing. It was bitter cold. The audience, it seemed to me in the first part of it, were all huddled like people trying to get close to each other to try to keep warm."[5] For weeks after the opening, the production did not do well at the box office. Audiences stayed away in droves. There was talk of closing the production, but the newspaper reviews had been laudatory. Claudia Cassidy, the critic for the *Chicago Tribune*, applauded the work, calling it a "tough little play."[6] Other critics joined in with expressions of admiration, and the play managed to survive its initial ten-week run.

In March 1945, the play headed to Broadway. Though Laurette Taylor was reportedly drunk during the Broadway opening, she held the New York audience spellbound. The cast was accorded 27 curtain calls, and Taylor was a star again. "Never before in my experience and never since and perhaps never again in my life will there be anything like it," Dowling said later. "It was really a thunderous, thunderous thing."[7] The show would run in New York for 563 performances. Young actors watched as Taylor provided a clinic in acting. Patricia Neal would later say that Taylor's was the "greatest performance I have ever seen in my life." Charles Durning was likewise blown away by Taylor's naturalistic acting style. "I thought they pulled her off the street," he said. "She was ... so natural."[8]

The Glass Menagerie also made Tennessee Williams a theatrical star. A few days after the New York opening, he sent a telegram to his parents' house, notifying them of his resounding success: "Reviews all rave.

L. to R.: Anthony Ross, Laurette Taylor, Eddie Dowling, and Julie Haydon in *The Glass Menagerie*, Broadway, 1945 (Billy Rose Theatre Collection; New York Public Library).

Indicate smash hit. Line block long at box office. Love, Tom."[9] He had gone from making $17 a week as an usher in a movie theater in 1943 to making a thousand dollars a week from royalties for his play in 1946. His career did not stop there. *The Glass Menagerie* was followed by a string of theatrical hits. *A Streetcar Named Desire* opened in New York in 1947. *Cat on a Hot Tin Roof, Orpheus Descending,* and *The Rose Tattoo* all premiered in the 1950s. His last big hit play was *The Night of the Iguana,* which opened in 1961.

Not everyone involved in the premiere of *The Glass Menagerie* lived happily into old age. Although Williams lived until 1983, his final decades were plagued with ill health and unhappiness. His plays began to flop. He was committed to psychiatric care for a brief period. He died of asphyxiation, according to one report, having choked on the plastic cap of his asthma inhaler. In his last will and testament, he left the bulk of his estate to the care of his sister Rose, who had been institutionalized due to her mental health issues since the mid–1940s and who lived until 1996.

Taylor's career, after the opening of *The Glass Menagerie,* would continue to be marred by alcoholism and sickness. As the run of the play progressed, she grew increasingly absent from the production, relying on an understudy to step into the role. Sometimes she would appear in the first act of the play and bring her understudy on for the second act. She nevertheless won the Drama Critics Award for Best Actress in 1946. It was in the same year, on December 7, that Taylor died of a heart attack, but not before her theatrical comeback had been realized.

Of everyone involved in that production, Eddie Dowling seems to have had the most joyous existence. While none of his future successes would come near to his work on *The Glass Menagerie,* Dowling was active in the theater until the early 1960s. He died on February 18, 1976, in a nursing home in Smithfield, Rhode Island.

CHAPTER 30

Waiting

Waiting for Godot, *San Quentin Prison, California, November 19, 1957*

Samuel Beckett's famous play *Waiting for Godot* had several openings in several different languages. Written originally in French, the play premiered at the Théâtre de Babylone in Paris on January 5, 1953. Pierre Latour played Estragon, Lucien Rinbourg played Vladimir, and Jean Martin played Lucky. Roger Blin, who directed the play, had to step into the role of Pozzo at the last minute when one of his actors left the production for more lucrative work elsewhere. Beckett also wrote the English-language version of the play. The English-language premiere took place in London at the Arts Theatre on August 3, 1955. Its 24-year-old director, Peter Hall, admitted to his cast in an early rehearsal that he didn't have "the foggiest idea what some of it means."[1] The play was also performed at the Lüttringhausen Prison, near Remscheid, in November 1953, after an inmate had obtained a copy of the original French edition and translated it into German. Perhaps the most famous opening of Beckett's play—and the one this essay will be focused on—occurred in 1957, when it played for one night in front of 1,400 inmates at San Quentin Prison in California.

Waiting for Godot is a flagship of the Theater of the Absurd, a movement which was first identified in Martin Esslin's 1960 essay "The Theatre of the Absurd," in which Esslin finds that absurdity is the common denominator in works by Beckett, Arthur Adamov, and Eugène Ionesco. Esslin later expanded his essay into a book entitled *The Theatre of the Absurd*, identifying four playwrights—Beckett, Adamov, Ionesco, and Jean Genet—as groundbreakers in the movement. In later editions of the book, he adds Harold Pinter as a fifth defining playwright. Esslin begins his book with a brief analysis of the San Quentin production of *Waiting for Godot*, describing the production and the enrapt captive audience. "Why did a play of the supposedly esoteric avant-garde make so immediate and so deep an impact on an audience of convicts?" Esslin asks.

179

"Because it confronted them with a situation in some ways analogous to their own? Perhaps. Or perhaps because they were unsophisticated enough to come to the theatre without any pre-conceived notions and ready-made expectations...."[2]

Inextricably tied to existential philosophy, the Theater of the Absurd sought to make humankind's alienation tactile to its audiences. Existential philosophers like Jean-Paul Sartre and Albert Camus articulated a landscape in which humankind, bereft of faith in God, is left to discern their own sense of purpose, their own sense of right and wrong. In this landscape, humankind is forced to deliberate on the often nauseating or paralyzing possibilities of a new-found personal freedom. What does it mean to exist? Is life important? Is communication important?

In his famous essay, "The Myth of Sisyphus," Camus located the specific moment of helplessness and frustration in an existential world. He described the mythical Sisyphus, doomed by the gods to roll a rock repeatedly up a mountainside and then to watch it roll back down again. In the moment after he's achieved the summit and just as the rock is once again pulled downward by gravity, Sisyphus experiences everything we need to know about a universe in which the gods have left humankind to its own devices. If people are alienated from God, in an existential universe, they are also alienated from their fellow human beings. The physical boundary of the human skull makes this alienation evident. How can I be sure, my brain encased within my skull, that the color I experience as blue is the same as the color you experience as blue?

Spurred on by the existentialists, absurd dramatists found new forms based, according to Esslin, on traditions of clowning, verbal nonsense, and the literature of dream and fantasy. Time and place are often generalized in absurd plays. Plots are circular. Dramatic irony is reversed; characters often know more than the audience knows; they sometimes lie to each other and to us. Language is downgraded, used as a smokescreen to cover the nakedness of the characters. People in life rarely reveal their deepest secrets and yearnings, Pinter later argued, so there is no reason why characters in plays should be more forthright in their communications than the people you might meet on the street. In "Writing for the Theatre," he argues,

> We don't carry labels on our chests, and even though they are continually fixed to us by others, they convince nobody. The desire for verification, on the part of all of us, with regard to our own experience and the experience of others, is understandable but cannot always be satisfied. I suggest there can be no hard distinctions between what is real and what is unreal, nor between what is true and what is false; it can be both true and false. A character on the stage who can present no convincing argument or information as to his past experience,

his present behaviour or his aspirations, nor give a comprehensive analysis of his motives is as legitimate and as worthy of attention as one who, alarmingly, can do all these things.[3]

Absurd theater defies genre and reverses dramatic irony, often riding the thin line between comedy and tragedy.

Beckett's *Waiting for Godot* offers us a blueprint for what an absurd drama might look like. The play is divided into two acts which mirror one another. In Act One, Vladimir and Estragon meet near a leafless tree, waiting for someone named Godot to arrive. They pass the time with idle conversation. Two other characters, Pozzo and Lucky, pass by on their way to market, where Pozzo intends to sell Lucky. At the end of the first act, a boy shows up, claiming to be Godot's messenger. He explains that Godot will not be arriving that night, that he will appear tomorrow instead. In Act Two, Vladimir and Estragon await the arrival of Godot the following evening, again near the leafless tree. They talk and wait. Pozzo and Lucky pass by again, but Pozzo is now blind and Lucky is dumb—evidence, if we need it, that Time is not the healer in absurd theater. The boy reappears at the end of the play and tells Vladimir and Estragon that Godot will not be coming. After the boy exits, Vladimir and Estragon consider suicide but find that they do not have a rope with which to hang themselves. The curtain falls.

In Paris when he wrote the play, Beckett (an Irishman) had experienced man's alienation from his fellow man in the homeland of the existentialists. Having worked as an assistant to James Joyce, he was a known personality among the left bank literati of the 1930s. In 1938, Beckett was accosted and stabbed by a notorious pimp nicknamed Prudent. After a time in hospital where he almost died, Beckett attended a preliminary hearing and asked his attacker to describe his motives. Prudent offered an existential response. "I do not know, sir," he said. "I'm sorry." Partly because he found his attacker to be likeable and well-mannered, Beckett dropped the charges.

During the Second World War, the French Resistance was largely covert and underground; writers like Camus, Beckett, and Sartre witnessed horrific violence and the inhuman treatment of French nationals at the hands of their German occupiers. Beckett served as a courier for the French underground and was nearly caught by the Gestapo on several occasions. At the end of the war, the French government awarded him the Croix de Guerre for his services in fighting the German occupation, but Beckett, in later life, dismissed his service as Boy Scout heroics.[4] Sartre also learned lessons about man's alienation from his fellow man while serving in the underground. In describing his wartime experiences, Sartre later emphasized the importance of communicating with speed and efficiency. "When each word might cost a life," he wrote, "you ought not take time off to play the 'cello."[5]

The 1957 production of *Waiting for Godot* at San Quentin Prison is the subject of a documentary film entitled *The Impossible Itself*. It is also described in detail in Russell Dembin's excellent essay "Nothing but Time." Beckett's play had met with a mixed reception in its initial Broadway run, partly owing to its promotional package which described the play as a laugh-riot. Even with Bert Lahr in the role of Estragon and E.G. Marshall as Vladimir, the production failed to wow audiences. The Broadway audience was not prepared for what it saw—a stark, unremitting, absurd universe. When Herbert Blau later directed the play at the Actors' Workshop in San Francisco, he decided to present it in an avant-garde style, much as his predecessors had done in Paris and London.

The Actors' Workshop production transferred for one night only to the North Dining Hall at San Quentin Prison. The transfer was organized by George Poultney, a representative of the Actors' Equity Association. While working as an actor, Poultney had made most of his living overseeing the ferrying of inmates between California prisons. He had also organized variety shows at Christmases and New Year's Eves in San Quentin Prison. It had been more difficult to bring traditional plays into the prison, owing to a rule that only male entertainers were allowed inside. Prior to the 1957 presentation of *Waiting for Godot*, the last traditional theatrical production offered at San Quentin had showcased Sarah Bernhardt in 1913, in a play about the French Revolution entitled *A Christmas Night Under the Terror*. Noting that the all-male cast of *Godot* met the modern requirement, Poultney had broached the idea of a transfer with Herbert Blau.

Dembin begins his essay with a description of the 24-year-old designer, Robin Wagner, getting ready for the San Quentin production. Setting up the lighting boards, Wagner forgot about his crew members— mostly prison inmates—who had been asked to erect a cyclorama. They were sitting on a scaffold, thirty feet in the air, awaiting further instructions. "I saw these eight guys sitting up there," Wagner later recalled, "and I said, 'Gee, I'm really sorry, you guys. I forgot that you were working on that, and I see that you finished.' And one of them said, 'It's okay—we've got lots of time.' They were accustomed to waiting."[6]

The production was presented to about 1,400 inmates on Tuesday, November 19, 1957. The audience of convicts was mesmerized by the play. As the anonymous writer in the prison newspaper put it,

> From the moment Robin Wagner's thoughtful and limbo-like set was dressed in light, until the last futile and expectant handclasp was hesitantly activated between the two searching vagrants, the San Francisco company had its

audience of captives in its collective hand…. Those that had felt a less contro-versial vehicle should be attempted as a first play here had their fears allayed a short five minutes after the Samuel Beckett piece began to unfold.[7]

According to Wagner, the audience responded as though they were inside the play. Ed Reed, an inmate of the prison who later found some mea-sure of fame as a jazz vocalist also enjoyed the evening. "*Godot* was pretty special," he said later. "Everybody loved it."[8] It is quite possible that the inmates' intense gut reaction to the play was based on their own lack of theatrical sophistication, as Esslin maintains, but the review in the prison newspaper suggests that there was at least one perceptive audience mem-ber in attendance. It is also more than likely that Beckett's play, with its absurd overtones, spoke to the inmates in a way that no other play of the era could have.

The production spawned an amateur theater movement in the prison. Rick Cluchey, who later became instrumental in the movement, had not been permitted to attend the November 17 performance of *Godot*. Serving a life sentence at the time, he had not been given clearance to leave his cell at night. He'd heard about the production, after the fact, from his enthu-siastic cellmate who described Pozzo whipping his slave. "Guess what the guy-whipping dude called him?" the cellmate said. "Lucky." Cluchey later became involved with the San Quentin Drama Workshop, directing and acting in productions, sometimes writing his own plays. His service to the Workshop contributed to his early release from prison in 1966. He became personal friends with Beckett and founded the Barbwire Theater. In 1970, Cluchey toured the U.S. prison system with his own play, entitled *The Cage*. Cluchey's story would later inspire the 1987 movie *Weeds*, with Nick Nolte in the leading role. "The thing that everyone in San Quentin under-stood about Beckett while the rest of the world had trouble catching up," Cluchey told a *Los Angeles Times* reporter the year the movie came out, "was what it meant to be in the face of it."[9]

Theater productions in prisons were not the norm when Her-bert Blau brought *Waiting for Godot* to San Quentin in 1957. Much has changed since then. Theater programs, and fine arts programs in gen-eral, have grown up inside the walls of many North American prisons. These programs have been lauded for their rehabilitative effect in recent years. The United States Department of Corrections and Community Supervision (DOCCS) has recently noted the personal growth of inmates involved in the fine arts during incarceration. "Artistic expression in gen-eral, and Rehabilitation Through the Arts (RTA) in particular, help to fulfill our mission in a profound way," writes DOCCS Acting Commis-sioner Anthony Annucci. "RTA participants develop life-changing skills that lead to personal growth and well-deserved praise for their hard work and accomplishments. The program's popularity, coupled with its strict acceptance criteria, influences positive behavior within our facilities, making them safer for everyone."[10] The 1957 *Godot* led the way; the production was an early sign that theater in prisons could make the waiting bearable.

The Angry 1950s

At the end of the Second World War, social change was on the horizon in countries like Great Britain and the United States. Having been inducted into the workforce during the war years, women were used to the notion of working outside the home. Changes in technology—automatic washing machines and electric stoves—meant that women were no longer chained to the traditional role of homemaker. Relaxed divorce laws made it easier for women to escape unhappy marriages. Especially in Britain, the fissure between the ruling class and the working class began to close. New government funding made it possible for working class youths to attend universities where they might be exposed to the socialist doctrines of the New Left. As the British Empire crumbled, and when it became apparent that postwar prosperity would not trickle down to the lower classes, there arose much dissatisfaction, again especially in England, among the under-privileged who worked in street stalls or drove taxicabs for a living.

It was only to be expected that new voices, which had been silenced in previous eras, would find their way onto the stage, and the decade of the 1950s saw the inclusion of these new voices in the theater, voices of women, of the working class, and of the under-privileged. New playwrights broke down the doors of the theatrical establishment and pushed their way in. They were brash and daring, and they did not often arrive in a particularly happy mood.

A major spokesman for the angry young man movement in Britain was John Osborne. His play *Look Back in Anger* arrived on stage at the Royal Court Theatre in 1956 and was greeted with mixed reviews. Most of the negative reviews focused on the lead character, Jimmy Porter, a sweets stall worker in an unhappy marriage. One reviewer found the character too self-pitying, while another compared Jimmy Porter to Strindberg's women-haters. But the influential Kenneth Tynan called Osborne's "the best young play of the decade."

Following close on Osborne's heels was a working-class playwright from East London named Harold Pinter. Like Osborne, Pinter had started out as an actor and had little intention of writing plays. In 1957, when his childhood friend, Henry Woolf, insisted that Pinter write a play for Woolf to use as his graduate directing assignment, Pinter quickly produced "The Room." It was the beginning of a long and successful playwriting career for Pinter.

While the angry young man movement was flourishing in England, a young African American playwright was making inroads into the theater in America. Lorraine Hansberry wrote a play about her parents' struggle to purchase a house in an all-white Chicago neighborhood. African American theater had been flourishing during the Harlem Renaissance of the 1920s and 30s, when actors like Paul Robeson began to appear and when, in 1925, Garland Anderson's *Appearances* was the first play by an African American to be produced on Broadway. Not until Langston Hughes' play *Mulatto* appeared in 1935 did a black playwright produce a major Broadway hit. After the Second World War, African American theater became more radical and more militant, seeking to abolish the racial stereotypes that had been prevalent on stage and in films in previous years. The time was right for a playwright like Lorraine Hansberry to appear. *A Raisin in the Sun* became the first play by an African American woman to be produced on Broadway. It opened at the Ethel Barrymore Theatre on March 11, 1959.

CHAPTER 31

Look Back

Look Back in Anger, *Royal Court Theatre, London, May 8, 1956*

When *Look Back in Anger* opened at the Royal Court Theatre in London on May 8, 1956, the play was a far cry from the type of theater to which London audiences had become accustomed. John Osborne's new play had none of the flippant upper-class humor of a Noel Coward comedy, none of the light religiosity of a James Bridie piece, none of the trappings of the well-made play that were evident in almost everything George Bernard Shaw had written. *Look Back in Anger* was set in a slummy attic apartment. Its protagonist was the lower-class sweets stall worker Jimmy Porter, who railed against the upper classes generally and who belittled his posh wife Alison specifically. Osborne's play signaled the beginning of what became known as the "angry young man" movement in British theater. It influenced a plethora of young playwrights, including Harold Pinter, Arnold Wesker, and Shelagh Delaney. As Dan Rebellato writes, in his introduction to the play, *Look Back in Anger* helped British theater rediscover "its artistic seriousness, its youth, its politics, its anger."[1]

At its opening, *Look Back in Anger* received mixed reviews. Philip Hope-Wallace, in *The Guardian*, took exception to the "self-pitying, self-dramatizing" tendencies of Jimmy Porter. "The trouble seems to be in the overstatement of the hero's sense of grievance," Hope-Wallace wrote; "like one of Strindberg's women-haters, he ends in a kind of frenzied preaching in an empty conventicle. Neither we in the audience nor even the other Bohemians on the stage with him are really reacting to his anger. Numbness sets in."[2] In the *Evening Standard*, Milton Shulman called the play "a self-pitying snivel."[3] The critic for the *Evening News* called it "putrid bosh."[4]

Other reviewers were more complimentary. In the *Sunday Times*, Harold Hobson called Osborne "a writer of outstanding promise." In the *Observer*, Kenneth Tynan's review may have single-handedly rescued the play from the dustbin of obscurity. Tynan admired the play for its forthright emotionalism, arguing that it presented "post-war youth as it really is." He ended his appraisal with two famous sentences. "I doubt if I could love anyone who did not wish to see 'Look Back in Anger,'" wrote Tynan. "It is the best young play of its decade."[5]

Osborne had written the play while working as an actor in the coastal town of Morecambe, in Lancashire. *Look Back in Anger* is based on Osborne's first failed marriage, to the actress Pamela Lane, which ended in 1957. In the evenings, at Morecambe, Osborne acted in a repertory company. In the afternoons, he sat on a deck chair on the pier, looking out at the Irish Sea, and committed his thoughts to a notebook. Still extant, the notebook offers close-up views of Osborne's relationship with Lane who, unlike Alison Porter, had a solidly middle-class background.

While Osborne's notebook was written in a prose style that was almost stream-of-consciousness, it did contain several lines that eventually made their way into the play. "All I ask for is a little enthusiasm," Osborne wrote on one page. "Dull and boring, she says, dull and boring," he wrote on another. "If only you would have a child and it would die."[6] The notebook listed several possible titles for what would become *Look Back in Anger*. They include *Farewell to Anger, Angry Man, Man in a Rage,* and *Bargain from Strength*. Clearly, the title he eventually picked was by far the best among all other prospects. He wrote *Look Back in Anger* in one month, between May 4 and June 3, 1955, while acting in Hugh Hastings' play *Seagulls Over Sorrento* at Morecambe.

Although the play was written hurriedly, its first draft was almost unchanged by the time it was presented professionally on stage. The fledgling English Stage Company had put out a call for new manuscripts, and Osborne's play was one of a handful of manuscripts that were chosen for production in the company's Royal Court space. Tony Richardson had agreed to direct Osborne's play.

The first order of business was to jump the hurdle of the Lord Chamberlain's Office, a hurdle that all theatrical manuscripts had to jump until the mid–1960s. The Lord Chamberlain's job was to censor any material that might offend public morality. In the manuscript of *Look Back in Anger*, the censor took exception to lines about defecation, homosexuality, and pubic hair. At the censor's bidding, Osborne agreed to change the song title in Act Two Scene One from "There's a smokescreen in my pubic hair" to "You can quit hanging around my counter Mildred 'cos you'll find my position is closed."

The Examiner of Plays, C.D. Heriot, reported that Osborne's "impressive and depressing play breaks new psychological ground," but took exception to a monologue in which Alison is compared to a python, seemingly on the grounds that the image of Alison devouring Jimmy whole, like a python, was too graphically violent. In a letter to Heriot, the director Tony Richardson begged for permission to include the python image. "What, however, is absolutely vital to the play," Richardson wrote, "and what I would ask you most urgently to try and help us over this, is for the 'python image'—which is central to the whole thought of the play, should be retained...."[7] In the end, Osborne agreed to soften the image slightly. He also slipped in an extra python reference, not present in the draft sent to the Lord Chamberlain, in a song Jimmy sings in the play's second act.

The production opened at the Royal Court in May 1956. The cast included Kenneth Haigh as Jimmy Porter, Alan Bates as his flat mate Cliff, and Mary Ure as Alison Porter. While the production was going on, Osborne embarked on a torrid affair with Ure, which led to a six-year marriage. After their divorce in 1963, Osborne was characteristically ungenerous in his appraisal of Ure and of her acting ability. "I had stopped concealing from myself, if I ever had, that Mary was not much of an actress," he wrote. "She had a rather harsh voice and a tiny range. Her appearance was pleasing but without any personal sweep to it."[8] Ure eventually left Osborne to begin a relationship with the actor Robert Shaw, with whom she was to have four children.

What was there to be angry about when Osborne wrote his play in 1955? As Dan Rebellato writes, Jimmy Porter's targets are "not carefully selected." He rails at the aristocracy, at poverty, at women. His misogyny, borne silently by his wife Alison as she irons his clothes or makes him lunch, is particularly unpalatable to a modern audience. More anarchic than constructive, Jimmy Porter's lament is, as Rebellato writes, about a "lack of feeling" in mid–1950s Britain. Porter even suggests that there is little to get excited about in contemporary society. "There aren't any good, brave causes left," he claims.

In fact, the 1950s were full of struggle, change, and hope for a new world order in England. After the Second World War, a new Education Act made it possible for men and women of the middle classes to attend universities. There arose several movements which would signal a strong leaning to the Left among educated youth. These included the New Left and Campaign for Nuclear Disarmament, both movements spawned at universities in the late forties and early fifties. Breakthroughs in technology resulted in labor-saving devices like electric stoves and washing machines, which reduced housewives' toil and created more leisure time. A large immigrant population was arriving in England in the late 1950s, particularly from Africa; England had become a multicultural society. And the stage was set for more permissive attitudes in the 1960s, for relaxed laws concerning the rights of homosexuals or the comparative ease of obtaining a divorce.

What becomes evident in Osborne's later plays is that England was also losing its status as a major global power in the 1950s. The Suez crisis, in 1956, demonstrated to the world that the British Empire was no longer in control of the world order. The crisis began when Egypt nationalized the Suez Canal, a waterway that controlled passage of two-thirds of the world's oil. The Israeli army invaded Egypt as a result, joined by forces from Britain and France. When the Soviet Union threatened to intervene, the British, French, and Israeli governments were forced to withdraw their troops in late 1956, having failed to receive support from the United States. It became apparent at that moment, if not before, that a new world order was in place, with Russia and the United States emerging as Cold War superpowers.

While Osborne's play spawned a new generation of playwrights, it also brought to prominence a new theater company. Situated in Sloane Square, the center of posh London, the Royal Court was to become known for producing dramas that challenged the political status quo. *Look Back in Anger* was the third play produced by the Royal Court in its inaugural season. The success of Osborne's play—which did not become entirely apparent until BBC television broadcasted a filmed version of the play in 1957—led to a much-needed early boost in the theater's reputation. In subsequent years, the Royal Court has produced the work of such luminaries as Arnold Wesker, John Arden, N.F. Simpson, Athol Fugard, Caryl Churchill, Timberlake Wertenbaker, and Nik Payne. Today, the Royal Court enjoys a sterling reputation as "a leading force in world theatre for cultivating writers—undiscovered, emerging and established."[9]

John Osborne continued to display his anger (and to incite anger) on stage and off until the end of his life. In 1966, when his play *A Bond Honoured* flopped at the National Theatre, Osborne was incensed about the negative press he'd received. He fired off a confrontational telegram to the critic for *The Times*, Irving Wardle:

> AFTER TEN YEARS I THINK YOU MIGHT ENTERTAIN THE POSSIBILITY THAT YOU ARE WRONG COMMA THAT I MIGHT BE RIGHT COMMA THAT THE THEATRE I WANT IS NOT A GYM FOR EGOS AND THAT I WROTE THIS PLAY WITH SOME INSTINCT FOR MY CRAFT WHICH MAY TURN OUT TO BE MORE PROPHETIC THAN YOUR OWN.[10]

Osborne went on to accuse Wardle of being "DEAF TO LANGUAGE" as well as "PURBLIND AND UNCHARITABLE." He concluded the telegram by declaring "OPEN WAR" on Wardle, who responded to Osborne's inflammatory words with a challenge of his own. "I don't know what you mean by open war," he replied, "but I'm told you used to be a boxer, and if you fancy a gentlemanly British punch-up I'm more than happy to oblige." Osborne's enthusiasm for open warfare quickly faded at this suggestion, and the proposed punch-up never materialized.

In 1992, two years before Osborne's death, he submitted a new play, entitled *Dejavu*, to several London theaters. A sequel to *Look Back in Anger, Dejavu* offered a portrayal of an older Jimmy Porter living, and arguing relentlessly, with his daughter Alison. Richard Ayre, the Artistic Director at the National Theatre, rejected the play. Max Stafford-Clark turned it down at the Royal Court, even though Tony Richardson had expressed his admiration for the play. Osborne then shopped the script around to various star actors. At one point, Peter O'Toole became interested in the project, but he dropped out after Osborne refused to make changes in the script. The play was eventually produced at the Thorndike Theatre, with Peter Egan in the role of Jimmy Porter. It ran for seven weeks and was revived at the Comedy Theatre in 1993. Peter O'Toole, who was also prone to the occasional angry outburst, attended a performance at the revival but was not amused. Apparently, the rewrites that O'Toole had called for were never made. As he stormed out of the theater in a huff that evening, O'Toole reportedly shouted, "Oi've never heard such fucking rubbish!"[11]

CHAPTER 32

The Man Who Discovered Pinter

The Room, *University of Bristol, England, May 1957*

University drama departments are not generally known for discovering new literary giants. Their repertoires are often filled with the greatest plays of other ages, classics from the Greeks, Shakespeare, and Molière. In May 1957, a postgraduate student named Henry Woolf bucked that trend by directing the premiere of Harold Pinter's one-act play *The Room* at the University of Bristol.

Founded in 1947, the Drama Department at the University of Bristol was the oldest degree-granting drama department in England, but it was run on a shoestring budget. When Henry Woolf arrived there in 1956, he was cast in a series of medieval passion plays on which the Department spent most of its budget. Woolf played a lot of shepherds and wicked Pharisees. He remembered those productions as being at once comedic and sinister. A line he'd uttered many times, "he beateth him some deal for his blasphemy," seemed to Woolf afterwards to have much in common with Pinter's comedies of menace. After the passion plays closed, each of the graduate students was assigned to direct a one-act play.

Woolf and Pinter had grown up together in the mean streets of East London. They had attended the same high school, Hackney Downs Grammar School, where they'd encountered an inspiring drama teacher named Joe Brearley. After high school, when Woolf went off to university, Pinter attended RADA (The Royal Academy of Dramatic Arts) and later acted with theater companies in the British provinces. Having written many poems and one unpublished novel (*The Dwarves*), Pinter was also limbering up as a writer.

Although he had chosen a profession in the theater, Pinter had never written a play. He was acting in a repertory company in Torquay, Devonshire, when Woolf called on him and asked, "Why don't you write a play for me to direct?" Pinter's response was, "I've never written a play.

I don't know if I can." Then Pinter proceeded to tell Woolf about an idea that might be the basis for something theatrical. He spoke in general terms about the play's premise: Bert and Rose Hudd, a couple who run a rooming house, are visited by a blind black man named Riley who has a message for Rose from her father.

Woolf went back to the University of Bristol and pitched the idea to the production committee. He had "a brilliant new play," he said, not mentioning that the play hadn't been written yet. How much would it cost to produce this play? Woolf knew that much would depend on his answer. "One shilling and nine pence," he replied, producing the numbers out of thin air. The production committee gave him its blessing. Woolf said later than the proposed budget "was pleasing to them."

Calling Pinter on the telephone that night, Woolf exhorted him to write the play at once. "No," Pinter said, "it would take at least six months." That would not be good enough, Woolf told him. "I need the play in two days." Two days later, Pinter's finished manuscript arrived in the post.

Rehearsals of Pinter's new script would have been daunting for most directors. "I was entering Pinterland," Woolf said later. "It was a strange land." It was a land of pauses and silences, words dangling from suspension ropes, torrents of language which were just another kind of silence. Woolf had some idea of Pinter's thought processes, having grown up with him. "I had read his poems and his novel," Woolf said later. "I had gotten used to the way he talked and the way he thought." The rhythms of Pinter's new play—the silences that grew out of the words—were something Woolf recognized. He was the right man to direct Pinter's first play.

Woolf's actors were also in the drama program at the University of Bristol. Claude Jenkins played Bert Hudd, and Susan Engel played his wife Rose. Engel would go on to a first-rate acting career in Britain. She would be best known for her television work in *The Lotus Eaters* and *Doctor Who*. Woolf himself played Mr. Kidd, the Hudds' landlord. Auriol Smith, who played Mrs. Sands, would later co-found the Orange Tree Theatre in Richmond with her husband Sam Walters. George Odum, who played Riley, afterwards embarked on a career in politics and served for a time as Deputy Prime Minister of Saint Lucia.

While he was rehearsing the play, Woolf got in touch with Duncan (Bill) Ross, principal of the Old Vic Theatre School across town in Bristol. "I've got a first-rate play," he told Ross. "Maybe you should do it." Ross was reticent. He was awfully busy at the moment, he told Woolf, and would not be able to involve himself with a new work by an unheard-of playwright.

Opening night came. The audience entered the university theater, prepared to witness an evening of high culture. "No one had written like that before," Woolf later claimed. "The theater of the time was largely a middle-class theater, for a middle class audience. [Plays] had a beginning, a middle, and an end. But the thing was, 'The Room' was a different play." Pinter's was the kind of play that didn't require the audience's approval. It didn't cater to the middle class.

Although it was in unfamiliar territory, the opening night audience was drawn into the mystery of the play. Who were these characters? What motivated them? Why did they not reveal their innermost thoughts, as characters in Ibsen and Chekhov frequently do? Where was dramatic irony? According to Woolf, that first night audience "found themselves immediately drawn into the play. It meant something to them … and it was so funny, and they leaned forward and had to laugh." Bill Ross was in the audience that first night, as well. He too was laughing. "But his laugh had a strangulated quality," Woolf said later. "He was clearly not enjoying himself at all. He knew he'd missed a first-rate opportunity to be the man who discovered Pinter."

A reviewer for the *Bristol Evening News* was in the audience too. In an article published the next morning, he signaled his approval. "One can never be sure about these private University productions," he began. "[T]he quality varies so much." The reviewer then commended the play's "macabre atmosphere" and "natural looking dialogue," giving Woolf and Pinter a high commendation for their work. "I'm so glad I didn't miss this production," he wrote. "[H]enry Woolf, whose work as a character actor has caught our

eye before, here introduces himself as an intelligent and sensitive producer. He introduces too, an old school friend of his, Harold Pinter, who as a writer, should go on writing."[1] Buoyed by observations such as these, Pinter did go on writing. In subsequent years, he produced some of the most startlingly innovative theater the world has known.

A few months after the premiere, Bill Ross decided to mount his own production of *The Room* for the National Student Drama Festival in London. Much to

Henry Woolf (photograph by Dave Stobbe).

Woolf's chagrin, Ross hired Susan Engel and George Odum (without asking Woolf's permission) to perform at the festival. Although it featured less humor than the original production, Ross' interpretation of the play nevertheless garnered the attention of the critic for the *Sunday Times*, Harold Hobson. "[The play] was a revelation and the directors of the London Arts Theatre and the English Stage Company should be after Mr. Pinter before they eat their lunch today," he wrote. "It is a brief excursion, in a slum room, into the nightmare world of insecurity and uncertainty."[2] Hobson wrote that Pinter's new play echoed the works of Beckett and Ionesco. Woolf's contribution to the original production was not mentioned in the review; the play's beginnings at the University of Bristol were alluded to as an afterthought. "I believe it was discovered, directly or indirectly, by the Department of Drama [at Bristol]," Hobson continued. "It is a matter for them of pride."

Pinter and Henry Woolf remained friends for the rest of their lives. Woolf went on to a marvelous acting career with the Royal Shakespeare Company and the Royal Court Theatre before turning his attention to academia. Pinter began work on *The Dumb Waiter* and *The Birthday Party* almost immediately after the premiere of *The Room*, but his success as a playwright was not overnight. When *The Birthday Party* opened, the critics were unkind. The production closed after one week. No one understood these characters who kept their innermost thoughts to themselves. Had Pinter's career ended there, this essay would likely not have been written. It did not end with unsatisfactory reviews for *The Birthday Party*. Instead, he scored a resounding success with *The Caretaker* in 1963, and his reputation was secured. He went on to write such masterpieces as *The Homecoming* and *Betrayal*. In 2005, he won the Nobel Prize for Literature. Nobody was happier for him than his friend Henry Woolf.[3]

CHAPTER 33

Hansberry

A Raisin in the Sun, *Ethel Barrymore Theatre, New York, March 11, 1959*

When Lorraine Hansberry's *A Raisin in the Sun* opened at the Ethel Barrymore Theatre on March 11, 1959, it was the first play written by an African American woman to be produced on Broadway. The process of getting the play produced had been arduous. The play's producer, Philip Rose, had found it difficult to raise enough money to assemble a production, largely because investors were worried that a play in which all the characters but one were African American would not attract an audience.[1] Previews of the play had garnered mixed reviews. Would Broadway's predominantly white, affluent audiences appreciate and understand a play about one African American family's experience of dealing with racist zoning laws in Chicago in the early 1940s?

Hansberry had originally entitled her play *The Crystal Stair*, but she later renamed it *A Raisin in the Sun*, which was a phrase she'd borrowed from the Langston Hughes poem "Harlem." She later quoted those lines in her autobiography *To Be Young, Gifted and Black*:

> What happens to a dream deferred?
> Does it dry up
> Like a raisin in the sun?
> Or fester like a sore—
> And then run?
> Does it stink like rotten meat?
> Or crust and sugar over—
> Like a syrupy sweet?[2]

Set in the South Side of Chicago, Hansberry's play is about an African American family trying to buy a house in a white neighborhood. A representative of the neighborhood association, Karl Lindner, offers to buy them out in order to alleviate tensions over a potential interracial mix. The African American family eventually refuses Lindner's offer, and the play ends with them leaving their squalid apartment for their new home in the white neighborhood.

The play was based on an actual court case in which Hansberry's father was the complainant. Back in 1940, when Hansberry was still a child, her father had sought his day in court over an effort to keep him from purchasing a home in Chicago's Washington Park area. He had bought the house from one James Burke, but the sale had been contested on the basis of a racially restrictive covenant that barred African Americans from purchasing land in the subdivision. While Lorraine Hansberry's father fought in court, her mother fought another kind of battle. In her autobiography, Hansberry wrote,

> My memories of this "correct" way of fighting white supremacy in America included being spat at, cursed and pummeled in the daily trek to and from school. And I also remember my desperate and courageous mother, patrolling our household all night with a loaded German Luger, doggedly guarding her four children, while my father fought the respectable part of the battle in the Washington court.[3]

Hansberry's father did win the case in court (Hansberry v. Lee, 311 U.S. 32 [1940]), and the Hansberry house at 6140 South Rhodes is now a historical landmark in Chicago.

A Raisin in the Sun defied expectations; it ran all summer long at the Ethel Barrymore and was transferred to the Belasco Theater on October 19. The initial production ran for a total of 530 performances. Two wonderful things happened. Broadway's predominantly white audiences embraced the play, and an African American audience began to emerge in large numbers. In June 1959, *Vogue Magazine* published a story about Hansberry's meteoric rise to fame. "Although caught in the pounce of publicity, she has remained a quiet woman who lives three flights up in a Greenwich Village walk-up with her husband, a song-writer and music publisher," the story tells us. "Her creation now brings her ten per cent of the weekly gross of $41,000, a big whack of the $300,000 that Columbia Pictures has paid for the movie rights, plus handsome financial arrangements as writer of the movie script."[4]

It had not hurt the production's chances when a rising film star by the name of Sidney Poitier accepted the part of the family patriarch Walter Lee Younger. By 1959, Poitier had already starred in two significant movies, *Blackboard Jungle* (1955) and *The Defiant Ones* (1958). Others in the cast of *A Raisin in the Sun* included Claudia McNeil as the mother Lena Younger and Ruby Dee as the daughter Ruth. The production was eventually nominated for four Tony awards: Sidney Poitier for Best Actor, Claudia McNeil for Best Actress, Lloyd Richards for Best Direction of a Play, and Lorraine Hansberry for Best Play. It also won the Drama Critics Award for Best Play of 1959.

L. to R.: Ruby Dee (Ruth Younger), Claudia McNeil (Lena Younger), Glynn Turman (Travis Younger), Sidney Poitier (Walter Younger), and John Fiedler (Karl Lindner) in *A Raisin in the Sun*, Broadway 1959 (Friedman–Abeles; Wikimedia Commons).

What is doubly remarkable about the success of *A Raisin in the Sun* is that its author was only 29 when it opened. Lorraine Hansberry's life, to that point and afterwards, was as remarkable as anything she had managed to put on stage. Having graduated high school in Chicago, she attended the University of Wisconsin in Madison, becoming involved in the Communist Party during her time there. She would later opine that the issues of white racism and African American poverty were interlinked. In 1950, Hansberry moved to New York City and began writing for Paul Robeson's *Freedom Newspaper*. One of the great African American actors of his time, Robeson served as a role model for Hansberry on stage and off. For Robeson's newspaper, Hansberry covered the Willie McGee case in Mississippi. McGhee had been convicted of the rape of a white woman in Hattiesburg, Mississippi, and was sentenced to death by an all-white jury in what many people viewed as a miscarriage of justice. His public execution, on May 8, 1951, was broadcast on radio.[5] Hansberry's involvement in the case would eventually spawn a poem entitled "Lynchsong."[6]

Hansberry married Robert Nemiroff, a Jewish publisher and political activist, on June 30, 1953. A musician as well as an activist, Nemiroff co-wrote the song "Cindy, Oh Cindy," under the pseudonym Robert Barron, the success of which afforded Hansberry the opportunity to begin a full-time career as a writer. As Hansberry's personal notebooks reveal, she was also a closeted lesbian. Her marriage to Nemiroff did not last long—they separated in 1957 and were divorced in 1962—during which time Hansberry began contributing letters (using her initials only) to the lesbian rights magazine *The Ladder*. In later life, Hansberry became more committed to her own homosexuality, taking lovers and surrounding herself with a circle of gay friends. She remained friends with Nemiroff through it all and, as her executor, he donated all Hansberry's notebooks and letters to the New York Public Library but blocked access to any materials related to her lesbianism.[7]

While Hansberry wrote many articles and essays, none of her other literary works matched the success of *A Raisin in the Sun*. She wrote one other play, entitled *The Sign in Sidney Brustein's Window*, which opened on Broadway at the Longacre Theatre on October 15, 1964. The play ran for 101 performances and closed on January 12, 1965, the night Lorraine Hansberry died of cancer at the age of 34.

After Hansberry's death, Robert Nemiroff adapted several of her essays into a play, entitled *To Be Young, Gifted, and Black*. It ran for 12 months in New York during the 1968–69 season. Nina Simone recorded a beautiful song, also by that title, in 1969. Paul Robeson gave a eulogy at Hansberry's funeral. Martin Luther King, Jr., could not attend but sent a message. "Her creative ability and her profound grasp of the deep social issues confronting the world today," King wrote, "will remain an inspiration to generations yet unborn."[8] In his introduction to Hansberry's posthumously published autobiography, James Baldwin wrote about the house Lorraine Hansberry's father fought for as it appeared in her famous play:

> But, in *Raisin*, black people recognized that house and all the people in it—the mother, the son, the daughter and the daughter-in-law, and supplied the play with an interpretive element which could not be present in the minds of white people: a kind of claustrophobic terror, created not only by their knowledge of the house but by their knowledge of the streets. And when the curtain came down, Lorraine and I found ourselves in the backstage alley, where she was immediately mobbed. I produced a pen and Lorraine handed me her handbag and began signing autographs. "It only happens once," she said.[9]

It was a house that Black people understood, and it brought them flooding into the theater.

A Raisin in the Sun was adapted into a feature film in 1961. The success of the play and the film led to the emergence of a strong African American theater movement in the 1960s and to the establishment of the Black Arts Repertory Theater in Harlem in 1965. Sidney Poitier went on to become the first African American to win an Academy Award in 1964, for his performance in *Lilies of the Field*. He later starred in several successful and excellent films, including *In the Heat of the Night*, *To Sir, with Love*, and *Guess Who's Coming to Dinner*. During the 1980s and '90s, a new generation of Black playwrights appeared, August Wilson and Suzan-Lori Parks among them, spurred on by the success Hansberry had achieved. In 2010, Bruce Norris' play *Clybourne Park*, a spin-off of *A Raisin in the Sun* told partly from the perspective of the white family that sells their house to the Youngers in Hansberry's play, opened at Playwrights' Horizon in New York. *Clybourne Park* won the Pulitzer Prize for Drama in 2011 and the Tony Award for Best Play in 2012.

True North [4]

Theatrical traditions were revived in French-speaking and English-speaking parts of Canada after the British conquest in 1763. As Gaëtan Charlebois and Ann Nothof write in *The Canadian Theatre Encyclopedia*, the first original English-language play written and produced in Canada was *Acadius; or, Love in a Calm*, staged in Halifax in 1774. Many productions emanated from amateur groups—often citizens and soldiers—and two companies came to the fore in the 1780s, Allen's Company of Comedians and Les Jeunes Messieurs Canadiens. The first purpose-built theaters began to appear in this era, as well. In 1789, the New Grand Theatre in Halifax opened with a production of Shakespeare's *Merchant of Venice*. Other theaters were soon built in central Canada as well as in Charlottetown and St. John. Once the theaters were in place, a tradition of playwriting began to grow. Writers like Charles Heavysege (*Saul*, 1857), Louis Frechette (*Félix Poutré*, 1860), and Sarah Anne Curzon (*Laura Secord*, 1887) flourished in the 19th century.

The touring companies that came through Canada in the early 20th century were largely foreign or producing foreign fare. As Charlebois and Nothof write, "[I]t took two world wars, radio and television, for Canadians to begin to insist on a vision of themselves in the theatres."[1] Until the 1950s, the amateur theater movement in Canada had been vibrant, but there was little in the way of resident professional theaters. Touring shows from some of the larger centers and from New York City played in the theaters and opera houses that dotted the countryside.

That all began to change in the 1940s and '50s. Theater departments began to grow up in Canadian universities. In 1949, Prime Minister Louis St. Laurent appointed Vincent Massey to investigate the anemic state of Canadian arts and the pervasive influence of American media upon Canadians. The Massey Commission report of 1951 led to the founding of the Canada Council for the Arts (an arts funding organization) six years later. The Stratford (Canada) Festival was founded in Ontario in 1953. A young entrepreneur named Tom Patterson had managed to attract Irish director Tyrone Guthrie to the project. Guthrie brought with him the stage designer Tanya Moiseivitch and the British star actor Alec Guinness. On July 13, 1953—four years before the Canada Council was established— Guinness appeared on the Stratford stage as Richard III opposite Canadian actress Amelia Hall.

In the 1950s and 1960s, regional theaters sprang up across the country. These included the Vancouver Arts Club (1958), the Manitoba Theatre Centre (1958), and the Neptune Theatre (1963) in Halifax. In Canada, 1967 is sometimes referred to as the year in which professional theater proliferated. It was the 100th anniversary of Canada's confederation, and the government of Pierre Elliott Trudeau was opening its purse strings in aid of the celebration. Theaters and symphony halls and skating rinks were built. Three productions from that year stand out in memory. John Herbert's play *Fortune and Men's Eyes* opened at the Actors Playhouse in New York. James Reaney's *Colours in the Dark* was produced at the Stratford Festival. And George Ryga's *The Ecstasy of Rita Joe*, starring Francis Hyland and August Schellenburg and Chief Dan George, was commissioned by the Vancouver Playhouse.

In the 1970s, small theaters emerged across Canada, often with a mandate to produce Canadian plays. Among these smaller theaters were Tamanhaus Theatre in Vancouver, Prairie Theatre Exchange in Winnipeg, 25th Street Theatre in Saskatoon, and Toronto Free Theatre. In Saskatchewan in 1977, tiny 25th Street Theatre produced a small play that was to become a big national hit. When *Paper Wheat* opened at St. Thomas Wesley Hall in Saskatoon, there was little intimation that the play would ever leave the province. It was, after all, about a very regional subject—the founding of the Saskatchewan Wheat Pool. After a provincial tour of the play was well received, the company decided to embark on a national tour. They played to packed houses, and the production received rave reviews across the nation. As Ted Johns wrote in the *Toronto Theatre Review*, "lucky Saskatchewan seems to be witnessing the birth of a new, muscular, and influential young theatre."

The seeds of modern Indigenous theater in Canada had been planted before Tomson Highway came along. They can be found in the performances of Chief Dan George and August Schellenberg in *The Ecstasy of Rita Joe* or in 25th Street Theatre's 1977 production of *Don'tcha Know— You and the North Wind in My Hair*. They can be found in the work of Maria Campbell and, especially, in her 1982 play *Jessica*, co-written for 25th Street Theatre with Linda Griffiths and Paul Thompson. Indigenous theater groups began to proliferate in the 1980s and '90s, with the development of Native Earth Theatre (1982) in Toronto, the Nakai Theatre Ensemble (1989) in Whitehorse, and the Gordon Tootoosis Nikinawin Theatre

(1999) in Saskatoon. Interesting playwrights like Drew Hayden Taylor and Tomson Highway soon followed.

Although he eventually became the Artistic Director at Native Earth Theatre, Highway had a particularly unlikely start as a playwright. He grew up on a trapline in northern Manitoba, receiving his formal education in a residential school. He had dreams of becoming a concert pianist but gave them up for a career in social work. He only got involved in a career in the theater so that he could help his younger brother, whose career as a choreographer had stalled. In 1986, when he produced his own play *The Rez Sisters*, Tomson Highway became a major voice in Canadian theater.

CHAPTER 34

Spittle in the Face

Richard III, *Stratford Festival,*
Stratford, Canada, July 13, 1953

On July 13, 1953, Canadian actress Amelia Hall spat in the face of British star Alec Guinness during a production of *Richard III*. Guinness calmly collected the spittle on his forefinger and thrust that finger into his mouth, savoring Hall's bodily fluids and her indignation. He was the devious Richard, after all, and she was Lady Anne. In that moment, the Stratford Festival of Canada was born.

The Festival had been the brainchild of Tom Patterson, a local Stratford, Ontario man who knew little about the theater. He'd served in the Canadian army during World War II, mostly in north-western Europe. When he returned to Canada after the war, he studied history at Trinity College in Toronto. After graduating, Patterson became the associate editor of a trade magazine called *Civic Administration*. He was covering a convention of the American Waterworks Association, in Winnipeg, when the idea of a Shakespearean festival came up. The mayor of Stratford also happened to be attending the convention and, over drinks one evening, Patterson spoke of his vision for a festival. Stratford's economy was dying. The small city had been a railway terminus and repair center, but now railway jobs had become scarce as other methods of transportation became more prominent. The city had entertained other plans to rejuvenate itself. One of them was to create an international hockey school since Howie Morenz, the famed Stratford Streak, had been born there. But on that night in 1951, the mayor encouraged Patterson to act on his idea.

In the winter of 1951–52, Patterson approached the Stratford Chamber of Commerce with his idea. The Chamber quickly gave its support for the formation of a "Shakespearean Week." Patterson's vision for the Festival was, at the time, minuscule. He advocated for a renovation of the city's bandshell, which is even now located across the street from the hockey rink on the banks of the Avon River. The idea was to cordon off the roads for a week or two and offer performances in the open air.

Even though his vision for a stage was not majestic, Patterson hoped to attract world-class actors to the site. On January 22, the Stratford City Council provided him with a grant of $125 (Canadian) to pay for a trip to New York City. Patterson was to use that money to secure a meeting with Sir Laurence Olivier who was working in New York at the time. Perhaps Olivier would agree to act in the Festival. If nothing else, he might lend his support to the project. For one reason or another, the meeting with Olivier didn't materialize, but Patterson received a tepid expression of interest from Olivier's personal secretary. He returned to Stratford a few days later with news that Olivier had been unwavering in his support. "Heartened by Sir Laurence Olivier's interest," an article in *The Toronto Globe and Mail* opined, shortly after Patterson's sojourn, "the citizens of Stratford have set up a committee to organize a Shakespearean drama for that city."[1] Patterson's trip to New York, and his supposed meeting with Olivier, made headlines in several newspapers and on a national news telecast.

The next step was to contact Mavor Moore, the newly appointed Head of Television Drama at the Canadian Broadcasting Corporation. Moore sent Patterson to see his mother Dora Mavor Moore, the maven of theater arts in Toronto who was, at the time, running a semi-professional company called the New Play Society. Mrs. Moore recommended that Patterson get in touch with Tyrone Guthrie, the famed British theater director. She offered to write a letter of support. Guthrie had been a friend of Dora Mavor Moore's since 1931, when he had been invited to direct a CBC radio show entitled "The Romance of Canada." His immediate fondness for the country was apparent. He liked to compare Canada to a strapping teenage boy, not overly eloquent, who would one day be a patriarch. "It is like an enormous young boy," Guthrie wrote in *Mayfair* magazine in October 1953, "perhaps the handsomest and strongest young boy ever created. He is probably destined to be the head of the family. But so far he has hardly spoken."[2]

Guthrie was a remarkable man with a chip on his shoulder. He was ready for a change. London critics had just savaged his production of *A Midsummer Night's Dream* at the Old Vic. His direction was superficial in their view; he had emphasized color and pageantry instead of interpreting the words of Shakespeare. This was a common charge against Guthrie. If the scene called for the appearance of a bishop in clerical uniform, the critics maintained, Guthrie would invariably put two bishops in the scene for the sake of added pageantry. While he was dealing with unkind critics, Guthrie was also perturbed that over thirty years of his work at the Old Vic had largely been ignored. Actors like Sir Ralph Richardson and Sir

Laurence Olivier had been knighted for their work. Where was Guthrie's knighthood?[3]

These slights aside, Guthrie had grown to dislike the fashionable British theater of his day because it was steeped in tradition and gentle ideas that were comforting to its audience. Mostly, Guthrie disliked the way Shakespeare had been staged in England during the first half of the 20th century. He was particularly dissatisfied with British theater's reliance on the picture frame stage which necessitated the addition of scenic elements in Shakespeare's plays.

Also remarkable was Guthrie's physical appearance. He was a tall man, mustachioed, six-foot-four, and quite slender. When he was about to collect Guthrie at the airport in Toronto, Tom Patterson was told to look for a guardsman on stilts. Guthrie came out of the concourse in a crowd of Mounties, who had been disembarking from their own flight at roughly the same time. Patterson later said he thought he'd encountered a convention of basketball players.

When he'd been asked to come to Stratford, Canada, Guthrie specified that he would do so only if he was given the right to design the Festival's stage and auditorium. With the help of Tanya Moiseivitch, who was to become a fairly permanent fixture in Stratford, Guthrie co-designed a raised platform for a stage, 11 feet deep by 18 feet wide. The stage had a balcony above it, in the shape of a ship's prow, supported by nine pillars. Guthrie also insisted on adding two runways down through the audience, which would make quick exits for processions and armies possible. Moiseivitch later suggested that Guthrie had gotten the idea from watching soccer matches, where players entered from dressing rooms below the stands.[4] In its first season, stage and auditorium were situated in a massive tent—billed as the second largest tent in the world—on the banks of the Avon River.

Rehearsals began for the two productions of the six-week season, *Richard III* and *All's Well That Ends Well*. Guthrie secured the participation of his friend Alec Guinness as Richard, further ensuring that the opening would be an event of international proportions. The company rehearsed in a long wooden shed in the local fairground, notable for its two deficiencies: bad acoustics which made it impossible for the actors to hear one another; and the dozens of sparrows who had made their homes in the rafters of the shed. In rehearsal, Guthrie was witty and familiar. When he learned that three of his actors were William Hutt, Peter Mews, and Eric House, he insisted on referring to them as "Your Eminent Residences." He told one actor that his wig looked like the pubic hair of a yak. Occasionally his wit turned caustic. Just before opening, he told House that "his performance was deplorable, his intonation was wrong, his meaning was wrong, and the way he held his hands was wrong." House replied, "Aside from that, was everything else all right?"[5]

Guthrie's love of extravagance and superfluity began to emerge in rehearsals. He had Guinness playing about with the head of the decapitated Hastings and tossing it like a football. He kept sending Henry's corpse, over which Richard woos Lady Anne, back to the properties department, so that it could be made as gory as possible. Tanya Moiseivitch later recalled that poor Henry "was really quite horribly dead."[6]

Publicity for the new Festival had created a buzz. On July 13, prospective theatergoers streamed into the small city by train and automobile. Hotels were full. Local restaurants were overwhelmed. At eight o'clock that evening, local church bells pealed for five minutes. Then the factory whistles of Stratford sounded out a welcome. Five trumpeters, at the entrance to the Festival tent, offered a fanfare. And then a cannon sounded. Robertson Davies describes the goings-on inside the theater tent, which were witnessed by 1,500 spectators: "The lights on the acting area rise quickly to full and there, not hastily, yet promptly, is Richard, Duke of Gloucester, coming slowly toward us, on the topmost balcony. He does not pretend that we are not there; he does not speak quietly, as though to himself: loudly, clearly, he speaks to us, after a long, considering look."[7]

Guinness delivered most of his first speech while sitting astride the balcony parapet and stabbing at the wood with a dagger. The marks of his dagger remained in the wood until the stage was remodeled some years later.[8] The play went on without a hitch. At the end of the performance, the crowd leapt to their feet in a standing ovation that lasted five minutes. As Nathan Cohen later wrote about the opening, "That first night at Stratford was the single most memorable experience I ever had in the theatre."[9]

Reviewers of Stratford's first production were not entirely overwhelmed. As Portman and Pettigrew write, "In general, leading critics—partly because they seem to have held over-solemn preconceptions about the play—tended to feel that Guinness and the production as a whole had been rather too lightweight, even too frivolous."[10] In *The New York Times*, Brooks Atkinson wrote that the production had been spectacular but that the performances were shallow. Walter Kerr wrote in *The New York Herald-Tribune* that Guinness had allowed his inner clown to get "the upper hand."[11] Then, as now, comedies fared better than tragedies on the Stratford Festival stage. *All's Well That Ends Well*, which opened one night later, got the best reviews, despite Guinness' star turn as Richard and despite his inventive business with Amelia Hall's spittle.

During the Festival's first week, almost all of the 10,339 available seats were sold. The productions played to sold-out houses at ticket prices that ranged from one to six dollars. On the weekend, Brooks Atkinson wrote a long article in *The New York Times* endorsing the festival, and a chorus of praise grew across North America. On July 26, the Festival's board announced that the season would be extended by one week. On August 8, the tent's canvas walls were moved back so that an extra row of seats could be added. The Board announced that the Festival would become an annual venture. By the end of the first season, which lasted six weeks, a total audience of more than 68,000 had viewed the two productions. Most amazing of all was the fact that little more than a year had passed since Tom Patterson had first broached the idea of a festival with the mayor of Stratford.[12] For his part, Guthrie admired the successes of the Festival but dreaded two possible outcomes:

> First, that the Festival may be abused by profiteers. Even last year there was a tendency for bed and breakfast to cost substantially more at the end of the Festival than at its start. Second, a refinement of the same old thing, that there will be an outbreak of Ye Olde. I heard a rumour that two ladies had bought land and proposed to erect an imitation of Anne Hathaway's cottage in which they would brew Daintye Teas.[13]

Certainly, with the continued success of the Festival, the first of Guthrie's fears has materialized. The costs of bed and breakfast in Stratford have risen appreciably, and it is well-known that meals in restaurants cost more when the Festival is running than they do in the off-season.

CHAPTER 35

1967

Fortune and Men's Eyes, Colours in the Dark, *and* The Ecstasy of Rita Joe, *Canada, 1967*

In Canada, 1967 was a banner year. It was the hundredth anniversary of the confederation that created a country north of the 49th parallel. There were celebrations of nationhood, including the World Exposition in Montreal (which cost taxpayers millions of dollars). The Montreal Expos, an expansion major league baseball club that got its start in 1969, was named after that exposition. Across the country, there was massive spending on sports, arts, and culture. Many hockey rinks in Saskatchewan were centennial projects as was the Centennial Auditorium in Saskatoon, a 2,000-seat roadhouse theater that is now known as TCU Place. Federal funds were used to create the St. Lawrence Centre in Toronto and Winnipeg's Centennial Concert Hall. As Don Rubin writes in his chapbook "Creeping Toward a Culture," by 1967 it was apparent that Canada had a viable theater in its midst. "The only question existing by this time, though," he continues, "was one of identity: most of the theatre being produced in Canada was clearly not Canadian."[1]

A watershed year for theater as well as other art forms, 1967 saw a celebration of Canadian nationalism on stages from coast to coast. Three specific theatrical events in that year signaled the rise of three very different English-language playwrights. These new plays were also the harbingers of a rising professionalism in Canadian theater. The three theatrical events that resounded, more than any others, during Canada's centennial year were the openings of *Fortune and Men's Eyes* at the Actors Playhouse in New York City, *Colours in the Dark* at the Stratford Festival, and *The Ecstasy of Rita Joe* at the Vancouver Playhouse.[2]

John Herbert's play *Fortune and Men's Eyes* was a searing portrayal of homosexuality and sexual slavery in Canada's prison system. Herbert had begun work on the script in 1964, but the play had been rejected by some of Toronto's leading theaters in the years following. Finally, the Stratford (Ontario) Festival agreed to mount a studio production of Herbert's play, starring Richard Monette and directed by Bruno Gerussi (who would later rise to fame on CBC's *The Beachcombers*). The Festival's management deemed the work too volatile for public performance, however, and the play was ultimately presented to an in-house audience of Stratford actors and actresses. Not able to find a Canadian theater company that was willing to produce his play, Herbert appealed to theater critic Nathan Cohen who, in turn, sent the script to New York producer David Rothenberg. The result was an Off Broadway production that opened at the Actors Playhouse on February 14, 1967.

The play was largely biographical. Born in Toronto in 1926, John Herbert began competing in drag pageants in the 1940s. In that decade, as well, he was the victim of an attempted robbery. In court, his male assailants claimed that Herbert, who was dressed as a woman at the time, had solicited them for sex. Herbert was subsequently charged with indecency, convicted, and sentenced to four months' incarceration at a youth reformatory in Guelf, Ontario. At the reformatory, he was beaten and raped. After his release, Herbert travelled across North America, taking occasional work in order to survive.

In the 1950s, he returned to Canada, studied at the National Ballet School for a time, and became a member of Dora Mavor Moore's New Play Society. In 1960, he co-founded the Garrett Theatre in Toronto, with his sister Nana Brundage. In later life, he lectured at Ryerson University, Glendon College, and the University of Toronto. His other works include *Born of Medusa's Blood* (1972), *Omphale and the Hero* (produced at Forest Hill Chamber Theatre in 1974), *Blanche and Rose's Dream Song* (1986), and *Marilyn at Seventy* (1995). Herbert died in Toronto in 2001.[3]

While none of his other plays were international successes, *Fortune and Men's Eyes* remains one of the most widely produced plays in the history of Canadian theater. In its New York debut, the play shocked audiences and critics alike with its bold depiction of sexual politics in male prisons. The reviewer for the *New York Tribune*, Norman Nadel, wrote that the play was otherwise so disgusting that reference to a character vomiting in an off-stage toilet "came like a breath of spring."[4] Nevertheless, the play saw numerous productions in the U.S., Argentina, England, South Africa, Israel, France and Sweden in the year that followed. Sal Mineo produced the play in Los Angeles, with a youthful Don Johnson in the lead. The Canadian film director Harvey Hart produced a cinematic adaptation of the play in 1971.

While *Fortune and Men's Eyes* was making a splash in New York City, another Canadian play had a less provocative opening in Stratford,

Ontario. James Reaney's early work *Colours in the Dark* opened at the Avon Theatre in Stratford on July 25, 1967. John Hirsch directed the production, which featured Douglas Rain as Pa, Martha Henry as Ma, and Heath Lamberts as Son. During that same summer, Reaney's own Alphabet Players performed his marionette plays *Apple Butter* and *Red Riding Hood* at the Stratford hockey arena.

Already an established poet and academic by the time *Colours in the Dark* was produced, Reaney had won three Governor General's awards for poetry: the first for his book *Red Heart*, published when he was still a student at the University of Toronto; the second, in 1958, when he released *A Suit of Nettles*; and the third for *Twelve Letters to a Small Town* in 1962. Having studied under the celebrated Northrop Frye, Reaney was teaching English at the University of Western Ontario by 1960.

Reaney never strayed too far from his southern Ontario roots in his writing, and *Colours in the Dark* is no exception to that rule. The play is, on one level, a love letter to Canada and to southern Ontario. It chronicles the spiritual growth of a character named Pa who, on his fortieth birthday, displays an uncanny ability to identify people and colors during a game of blind man's buff. Reaney flashes back to Pa's childhood when, diagnosed with measles, his eyes bandaged, he learns to color with crayons in the dark.

With references to Biblical and historical events, the play seeks to merge Pa's reality with a larger, more universal mythology. Northrop Frye's influence can be seen throughout. Frye's method, in books like *Anatomy of Criticism* and *The Educated Imagination*, was to demonstrate the connection between literary works and mythological archetypes, sometimes found in older literary works.

The mythopoeic approach, in *Colours in the Dark*, is not manifested entirely in its reference to older literatures but also to Ontario landscapes and history. As George Bowering wrote, in 1965, Reaney "has in most recent years broken loose to make myth from local materials rather than spooning it on from the golden bowl of literary materials. In the later poems and theatrical experiments he has sought a way of understanding myth and myth-making not as alternative to history and politics and commerce and city-planning, but as the register made on the emotions and unreason by all those things."[5] In *Colours in the Dark*, Reaney's characters frequently refer to the Bible and Greek mythology but also to the 1850 Criminal Records for the Huron and Bruce District.

While 1967 was a big year for James Reaney, it was not his biggest year. *Colours in the Dark* and his earlier play *Listen to the Wind* were important steps in preparing Reaney to write his masterpiece, *The Donnelly's Trilogy*. "While people found [Reaney's] earlier plays original, striking and not

James Reaney (Mohan Juneja; Wikimedia Commons).

without potential," Moira Day suggests, "there was a general feeling that there was a mismatch between his sweeping mythopoeic vision and the realistic dramaturgy and conventional structures into which he was trying to shoehorn his vision."[6] Reaney rectified that disconnect between mythopoeic vision and dramaturgy in his later work. Between 1973 and 1975, he wrote *The Donnelly's Trilogy*, which debuted at Toronto's Tarragon Theatre and which toured nationally. The second installment of the trilogy, *The St. Nicholas Hotel*, won a Chalmers Award. Reaney was invested as an Officer of the Order of Canada in 1975 and elected a Fellow of the Royal Society of Canada in 1978. He died in London, Ontario in 2008.

The last theatrical milestone of 1967 was the opening of George Ryga's *The Ecstasy of Rita Joe* at the Vancouver Playhouse on November 23. Directed by George Bloomfield, the play had been commissioned as part of an all–Canadian season to celebrate the country's centennial. The production starred Frances Hyland as Rita Joe, Chief Dan George as her father, and August Schellenberg as Jamie Paul. The interracial casting of the play was unusual for its time. A graduate of RADA, Hyland came from Canadian prairie settler stock while George and Schellenberg were Indigenous. All three of the stars went on to wonderful careers in cinema and television, Hyland in *Anne of Green Gables* on CBC, George in the movie *Little Big Man*, and Schellenberg in *The Robe* and the *Free Willy* franchise.

The Ecstasy of Rita Joe is a study of systemic white racism and the lot of First Peoples in Canadian urban life. The play follows a young Indigenous woman named Rita Joe as she navigates her way through public schools, homeless shelters, and the Canadian legal system. Its original setting consisted of two circular ramps: an outer circle representing the external realities of Rita Joe's life, and an inner circle representing the cloistered views of mainstream (white) society. With a nod to Brecht, Ryga included a narrator, a singer who commented on the action of the play. Ann Mortifee composed the music and played the Singer in the Playhouse production. The Caucasian characters are stereotypical, representatives of professions and positions of authority. While they think they might be helping Rita Joe navigate her way through mainstream society, they inevitably defeat and destroy her. The play begins with Rita being sentenced to 30 days in jail and ends with her rape and murder at the hands of nameless thugs.

Ryga's play was ground-breaking and audacious. It took the plight of Canada's Indigenous population seriously and, owing to its Brechtian leanings, its message was clear. Before *The Ecstasy of Rita Joe*, not many of Canada's major theaters had produced high-profile plays dealing with the violence visited upon an Indigenous population by white settlers. With its unflinching portrayal of marginalization and social injustice, the play was a particularly interesting choice for a celebratory centennial year. According to several observers, the Playhouse production was met with stunned silence by its predominantly white audience. The Artistic Director of the Playhouse, Joy Coghill, wrote that the production "was such a moving experience that the people didn't want to clap." CBC Radio producer Ben Metcalfe said, "The silence it commands in the theatre is perhaps the echo of shame and guilt, even momentary contrition."[7]

Virtually all reviewers commented on the play's raw power. A reviewer for *The Vancouver Province* later wrote that the play "was a landmark in more ways than one. It was—and remains—a play for all seasons and for all peoples."[8] But the production did not receive entirely glowing reviews in its own day or any other. The *Vancouver Sun's* reviewer, Jack Richards, wrote of the premiere, "I don't know if it is a great play," but then added that Ryga and his director had accomplished their purpose if their purpose was to communicate a systemic problem in Canadian society.

More recently, the Indigenous playwright Kenneth T. Williams has referred to the play as "poverty porn." He suggests that it is "as destructive as the forces of colonization Ryga decries."[9] Other Indigenous voices in Canadian theater have not shared Williams' view. After directing a 2009 National Arts Centre production of the play, Yvette Nolan wrote,

> In my estimation, George Ryga got a lot of *Rita Joe* right. He knew the poverty and despair that so many Indigenous people confronted when they moved to

the city. He identified the racism, both overt and insidious, that Indigenous people dealt with on a daily basis. He traced the system that criminalizes the poor and the marginalized. With his 1967 centennial play, he challenged the mainstream, the settler population, Canadians, to actually see the relationship that they had with the first people of this land.[10]

The play has been produced internationally and continues to be performed in Canada.

While some might argue that *The Ecstasy of Rita Joe* represented the pinnacle of George Ryga's fame, he did have a long career as a writer both before and after the 1967 opening. His first collection of poetry, entitled *Song of My Hands*, was published in 1956. Ryga wrote several novels and many plays, including *Captives of the Faceless Drummer* (1971), *Sunrise on Sarah* (1972), and *Ploughmen of the Glacier* (1977). I met Ryga at a party in 1986. He was an affable, kind-hearted man but, by then, somewhat disillusioned with the state of Canadian theater. His iconoclastic nature had made him impatient with the compromises that theater-makers of the time were making to create critically and financially successful theater. I told him I was interested in how one goes about writing the Great Canadian Play. "It isn't difficult," he replied.

With those three productions, Canadian theater came of age. Herbert, Reaney, and Ryga helped to pave the way for such luminaries as Michel Tremblay, John Murrell, David Fennario, and Judith Thompson. After a hundred-year history that was largely devoted to amateur theater, some of Canada's best-known professional companies began to spring up. In Toronto, the Factory, the Tarragon, Theatre Passe Muraille, and the Toronto Free all got their start in the early seventies, as did Persephone Theatre in Saskatoon, the Globe in Regina, Green Thumb in Vancouver, and the Great Canadian Theatre Company in Ottawa. For Canadian theater, 1967 had been a good year indeed.

George Ryga (photograph by Norma Ryga).

CHAPTER 36

Dogged Intrepidity

Paper Wheat, *St. Thomas Wesley Hall,*
Saskatoon, March 18, 1977

Like much of 25th Street Theatre's previous work, its production of *Paper Wheat* was created in an atmosphere of hurried confusion. The production was originally supposed to open in March 1977 in Saskatchewan's capitol city, Regina, but the company's artistic director Andy Tahn decided, late in the rehearsal period, to open in Sintaluta instead. The actors were transported to the small prairie town, 85 kilometers east of Regina. The set, which consisted of a prairie mural and an outline of a map of Canada, arrived in Sintaluta while the audience was lined up outside, waiting to be admitted to the hall. There is, unfortunately, no newspaper account of the Sintaluta presentation, but an anonymous newspaper reviewer in Eston, where the production was mounted a few days later, called the play "a fine dramatization" and wrote: "These young players exhibit great versatility by assuming various roles and dialects and appeared to have a genuine feeling of the actual situations. The play moved along with no dull moments."

When *Paper Wheat* was performed at St. Thomas Wesley Hall in Saskatoon on March 18, 1977, there was little indication that the play would become a Canadian theater phenomenon. The hall, located in a neglected part of Saskatoon's Riversdale community, was not much like a theater. It boasted a scratched linoleum floor, folding tin chairs, and plain walls. In his review of the 25th Street Theatre production, Don Kerr commented that he had previously attended political meetings at St. Thomas Wesley Hall. "Nobody in charge of the world would meet here," Kerr wrote, "but it's a very serious place. The kind of hall early co-operators must have met in. But not the place for theatre, aesthetics, beauty. Holding a play here is like hanging an art show in a Saskatchewan Liquor Board Store."[1] The play opened to an audience of 132, and the *Star-Phoenix's* Jean Macpherson predicted capacity crowds for the rest of the run. She gave the show a rave review:

It's also a fairly safe prediction that every one of the 132 first-nighters will tell
at least a couple of friends each that *Paper Wheat* by 25th Street House Theatre is a show that shouldn't be missed. *Paper Wheat* has every kind of appeal:
it's homegrown, it's dramatic, it's funny and it's true. It is also a well-acted and
well-produced performance.[2]

Ted Barris, of CFQC Radio, was similarly enthralled. He maintained that
Paper Wheat "succeeds like no other 25th Street work to date" and that the
company had "honed their production into a finely tuned piece of drama
and humour."

The company's artistic director, Andy Tahn, was not yet thirty when
Paper Wheat found its way to the stage. None of the plays produced in the
previous years had come close to the success of *Paper Wheat*. The company had become used to negative newspaper reviews which characterized it as "a nice group of children" or commended it for "a special brand
of dogged intrepidity." Tahn had fought tooth and nail for grants from the
Saskatchewan Arts Board and the Canada Council. The company, which
eventually became known for its early forays into devised theater, did not
begin to develop that mandate until 1975. With help from Paul Thompson, the artistic director of Theatre Passe Muraille in Toronto, the 25th
Street company had devised a show entitled *If You're So Good, Why Are
You in Saskatoon?* in that year. Emboldened by their work with Thompson,
the company then decided to adopt a similar approach to a play about the
founding of the Saskatchewan Wheat Pool.

Although 25th Street Theatre was finally receiving positive reviews
for its production of *Paper Wheat*, there were rumors of "insurrection"
against Tahn by his own company. According to Alan Filewod, Tahn was
forced to hire another director for a proposed tour of *Paper Wheat* "when
his cast refused to work with him again."[3] Tahn met with several of the
cast members to discuss their concerns about his direction of the play, and
he agreed to hire another director who might be more well-versed in the
art of collective creation. As a result, the Montreal director Guy Sprung
was called in to re-direct the show for a national tour.

Sprung felt little obligation to follow the original script for *Paper
Wheat*; he'd been hired on the condition that he would have control over
both script and casting. While he maintained the original two-act structure of the play in his revision, with the first act focusing anecdotally on
the experience of the sodbusters and the second act on the founding and
growth of the co-operative movement, he also composed a radically different play.

Sprung began the research process all over again, this time with new
actors.[4] He reduced the number of major characters in the first act from 14
to five, so that each actor might concentrate on one character and so that

the audience might more easily follow the trajectory of each character. He made use of the ethnic background of each of the actors, having David Francis play an English immigrant named William Postelthwaite, having Lubomir Mykytiuk play the Ukrainian Vasil Havryshyn, having Michael Fahey play an Irishman named Sean Phalen, and so forth. Sprung tightened up the historical second act, as well, including six new scenes which were meant to show how the co-operative movement had changed over the years. Sprung was interested in setting up the second act as a political dialectical whereas Tahn had been more interested in presenting the human story of the homesteaders and of the founders of the co-operative movement. At Sprung's insistence, Tahn went out in search of a fiddle player who could provide background music for the tour, and he eventually discovered Bill Prokopchuk, a farmer from Springside, Saskatchewan. Prokopchuk also happened to be the Western Canadian Fiddle Champion.

On September 29, 1977, Sprung's version of *Paper Wheat* opened at the Saskatoon Theatre Centre, a church hall at 808 20th Street West, before transferring to Toronto and then embarking on a tour of Saskatchewan. In her *Star-Phoenix* review, Jean Macpherson noted some changes in the script but attributed the further success of Sprung's production to changing attitudes and economic conditions: "Last year's version of *Paper Wheat* was good entertainment; this year, in view of altering attitudes due to altering economic conditions, it is even more relevant, and therefore even more entertaining."[5] The production ran in Saskatoon until October 8 before transferring to Café Soho in Toronto.

Nothing sells in Saskatchewan so well as success elsewhere, and 25th Street Theatre eventually got a boost from *Paper Wheat's* Toronto transfer. The *Toronto Star* review, which came out a day after the October 11 opening, was not particularly glowing. While praising the plain-spoken acting and down-to-earth production values, Brian Freeman was also cognizant of the production's meandering lack of pace. "It's just too slow!" he wrote, adding, "Actors wander in and out of scenes as though out on a Sunday stroll. Nothing is ever really allowed to build a head of steam."[6] Ted Johns published a much more favorable article in the *Toronto Theatre Review* in December. Johns gave the production high marks, suggesting that "[l]ucky Saskatchewan seems to be witnessing the birth of a new, muscular, and influential young theatre."[7]

As an added dimension to the tour of Saskatchewan that followed the Toronto opening, the theater was able to negotiate a film deal with the National Film Board. Sprung made the initial contact with Albert Kish, who eventually agreed to direct a documentary about the production. The film displays the sometimes hilarious hardships of a touring production in Saskatchewan during an early winter. In one scene, Tahn, who was still involved with the production as the theater's Artistic Director, arrives in Swift Current to distribute posters a day before the play opens there. After filling his rickety vehicle with gasoline at a local station, Tahn asks the cashier to put a poster on her wall and then proceeds to get his vehicle stuck in the snow and ice as he is pulling away from the gas pumps.

It was Guy Sprung's production of *Paper Wheat* that toured to Montreal's Centaur Theatre in the autumn of 1978. The eastern critics were fonder, perhaps, of the performances than of the script. Writing for the *Ottawa Review*, Michael Carroll was especially complimentary about the acting ensemble. "As a chronicle telling of the advent of diverse immigrants to Canada at the turn of the century, and a witty documentation of the rise of the co-operative movement in Saskatchewan," he wrote, "*Paper Wheat* has everything going for it. The cast of the production, as good an ensemble as I've ever seen, comes across with a uniformly splendid piece of work—not one weak link."[8]

It was also Sprung's production, with Peter Meuse replacing an unavailable Michael Fahey in the cast, that began touring nationally in the spring of 1979. As Alan Filewod writes, national audiences did not fall in love with the play's razor-sharp analysis of the founding of the co-operative movement; instead, they fell in love with the actors' retelling of the story, with the intersection of reality and artifice in the play, and with the play as "heroic myth." Reviewers of the national tour almost invariably referred to the production's acting virtuosity and usually commended the ensemble for capably employing mime, song, dance and other theatrical elements in performance. Ray Conologue's review in the *Toronto Globe and Mail* refers repeatedly to these moments of virtuosity:

> Inventive and delightful moments come tumbling back in memory after seeing the show: a prairie couple who recount their first years of famine, drought, wind and frost by rolling and unrolling a blanket which symbolizes their beloved land; two tap dancers, each with only one shoe, who learn to make a complete melody by dancing together (a lesson in the virtues of prairie co-operatives); the exploitation of farmers by grain speculators wittily rendered as an old fashioned radio thriller, complete with sound effects.[9]

The virtuosic telling of the story was at least as important as the story itself.

The intersection between reality and artifice, signified by the authenticity of the actors, was also highly seductive to audiences during the national tour. Arnold Edinburgh did not hesitate to mention this intersection in his review of the production for the *Financial Post*:

> The company in the present 25th Street House cast are a remarkable bunch. Skai Leja, of Latvian origin, is striking to look at, delicious to listen to and has

a variety of accents which, together with her acting ability, make her a remarkable personality on stage. Sharon Bakker, raised on a Saskatchewan farm, is equally good as a thieving elevator agent or a flustered, pregnant settler's wife. Lubomir Mykytiuk is a Ukrainian who starts the play off with a flood of Ukrainian talk, but after that dazzles both by his linguistic ability and, in one magnificent scene, his juggling.[10]

Bill Prokopchuk's presence on stage seemed to provide the production with a degree of authenticity it otherwise would not have had. In the *Vancouver Sun*, Wayne Edmonstone was rapturous about Prokopchuk's performance:

> Bill Prokopchuk, himself a retired wheat farmer and the only member of the group old enough to have first hand knowledge of the period of the piece is— thank God—a genuine Canadian old time fiddler. Which is to say, his music is based on the folk-fiddle tunes people actually used to play at square dances in rural Canada, and not some imported bluegrass derivative. Like most things about this play, it's a treat.[11]

For several reviewers, Prokopchuk was living testimony of prairie hardship, cunning, and resilience.

The phenomenon of *Paper Wheat* catapulted 25th Street Theatre into the national consciousness. Two years earlier, Tahn would not have imagined that any play of his theater's making might be touring nationally. He would have scoffed at the idea that any of his theater's productions might be reviewed in the *Toronto Globe and Mail* or the *Vancouver Province*. But there was seemingly no end to the popularity of the production, and 25th Street Theatre revived the play for successful runs in 1981 and again in 1982. There were even rumors of a yearly remount in the style of *Anne of Green Gables*, but those rumors died when Tahn resigned as the theater's artistic director in 1983.[12]

CHAPTER 37

Highway

The Rez Sisters, *Native Earth Theatre,* *Toronto, November 26, 1986*

Judging by his humble beginnings, few would have suspected that Tomson Highway might become a playwright of international stature. He was born on a trapline in northern Manitoba. Sent to residential school at an early age, Highway had dreams of becoming a concert pianist. When his musical dreams didn't work out, he embarked on a career in social work. His involvement in theater was casual and happenstance, at first, an attempt to help out a younger brother whose career in choreography had stalled.

On November 26, 1986, Highway's play *The Rez Sisters* opened in Toronto. It was a co-production of two small performance companies—Native Earth and Act IV—that had pooled their meagre resources to pay for actors and sets. In the first week of its three-week run, the play was not well-attended. The producers had to offer free tickets on the street in front of the theater, on one particular evening, because an Actors' Equity ruling disallowed performances in cases where the play's cast outnumbered the audience.[1] In the second week of the run, something wonderful happened. A reviewer for one of Toronto's newspapers gave *The Rez Sisters* a glowing notice. Prospective spectators read the review and decided to attend. On the final night of the run, two hundred people had to be turned away at the door. The Native Earth Theatre only held a hundred spectators.

The production soon garnered national and international attention. It won the Floyd S. Chalmers Award for Outstanding Canadian Play of 1986 and the Dora Award for Best New Play in Toronto's 1986–87 season. A national tour played in five cities across Canada between October 1987 and February 1988. The Native Earth company was invited to perform the play at the Edinburgh Festival in the summer of 1988. Highway's playscript was published by Fifth House Press later that fall, and it won the Governor General's Award for Drama.

Founded in 1982, Native Earth's early output consisted largely of unscripted plays based upon improvisation. In its first seasons, Native Earth usually produced one production per year with the limited project funding it was afforded. The company's first production was a show based on a painting by Indigenous artist Daphne Odjig. Entitled *Native Images in Transition*, the show played October 2–10, 1982, in Toronto. The company's second production was a collective creation entitled *Wey-Can-Nee-Nah or Who Am I*. The story of an Indigenous girl brought up by settler parents, the play toured reserves in Ontario in April and May of 1983. The next show was *Double Take/A Second Look*, which examined various myths about Indigenous people. Tomson Highway was hired as musical director for the production, which opened in December 1983 and toured to New York in February of the following year. Other productions included *Give Them a Carrot for as Long as the Sun Is Green* (1984) and *Trickster's Cabaret* (1985).

Highway had become the Artistic Director of Native Earth Performing Arts by 1986, when *The Rez Sisters* was first performed. Conceived the previous winter, when Highway was working with De-ba-jeh-mu-jig Theatre Group on Manitoulin Island, the play deals with seven women from a fictional reserve. As Ann Nothof writes, *The Rez Sisters* "follows the pattern of the journey motif."[2] The seven women embark on a trip to Toronto in order to play in the world's biggest bingo game. One of the women wins six hundred dollars; another dies of cancer. The Trickster, Nanabush, appears throughout the comedy, sometimes transforming himself into a seagull or a nighthawk or a bingo caller. The original production was directed by Larry Lewis. It featured Gloria Miguel and Muriel Miguel as the sisters Pelajia Patchnose and Philomena Moosetail, Anne Anglin as Annie Cook, and Sally Singal as Zhaboonigan Peterson. Tomson Highway's brother René, a dancer of note, played Nanabush. I saw René Highway in the role of Nanabush during the national tour of *The Rez Sisters*. What I remember of his performance was not only the extreme grace of his dancing but also the joy with which he performed. Balletically trained, he moved with precision and ease through the many transformations of Nanabush. He was also hilarious as the Bingo Master at the top of Act Two.

In subsequent appraisals of *The Rez Sisters*, much attention has been focused on the character of the Trickster. Jennifer Preston concentrates on the genderlessness of the Trickster in Tomson Highway's work. The character is performed by a male actor in *The Rez Sisters* and by a female actor in Highway's companion piece *Dry Lips Oughta Move to Kapuskasing* (originally entitled *The Rez Brothers*).[3] In Alan Filewod's view, the Trickster in Highway's work functions as an expression of difference between settler and Indigenous cultures "by upsetting the cartesian causality in drama."[4] Nanabush turns the logical world of the well-made play upside down, shifting time periods, changing shapes at will.

Throughout his playwriting career, Highway has been willing to grapple with the theme of homosexuality in Cree culture. *The Rez Sisters* is written in a camp, over-the-top style, with brash character portrayals that are meant to shock audiences. The biker chick Emily Dictionary admits, in the play's second act, that she is grieving the death of her former lover, Rose. In a later autobiographical novel, *Kiss of the Fur Queen*, Highway deals head-on with the tensions between Cree culture and an LTBQ lifestyle. The novel's central character, Gabriel, is a promiscuous gay man who has sex while he is HIV positive. The character is reportedly based on Tomson Highway's brother René, who died of AIDS complications in 1990.

The bond between the Highway brothers was a close one. Tomson Highway later recalled his start in theater as an effort to help his younger brother:

> I didn't really have a primary goal when I started. My first impulse was to help my brother, Rene Highway, to put on shows. He was stuck in Toronto with a stalled choreography career and so I helped him put shows together and they were painful experiences: there was never any money in them and I ended up paying for most of them myself. But when the plays started working, and I realized I had the chops for it, I just kept on going.[5]

The last thing René Highway said to his brother, before he slipped into a coma and died of HIV complications, was "Don't mourn me, be joyful." At that moment, Tomson Highway resolved to be twice as joyful as ordinary people, because he was being joyful for his brother as well as himself. This all-consuming joy is apparent in Highway's work. In her essay on *Kiss of the Fur Queen*, June Scudeler demonstrates how Highway links social interdependence with the land and the cosmos in the spirit of wahkotowin, or kinship.[6] While he writes about the evils of colonialism and racism, Highway does so with joy and forgiveness. All humanity, in his view, is interconnected.

The Rez Sisters signaled the beginning of an Indigenous theater renaissance in Canada. After Highway's groundbreaking work, Indigenous theater groups quickly sprang up across the country. Nakai Theatre Ensemble, an Inuit theater in the Yukon, has been producing plays by First Nations playwrights since 1989. In 1996, Métis playwright Ian Ross won a Governor General's Award for his play *fareWel*, which premiered at Winnipeg's Prairie Theatre Exchange. The Centre for Indigenous Theatre in Toronto now offers training for First Nations performers. In Saskatoon, the Gordon Tootoosis Nikaniwin Theatre was founded in 1999. Urban Ink productions, in Vancouver, founded in 2001, develops and produces new Indigenous work on a regular basis. In Edmonton, Alberta Aboriginal

Tomson Highway (photograph by Sean Howard).

Arts was created in 2009. In the meantime, Native Earth Performing Arts has grown from a shoestring budget company to become "a formidable artistic hub for all things related to contemporary Indigenous performing arts."[7] Now the oldest professional Indigenous theater company in Canada, Native Earth has spawned the talents of playwrights like Daniel David Moses, Drew Hayden Taylor, and Cliff Cardinal.

The Native Earth production of *The Rez Sisters*, back in 1986, also signaled the beginning of an explosive career in theater for Tomson Highway. In subsequent years, Highway's fame has grown with productions of other plays, including *Dry Lips*, *Rose*, and *The (Post)Mistress*. In 1998, *Macleans* magazine named Highway one of the 100 most important people in Canadian history. Currently a member of the Order of Canada, he continues to write and produce for the theater.

After 2000

The first twenty years of the 21st century have been marred by terrorism, war, and plague. On September 11, 2001, the terrorist attacks in New York and Washington set off a chain of events that led to wars in Iraq and Afghanistan. Further acts of terror occurred in London, where the Underground was bombed in 2005, and in Paris, where an attack at the Bataclan Theatre killed 90 people in 2015. In December 2019, the Covid virus spread worldwide, causing an international pandemic which has resulted in loss of jobs, financial insecurity, rising inflation, and product scarcity. In 2021, Russia invaded Ukraine, and the war in that country has lingered into the present day. Naturally, the violence and unhappiness of the age has been reflected in its theater, especially in the work of the in-yer-face movement, but the theater of the 21st century has also reacted by celebrating victories in the areas of human rights and international friendships. Two of those victories will be discussed below.

The premiere of Sarah Kane's play *4.48 Psychosis* is included here because it provides an apt introduction to the violence of the 21st century. Kane quickly became a representative of the in-yer-face movement with several earlier plays staged at the Royal Court Theatre in London. Despite Kane's suicide a year before *4.48 Psychosis* opened, and despite the fact that some critics considered it an extended suicide note, the play has become a classic of the modern theater.

One of the most blatantly political events in recent theatrical history occurred on November 11, 2016, as the cast of the hit musical *Hamilton* was taking its curtain call. Vice President–elect Mike Pence was in the audience that evening. One of the actors, Brandon V. Dixon, quieted the audience and launched into a prepared statement, co-written by the show's cast and its creator Lin-Manuel Miranda and its producer Jeffrey Seller. The statement reflected the diversity of the cast and called upon the Vice President–elect to renounce the divisive rhetoric of the presidential election campaign. Although he was not in attendance that evening, President-elect Donald Trump was infuriated by the incident. He quickly incited a Twitter campaign to boycott the show, but the campaign back-fired when it was learned that the show had already been sold out several years in advance.

Unlike *Hamilton*, the musical *Come from Away* seemed likely to become, at most, a regional hit. The play was initially workshopped at a small college theater in Toronto. When a New York production company called Junk Yard Dog saw the play and liked it, good things began to happen. First produced professionally by the La Jolla Playhouse and the Seattle Repertory Theatre, the show transferred to Broadway in 2017 and then to the West End of London. It was a happy turn of events for a husband-and-wife writing team who thought their play would never be produced outside of Canada.

CHAPTER 38

Howl of Pain

4.48 Psychosis, *Royal Court Theatre, London, June 23, 2000*

In a rehearsal room at the Royal Court Theatre in London, on a June evening in 2000, three actors and a director grappled with a difficult text. In the play they were working on, there was no cast list, and none of the speeches were attributed to a character. It might have been performed by a dozen actors or by one. Stage directions were absent. In one scene, a seemingly haphazard list of numbers danced across the page, there to be recited by an unspecified actor. How could such a play, if indeed it could be called a play, be staged?

The three actors—Daniel Evans, Jo McInnes, and Madeleine Potter—all memorized the entire text. The director, James Macdonald, wanted to retain the script's lack of specificity, and he decided that some moments would be left to the actors' whim. A particular speech would be spoken by one actor on a given night and by a different actor the next. After a time, the playwright's brother began to attend rehearsals, relaxing on a mattress at the back of the rehearsal hall. The play dealt with difficult subject matter around the topic of mental health, but the rehearsal period was full of levity. "The strange thing is that it was the funniest rehearsal period I've ever had," actor Daniel Evans said later. "It was probably some strange coping mechanism. We howled and howled with laughter."[1]

One of the reasons why a laughter-filled rehearsal period might have seemed odd was that the playwright, Sarah Kane, had committed suicide a year earlier. The play *4.48 Psychosis*, found in her desk shortly after her death, has been called an extended suicide note. It featured a very personal account of the despair and insomnia that Kane had been going through when she wrote the play. During that period, she would often wake, tired and depressed, at precisely 4:48 a.m.

Kane was born in 1971 in Brentwood, Essex. Her parents were devout Christians, and Kane was also devout in her youth. She studied drama at

University of Bristol and received an MA in playwriting at the University of Birmingham. Her mentor, at Birmingham, was David Edgar. She landed an agent while still attending university. After graduating, Kane worked as a literary associate at the Bush Theatre in London as well as a writer-in-residence at Paines Plough.[2] She wrote prolifically.

Her first play, *Blasted*, which was staged at the Royal Court in 1995, featured scenes of anal rape and cannibalism. It was attacked by members of the press but praised by playwrights like Edward Bond and Martin Crimp. Harold Pinter later said that he'd never heard a voice like Kane's in the theater. "It was a very startling and tender voice," he maintained, "but she was appalled by the world in which she lived and the world within herself." Kane was in the theater on the night that Pinter saw the play, and she was upset with the audience's response. Pinter told her that he thought the play was terrific and agreed to meet with her later to discuss her work. Kane and Pinter soon became friends.[3]

Kane's next two plays were marked by their excessive violence. *Phaedra's Love* was commissioned by the Gate Theatre in London and produced in 1996. It was loosely based on Seneca's *Phaedra*, but Kane chose to show the violence on stage rather than off. Pinter later wrote that the world view in *Phaedra's Love* terrified him: "What frightened me was the depth of her horror and anguish…. I think she had a vision of the world that was extremely accurate, and therefore horrific."[4] According to Pinter, the violence of *Phaedra's Love* jumped right off the page at him. Her next play, *Cleansed*, premiered at the Royal Court in 1998. Critics suggested that the violence in the play was gratuitous and over-the-top, but, as Simon Hattenstone writes, violent incidents in the play are based closely on real incidents. For example, he suggests that the prisoner who, after discovering how much time he has left to serve, hangs himself in *Cleansed* is based on a man who served time with Nelson Mandela on Robben Island.[5]

Produced in 1998 by Paines Plough, Kane's fourth play, *Crave*, was devoid of plot, setting, and stage directions, and was a work Kane regarded as her most despairing. It was also generally regarded as her best work. She wrote it under the pseudonym Marie Kelvedon—Marie was her middle name and Kelvedon was a village near her birthplace—so that the play could be judged by its merits, irrespective of who wrote it. The critics seemed to like this new work, comparing it to Eliot's "The Wasteland." Kane's agent Mel Kenyon later said that she craved approval, and that it was "not a mistake that the last play but one was called *Crave*…."[6] According to Kenyon, this yearning for the approval of her audience was something that Kane felt deeply.

Together these four plays managed to put Kane at the forefront of the in-yer-face movement, which is characterized by a concentration on violent, emotional, and sexual subject matter, by onstage violence, by confrontation, and by a breaking away from the conventions of realism and naturalism. The movement began in Britain in the 1990s and has continued to the present day. Other playwrights in the movement include Joe Penhall, Anthony Neilson, Martin Crimp, and Mark Ravenhill.

Suicide was Kane's constant preoccupation, in her plays and outside of them. Harold Pinter spoke of her preoccupation after Kane had died. "She talked about it a great deal," he said. "She just said it was on the cards, you know, and I had to say, 'Come on, for God's sake!' I remember a line in *Crave*: 'Death is my lover, and he wants to move in.' That's quite a line, isn't it? She felt man's inhumanity to man so profoundly. I believe that's what finally killed her."[7] Kane first attempted suicide on February 17, 1999, over-dosing on sleeping pills and antidepressants, but her flat mate found her, and she was taken to King's College Hospital where she stayed for three days. In the middle of the night on February 20, a nurse discovered that Kane was not in her bed. She had managed to hang herself with her own shoelaces from a hook inside the toilet door.

After *4.48 Psychosis* had been rehearsed for several weeks at the Royal Court, it was presented to an audience of family, friends, and fellow playwrights. Harold Pinter attended, as did Joe Penhall. The actors felt the strangeness and the sense of loss palpably in the theater that evening. "It was strange," Jo McInnes said afterwards, "but it was also potent. It felt like we had a responsibility to give breath and life to this amazing thing that Sarah had created." The final line, at the end of the play, is "please open the curtains." At that moment, McInnes and Daniel Evans opened a window in the roof of the theater, allowing the summer evening to invade the space. "All of a sudden you could feel a warm breeze and the noise of the traffic," Evans said later. "It was like the world being invited back in."[8]

4.48 Psychosis opened at the Royal Court on June 23, 2000. The play has since been produced in France, Belarus, the United States, Canada, New Zealand, and Ukraine. It ran for a full six months in São Paulo, Brazil. A Polish adaptation played, with surtitles, at the Edinburgh Festival in 2008. The British composer Philip Venables turned the play into an opera which was staged at the Lyric Hammersmith in 2016. Critics have been largely responsible for the notion that the play is little more than an extended suicide note. In *The Guardian*, Michael Billington wrote of the first production, "How on earth do you award aesthetic points to a 75-minute suicide note?"[9] In *The Telegraph*, Charles Spencer called the play "a deeply personal howl of pain."[10]

Among Kane's defenders are her own brother and the actors who performed in the play's first production. "At the time, the last thing I would have wanted to say is that it's a suicide note," Simon Kane said in 2016. "I knew it wasn't just that, that was the point." Similarly, actor Jo McInnes found more in the play than a mere suicide note. "People take her story on, and then they infuse her work with that," McInnes said recently. "I find that really frustrating. To me the heart of it is a love story—what does it mean to love, can we love, all those questions."[11]

CHAPTER 39

The Revolution

Hamilton, *Richard Rodgers Theater, New York, November 11, 2016*

On November 11, 2016, the cast of the hit Broadway musical *Hamilton* took their curtain call. The actor Brandon V. Dixon quieted the applause and read a prepared statement to the Vice President–elect of the United States, who was in the audience. Co-written by the show's cast and its creator Lin-Manuel Miranda and its producer Jeffrey Seller, the statement called on the Vice President–elect to renounce the often-divisive rhetoric of his election campaign. "We, sir—we—are the diverse America who are alarmed and anxious that your new administration will not protect us, our planet, our children, our parents, or defend us and uphold our inalienable rights," said Dixon. "We truly hope that this show has inspired you to uphold our American values and to work on behalf of all of us."[1] The cast of the play standing before Vice President–elect Mike Pence that evening was composed of talented actors of many ethnicities, and their references to American values brought to mind his administration's controversial election promises, which included building a wall across the Mexico-U.S. border, deporting millions of immigrants, and registering Muslims.

From its inception years earlier, *Hamilton: An American Musical* was a project with a distinct political edge. The show's creator, Lin-Manuel Miranda, was an American librettist, actor, and hip-hop artist of Puerto Rican descent. He had written an earlier play, *In the Heights*, about immigrants living in Upper Manhattan, which had premiered Off Broadway in 2007. While on vacation from that production, Manuel had read Ron Chernow's biography of Alexander Hamilton and had decided to write some songs based on Hamilton's eventful life. These songs were eventually included in a project entitled *The Hamilton Mixtape*. When Miranda was invited to perform music from *In the Heights* at a White House gala in 2009, he decided instead to perform the first song from *The Hamilton Mixtape*. The program made good then–President Barack Obama's pledge to highlight the nation's artists, and Miranda was featured as the closing act. "I'm actually working on a hip-hop album," he said into the microphone, "a concept album about the life of someone who embodies hip-hop." He proceeded to sing the song, and the First Lady snapped her fingers to the beat. When the song ended, the President led a standing ovation. As Jeremy McCarter later wrote,

> That night, Lin reintroduced people to the poor kid from the Caribbean who made the country rich and strong, an immigrant who came here to build a life for himself and ended up helping to build a nation. He is the prototype for millions of men and women who followed him, and continue to arrive today. You can look up the facts and figures that demonstrate the vast and growing importance of immigrants to our national life: that 13 percent of the population is foreign-born, which is near an all-time high; that one day soon, there will no longer be majority and minority races, only a vibrant mix of colors.[2]

The vast contributions of a talented immigrant were fully evident in the White House that evening.

After the White House gala, Miranda resumed work on other songs for *The Hamilton Mixtape*. When he had amassed a variety of songs, he organized a workshop production of the show, still titled *The Hamilton Mixtape*, at Vassar College in Poughkeepsie. Directed by Thomas Kail, the workshop production consisted of songs from the first act of the play and parts of the second act. It played before an invited audience on July 27, 2013. The young actor Leslie Odom, Jr., was among the spectators that evening. After the performance, he sent Miranda a text saying "he would be the show's biggest cheerleader when it got staged."[3] Miranda did not want Odom Jr. as a cheerleader, however; he wanted the *Grey's Anatomy* star to act in an eventual production. Odom Jr. was eventually signed to play Aaron Burr on Broadway.

A more complete version of the play, now titled *Hamilton: An American Musical*, received its Off Broadway premiere at the Public Theater in New York on February 17, 2015. The play's producer, Jeffrey Seller, wanted to move the show to Broadway before the end of the 2014–15 season, but Miranda lobbied for more time to make revisions. Several musical numbers were cut after the Off Broadway run, and the revised musical previewed on Broadway, at the Richard Rodgers Theater, on July 13, 2015.

The play unfolds in two acts, taking us from Alexander Hamilton's beginnings on the Caribbean island of Nevis to his death in 1804. In Act One, the young Hamilton becomes George Washington's aide-de-camp and helps plan the decisive American victory at Yorktown. Developments in Hamilton's personal life are also chronicled. He meets Eliza Schuyler at a ball. The two fall in love and marry, and Eliza bears their first child, Philip. The United States of America achieves its independence, and the newly elected President George Washington appoints Hamilton as his Secretary of the Treasury.

In Act Two, Hamilton's professional and personal lives unravel. He embarks on an affair with the married Maria Reynolds which would eventually result in America's first political sex scandal. George Washington steps down as president, opening the door for John Adams to replace him. After Hamilton publishes a critique of the new president, Thomas Jefferson, James Madison, and Aaron Burr confront him about his extra-marital affair. When Hamilton admits to the affair publicly, a heartbroken Eliza burns all of her correspondence from him.

Hamilton endorses Jefferson in his bid for the presidential election of 1800, which is the last straw in his fractured relationship with Aaron Burr. The two men fight a duel, with Burr firing first (the play takes many liberties with actual historical accounts). Hamilton chooses to waste his first shot, as was common practice at the time, and Burr fires a second shot, hitting Hamilton in the abdomen. Burr is immediately remorseful, cognizant of the fact that he will be remembered as a villain.

The Broadway run benefited from the hype created during the popular Off Broadway engagement. Even before the play opened on Broadway, it had reportedly sold more than 30 million dollars' worth of advance tickets. In response to the show's popularity, the company instituted a "Ham-4Ham" lottery. Under the rules of the lottery, eager theatergoers could line up outside the theater for a chance to win ten-dollar seats in the front row. On July 13, before the first preview, 697 people had entered the draw, in a line stretching nearly to Eighth Avenue. Five days later, on the afternoon of July 18, President Obama attended the show, receiving a rapturous ovation. At the intermission, Obama came backstage to greet the cast. "It's really good!" he exclaimed. "Sometimes it takes a while until people know something is good. Here, people know."[4]

The reception Mike Pence received in the theater more than a year later was decidedly less enthusiastic. In fact, several audience members booed when it became known that Pence was in attendance. The Vice President–elect was not overly offended. He turned to his daughters as the booing continued and said, "That is what freedom sounds like." In a later interview on *Fox News Sunday*, Pence did not criticize the cast for addressing him from the stage. "I did hear what was said from the stage," he said. "I can tell you I wasn't offended by what was said. I will leave it to others whether that was the appropriate venue to say it."[5]

President-elect Donald Trump had a different view of the incident, and he demanded action. "Apologize!" he demanded in a tweet the next morning. A day later, the President-elect tweeted again. "The cast and producers of Hamilton," he wrote, "which I hear is highly overrated, should immediately apologize to Mike Pence for their terrible behavior." For his part, Pence tried to reassure the American public that minorities would be cared for. "I just want to reassure every American that in the days ahead," he said, "I am very confident that they are going to see President-elect Trump be a president for all the people and we embrace that principle." Former Republican speech writer Peter Wehner summarized the polarizing effect of the incident and of the President-elect's reaction to it as follows: "It was this collision of two different Americas and two different visions and two different sets of experiences, happening at once, and happening in a rather dramatic way."

Meanwhile, Trump's tweets led to an online campaign to boycott the production. The online campaign, labelled #Boycott-Hamilton, became the subject of much derision, especially because the show had been sold out months in advance. Historian Robert Dallek reportedly characterized Trump's tweets as "a striking act of divisiveness by an incoming president struggling to heal the nation after a bitter election."[6] Not often has a President-elect of the United States taken so much exception to the actions of a Broadway cast.

Hamilton: An American Musical nevertheless went on to win 11 Tony Awards and the Pulitzer Prize in Drama. The production eventually transferred to the West End of London, where it won the Laurence Olivier Award for Best New Musical. The play has spawned a documentary film and a traveling museum exhibition. In 2015, the U.S. Treasury Department announced a plan to redesign the ten-dollar bill, replacing Hamilton's image with that of another historical figure. Perhaps because of the play's popularity, the Treasury reversed its plan, deciding instead to replace the image of Andrew Jackson on the twenty-dollar bill with that of African American abolitionist Harriet Tubman.

CHAPTER 40

One of Those Stories

Come from Away, *Gerald Schoenfeld Theatre, New York, March 12, 2017*

On the tenth anniversary of the terrorist attacks on the World Trade Center, the musical writing team of Irene Sankoff and David Hein visited Gander, Newfoundland, a small city of ten thousand people on the east coast of Canada. There was a reunion of the many people who were involved in Operation Yellow Ribbon, both locals and those who came from away, on that day, and Sankoff and Hein were able to interview the key participants. The idea of writing a feel-good musical about such a horrific event might have seemed unlikely—especially as the writers had experienced only minor success with their work until that date. But after conducting interviews with passengers and hosts who had participated in the diversion of civilian airline flights to Gander, they penned a musical, infused with a particular brand of east coast Celtic songs, that would open on Broadway on March 12, 2017.

The project was first conceived by theater producer Michael Rubinoff, who was the Associate Dean of Visual and Performing Arts at Sheridan College in Toronto. He had shopped the idea around to various writing teams before settling on Sankoff and Hein. A young husband-and-wife team, Sankoff and Hein had little Broadway experience, and they did not think that their work on a musical about 9/11 would ever see the light of day outside of Canada. Their most significant work before that date was a brief musical, produced at the Toronto Fringe Festival in 2009, entitled *My Mother's Lesbian Jewish Wiccan Wedding*.

Based on the exhaustive interviews conducted in Gander, the writers produced a 45-minute workshop script for the Canadian Music Theatre Project. When the workshop was done, Rubinoff was sufficiently buoyed by its success to produce a fuller version of the play at Sheridan College in 2013 as part of the Theatre Department's regular season. While Rubinoff was not able to attract a Canadian producer for the play, he and the authors had better luck south of the border. Goodspeed Musicals, a nonprofit organization dedicated to the advancement of musical theater, included the play in its workshop season at East Haddam, Connecticut. Having seen the results of that workshop, the National Alliance for Musical Theatre selected the play for a showcase presentation in the autumn of 2013. Junkyard Dog Productions, a New York company that had previously produced the musicals *Memphis* and *First Date*, optioned the play shortly thereafter.

The play is a celebration of the friendships and compassion that grew out of Operation Yellow Ribbon. It is a story of human resiliency and of people coming together at a time of great fear and loss. The play begins on the morning of September 11, 2001, as the Gander townsfolk begin to learn of the terrorist attacks in New York, Washington, and Shanksville. When the U.S. closes its airspace, 38 civilian planes are diverted and forced to land in Gander. The townsfolk scramble to house, feed, and comfort the stranded passengers who are initially wary of such uncommon hospitality. Over the following night and day, the guests begin to bond with the townsfolk and are invited to be "screeched in" at a local bar—a process that involves drinking a glass of Newfoundland "screech" rum and kissing a codfish. People fall in love. Long-time relationships fall apart.

Although the play is largely about the friendships that result from these encounters, it does not shy away from the darker realities of the terrorist attacks. One of the passengers, Hannah, discovers that her firefighter son has lost his life in rescue efforts back home. As the passengers prepare to fly back home, near the end of the play, one Muslim passenger is forced to undergo a humiliating strip-search.

There are two sets of protagonists in *Come from Away*, one based on the locals from Gander and one based on the international passengers who arrive on that fateful day. The play seeks to tell its story from both sides of the international border. It also comes close to docudrama in its retelling. Characters are often given the same names as their real-life counterparts or, sometimes when they are conflated, the first name of one real-life person and the last name of another. Among the diverted airplanes is one piloted by Captain Beverley Bass who was the first female captain of an American Airlines commercial plane and whose Boeing 777 was enroute from Paris to Fort Worth. Bass becomes a major character in the play, and Jenn Colella's portrayal of the character eventually won her a Drama Desk Award. Part of the charm of the show is that it does not seek to stereotype any of the characters in the play; both sets of protagonists are presented with a deep sense of respect.

Come from Away was first produced professionally in 2015 as a collaboration between the La Jolla Playhouse and the Seattle Repertory Theater. Directed by Christopher Ashley, the production featured Joel Hatch as the

Mayor of Gander, Chad Kimball as Kevin, and Jenn Colella as Beverley. Ashley, Hatch, Kimball, and Colella would all be included in the Broadway run of the play, which opened at the Gerald Schoenfeld Theatre in 2017.

Three days after the play opened on Broadway, on March 15, Canadian Prime Minister Justin Trudeau addressed the audience, which included several Canadian politicians as well as Ivanka Trump. Trudeau received a great deal of press coverage as a result of his appearance; *Come from Away* became known as Trudeau's *Hamilton*. Trudeau used the occasion to highlight the importance of a strong U.S./Canada relationship. His address to the audience, and to Ivanka Trump, was particularly pointed because Trudeau's relationship with President Donald Trump had already been strained by dealings over the NAFTA Free Trade Agreement.

The critical reception for the Broadway production was glowing. In *Newsweek*, Joe Westerfield wrote that the attacks of September 11, 2001 evoked strong feelings of fear and sadness but that *Come From Away* managed to inject intelligent humor into its aftermath. He refered to a scene in which an African American man named Rodney Hicks is told to help prepare for a barbecue by going unannounced into local peoples' backyards and taking their grills. With visions of being gunned down by the local police, Hicks "gets perhaps the biggest laugh of the show with a raised eyebrow and a half-stifled gasp."[1] Westerfield ended his review with the suggestion that the musical was one of the best ensemble pieces Broadway had seen in years. "In one act, at one hour and 40 minutes, *Come from Away* moves at a brisk, entertaining pace and easily passes the wristwatch test: I never once checked the time," he wrote, suggesting that the play accomplishes what all great musicals accomplish. "[I]t takes you to a place where you didn't know you wanted to go, and makes you not want to leave."[2] In *The Huffington Post*, Steven Suskind wrote that the play was "brave and new and unusual and overwhelmingly heart-tugging."[3] In *The New York Post*, Johnny Oleksinski similarly raved about the play's message of compassion and hope. "The best stories of real-life tragedy shine a light on humanity's capacity for goodness, in spite of enormous odds," he wrote. "This is one of those stories."[4] Written the day before Justin Trudeau made his appearance at the Broadway show, Oleksinski's article made reference to the Canadian Prime Minister. "And like a reincarnated JFK, the nation's prime minister, Justin Trudeau, has skyrocketed to A-list celebrity status," Oleksinski wrote. "Every one of his manly likes, smoldering glares and competent explanations of quantum computing sets the internet ablaze."[5]

Because of the Covid-19 pandemic, the Broadway production closed temporarily on March 12, 2020, but reopened again on September 21, 2021. Subsequent productions of the musical have played well in North America and elsewhere. The Royal Manitoba Theatre Centre, in Winnipeg,

Canada, presented a four-week run in January 2018, and then the production proceeded to a longer run at the Royal Alexandra Theatre in Toronto. Another production ran at the Abbey Theatre in Dublin for two months before transferring to London's West End on January 30, 2019. An Australian production of the musical opened in Melbourne on July 20, 2019. The play has won several major awards, including a Tony for Best Direction of a Musical and a Drama Desk Award for Outstanding Musical. The cast album was nominated for a Grammy in 2018. In England, the play won Laurence Olivier Awards for Best New Musical and Outstanding Achievement in Music.

In October 2016, the cast of the musical traveled back to Newfoundland to perform a benefit concert in the local hockey arena in Gander. It was a homecoming of sorts, attended by about five thousand locals and by some of the international travelers who had arrived in Gander fifteen years earlier. Going back to the local roots of the play only seemed right. Proceeds from the performances were donated to charities like the Salvation Army Foodbank in Gander, the Lewisporte Heritage Society and the Norris Arm Lions Club. In subsequent years, a scholarship fund has been created for students from Gander. A feature film adaptation of the play, which will be played by lesser-known actors and will include appearances by Gander townsfolk, is currently in pre-production.

Ilene Sankoff and David Hein have risen from their Toronto Fringe Festival roots to become the toast of Broadway and the West End. Not bad for a writing team who thought the show would never be produced outside of Canada. Not bad for a show that got its start with a student cast at a small college in Toronto. And not bad for a show about some hospitable Newfoundlanders opening their hearts and homes to complete strangers in the wake of a tragic event that would have world-wide implications.

Epilogue

My own favorite opening night took place on September 14, 1980, in Stratford, Canada. On that date, *King Lear* premiered at the Avon Theatre. The revival of a 1979 production, starring Peter Ustinov in the title role and directed by Robin Phillips, it featured several actors who had not been in the cast the previous year. I was one of them.

Acting in a production with Peter Ustinov was the realization of an unlikely dream for me. A year earlier, I was a drama student at the University of Saskatchewan. I was, in fact, still enrolled in graduate studies there and had absconded to act in Stratford without alerting my thesis supervisor. My knowledge of Ustinov, until that time, was limited to watching him play the ghost of Edward Teach in a Disney production, entitled *Blackbeard's Ghost*, that had delighted my friends and me when we were in seventh grade. We used to run around the schoolyard, in my rural Saskatchewan hometown, shouting Ustinov's lines to one another.

How I even got a job at Stratford is a story that seems worth telling. Having pooled my resources in the late autumn of 1979, I bought a train ticket to Ontario so that I could audition for all the theaters there, although I hadn't even bothered to get in touch with those theaters before I breezily hopped on the train. I practiced my audition pieces in the sleeper car along the way. On the second morning of the three-day journey, a lady in the next sleeper complained that she'd heard voices coming from my compartment in the night and that it sounded like I was partying with fifteen people in there.

When I arrived in Toronto in late November, I found to my dismay that there were only a limited number of artistic directors who wanted to meet with me on such short notice. Luckily, I had free room and board at my Aunt Edna's apartment in Scarborough. I thought I could wait these stalling artistic directors out but, two weeks into the audition tour, it became apparent that I was running out of money. Was there anybody I'd missed? Stratford, of course. I found a telephone number and gave the theater a ring. It was likely the stage doorman who answered. I asked if I could audition. He informed me that the Festival was closed for the winter.

I hopped on a bus for Stratford early the next morning. Buses were less expensive than trains. It was a dreary, overcast day. I remember walking on sidewalks littered with leaves. I banged on the glass doors at the front of the theater. Then I went around to the stage door and asked to see the artistic director. The doorman told me that the artistic director wasn't there. The only administrator in the building, he said, was the literary manager. I said I'd like to talk to him. The doorman made a phone call and told me to wait.

A half hour later, the literary manager Urjo Kareda came down the stairs and met me at the stage door. He gave me a wry look when I told him I wanted to audition. He said there was nobody there who could give me a job, but I insisted on auditioning for him. He shook his head and smiled. "Okay," he said, "if that's what you want. But nothing will come of it."

We went up to the backstage area. Kareda escorted me out onto the famous apron stage that Sir Tyrone Guthrie and Tanya Moiseivitch had designed. While I was largely ignorant of what went on at Stratford, I did know that Alec Guinness and James Mason and Christopher Plummer had performed on that stage. Kareda told me to warm up while he attended to some other business. I wondered, later, if he'd been watching me on the live television feed from the theater to see how I responded to that hallowed space. When Kareda came back into the theater, I performed my best pieces for him, Mercutio from *Romeo and Juliet* and Bishop from *Billy Bishop Goes to War*. He didn't seem underwhelmed but, when the audition was finished, he thanked me for dropping by and made no other promises.

I returned to Saskatchewan a few days later, thinking what a waste of time the audition tour had been. A week later, I auditioned for the Globe Theatre school tour, which would be rehearsed in Regina. They gave me a job. We toured through northern Saskatchewan in a passenger van that was sprayed, on the inside, with a suspicious-looking foam insulation. I played Oberon in *A Midsummer Night's Dream* and various roles in Rex Deverell's *The Copetown City Kite Crisis*. We were in Green Lake in frigid January when I got the phone call. Stratford wanted to hire me.

My first impulse was to turn them down. I was under contract to do the Globe tour, after all, which did not finish until spring. A day later, Tom Kerr, the head of drama at the University of Saskatchewan, called me to ask if I'd lost my mind. "Are you kidding?" he said. "This is a once in a lifetime offer." I was on an airplane, bound for Stratford, one month later.

Peter Ustinov had a dream, as well, and that dream was to play Lear. As Robert Cushman wrote in an obituary in 2004, Ustinov "had been obsessed with Lear for years" before taking the role in Robin Phillips' production.[1] Not only would he sign contracts to play Lear at Stratford, Canada, in 1979 and 1980—and contracts for single roles at the Festival were not the norm—he would also lobby to play the character at the Haymarket Theatre in London in a Stratford Festival tour at the end of the final run. His hiring was clearly a throwback to the bad old days when British stars journeyed to a Canadian city to surround themselves with lesser-known Canadian actors.

For the 1980 production, I was contracted to play the Captain, both at the Avon Theatre and during the Haymarket tour. I had one scene as the Captain. After Edgar (played by Richard Monette) handed me a written order to murder Cordelia, I was fortunate enough to declaim two evocative lines that capture the debasement of a war-worn soldier. "I cannot draw a cart nor eat dried oats," I growled after reading the note in rehearsals. "If it be man's work, I'll do it." The lines have stuck with me until today; they are almost my favorite lines in all of Shakespeare. Having spoken the epigram of a character more used to action than to words, I executed a precise military about face—rehearsed ad nauseum because I'd never been in the military—and marched offstage where Cordelia would be dispatched. Phillips did not over-direct. At the final dress rehearsal, he offered me one piece of advice. "Don't read that piece of paper with the order written on it," he said. "You're willing to do whatever is asked of you." Of course, he was right.

I was also William Hutt's understudy as the Fool. If Hutt had ever taken ill—and he was not a young man in 1980—I'm sure I would have been booed off the stage at my first entrance. Having dutifully rehearsed the part in the confines of my apartment, I went to Hutt for advice in the middle of the run. "Let's hope you never have to play it," he intoned. "The only thing to know about the Fool," he added, "is that he's deathly ill."

Ustinov was a delight to be around, both on and off stage. Through most of that summer, he was ubiquitous at grocery stores and restaurants around town. My landlady, Jo Aldwinkle, had a friendly conversation with him once at a supermarket till. When she told me about it later, she referred to him as "Oosti-Boosti." If Ustinov saw his fellow actors in a restaurant, he'd come over and say hello. He spoke about twenty languages. One of my good friends was a fellow actor of Italian origin. Backstage, Ustinov would only speak Italian to my friend. When Ustinov asked me about my ancestry, I was reticent to tell him because I didn't speak a word of Norwegian. He refused to speak English to me after he'd pried that information out, starting every halting conversation with "Can du snakker Norsk?" On opening night, American Express threw a big party for the cast because Ustinov was their spokesperson at that time. I drank scotch and beer all evening. It was the first time I'd ever tasted caviar.

It was apparent, early on, that Ustinov's Lear would not be a conventional portrayal. He believed the play to be "about senility," as Robert Cushman later wrote. "This was the cause of Lear's capricious behavior toward his daughters in the first scene; this was the real diagnosis of his madness in the central scenes." I remember watching Ustinov in rehearsals, picking lint off someone's tunic in the tense first scene. Privately, some of the actors referred to the production as "Uncle Lear" due to the softness of Ustinov's characterization. His vocal power had likely diminished since the heydays of his early stage career. According to Robert Cushman, Ustinov's vocal shortcomings for the stage were evident in his vocalizations. "He made no attempt to outroar the storm or to create it with his voice," Cushman wrote. "'Blow winds, and crack your cheeks,' he modestly suggested, and left the winds to get on with it."[2] Still, the reviews were not entirely unfavorable. "But always one comes back to Ustinov's Lear," Ralph Berry wrote in *Shakespeare Quarterly*, "a marvelous and moving, deeply felt study of the being in decay."[3]

Near the end of the run, the actors were summoned to a townhall meeting with Robin Phillips. It was the first time I knew that the tour to the Haymarket was in doubt. The meeting was tense and unhappy; there were questions about whether a tour bond had ever been posted with Canadian Actors' Equity, about whether the company had ever been serious about letting the tour go ahead. We were assured that, if the tour did not go ahead, all of the actors would be bought out of their contracts. Nobody looked happy by the time the meeting ended.

There has been much speculation as to why the tour did not proceed. One explanation was that Phillips had been haggling with the Festival's board about escalating production costs all season long and that the Haymarket tour was caught in the crossfire. While Ustinov was committed to the Haymarket run—indeed, it had been in his contract that he would only perform in Stratford if the production was later mounted at the Haymarket—some of his supporting cast had not yet been signed to contracts. Douglas Rain, who played Gloucester, was worried about leaving his elderly mother who had moved to Stratford so that Rain could look after her. Martha Henry, who played Goneril, had other commitments but eventually agreed to be part of the tour.[4]

According to Martin Knelman, Ustinov was convinced that Phillips was sabotaging the tour. "I think he's afraid the production will fail and the critics won't like it," Knelman quotes Ustinov as saying. "It's his first production back in London since he left for Canada. If it's successful, I guess he's concerned I'm going to get the credit."[5] There were rumors that Ustinov wanted to sue the Festival for breach of contract. Eventually, Ustinov settled his claim against the Festival for $45,000.[6]

Thirty-four years later, as a professor at the University of Saskatchewan, I was organizing and leading a course entitled Theatre Studies in London. The University had offered the course for over a decade, ferrying

Canadian students across the Atlantic for two weeks of lectures, workshops and theatergoing. In May 2014, my students and I attended a performance of *One Man, Two Guv'ners* at the Haymarket Theatre in London. Having read the play beforehand, we knew that audience participation was a requirement, so I was a little uneasy when the box office gave us front row seats. Twenty minutes into the show, Rufus Hound stepped out of the set and scampered into the stalls. He took me by the hand and led me on to the stage. He asked me what I did for a living. I announced that I was a theater professor. "That's good," he said. "This lot could use a lesson in acting." For the next five minutes, I was given embarrassing tasks to perform, much to the delight of my students and the rest of the sold-out audience. After hurling an accusation of sexual impropriety at me, Hound sent me back to my seat. At intermission, another audience member approached me at the bar and asked if I was a plant.

The next morning, my students and I were taking part in a puppetry workshop with one of the actors from *War Horse*, which was also playing in London at the time. When I walked in the door of the rehearsal hall, the workshop leader shouted across the room, "Hey, you were on stage at the Haymarket last night." I admitted that, yes, it had been me. I must have looked downtrodden. "I know how you feel," the workshop leader commiserated. "Being called up onstage as an audience member is my worst nightmare too."

I nodded woefully, not bothering to inform him that I'd once had a contract to perform on that stage with no less an actor than Peter Ustinov. It was difficult to be too sad. We were in London, after all, with a group of enthusiastic theater students, learning puppetry skills at a National Theatre rehearsal hall. And somewhere deep inside, I sensed that my world had come full circle; I'd finally gotten my Haymarket debut.

Chapter Notes

Chapter 1

1. Katie Freeman, "Letter Threatening Jackson's Life Determined to Be Written by Father of Man Who Killed Lincoln," knoxnews.com/news/2009/jan/25/letter-threatening-jacksons-life-determined-writte.
2. Ward Hill Lamon, *Recollections of Abraham Lincoln 1847–1865*, Washington, D.C.: Dorothy Lamon Teillard, 1911, p. 116–117.
3. Quoted in "Assassination of Abraham Lincoln," Wikipedia.
4. Doris Kearns Goodwin, "The Night Abraham Lincoln Was Assassinated," *The Smithsonian*, April 18, 2015, smithsonianmag.com.
5. Quoted in Edward Steers, Jr., *Blood on the Moon*, Lexington: Univ. Press of Kentucky, 2001, p. 101.
6. *Ibid.*, p. 98.
7. *Ibid.*, p. 109.
8. Quoted in "Assassination of Abraham Lincoln," Wikipedia.
9. *Ibid.*
10. Steers, p. 114.
11. Samuel J. Seymour, as told to Frances Spatz Leighton, "I Saw Lincoln Shot," *The American Weekly, Milwaukee Sentinel*, February 7, 1954.

Chapter 2

1. Quoted in "William Terriss," Wikipedia.
2. Jessie Millward, *Myself and Others*, London: Hutchinson, 1923, p. 232.
3. Alice Johnson, "Examination of a Premonitory Case: Mr. Lane's dream of the death of Mr. Terriss," *Proceedings of the Society for Psychical Research* (Great Britain), p. 313.
4. *Ibid.*, p. 310.
5. Millward, p. 231.
6. Dan Gilloy, "The Murder of William Terriss," stagebeauty.com.
7. Millward, p. 231.
8. *Ibid.*
9. Quoted in George Rowell, *William Terriss and Richard Prince: Two Players in an Adelphi Melodrama*, London: Society for Theatre Research, 1987, pp. 78–79.
10. Quoted in https://www.jack-the-ripper-tour.com/generalnews/the-murder-of-william-terriss.
11. Millward, p. 233.
12. *Ibid.*, p. 234.
13. Rowell, pp. 79–80.
14. Millward, p. 240.
15. Rowell, p. 83.
16. *Ibid.*, p. 89.
17. Millward, pp. 237–238.
18. Quoted in "William Terriss," Wikipedia.
19. https://paranormalfact.fandom.com/wiki/William_Terriss_(Ghost).
20. *Ibid.*

Chapter 3

1. Perriton Maxwell, "The Editor Goes to the Play." *Theatre Magazine*, November 1928, p. 46.
2. Patricia Arechiga, "Woman Made of Stone: The Murder of Albert Snyder," November 12, 2019, stmuhistorymedia.org.
3. Landis MacKellar, *The "Double Indemnity" Murder*, Syracuse, NY: Syracuse Univ. Press, 2006, p. 72.
4. *Ibid.*, p. 98.
5. *Ibid.*, p. 99.
6. I am indebted to Patricia Arechiga for

her account of the murder and the events leading up to it, in "Woman Made of Stone: The Murder of Albert Snyder," November 12, 2019, stmuhistorymedia.org.
  7. MacKellar, p. 368.
  8. *Ibid.*, p. 371.
  9. *Ibid.*
  10. Maxwell, p. 46.
  11. Brooks Atkinson, "The Play," *New York Times*, September 8, 1928.

Chapter 4

  1. Sudhanva Deshpande, *Halla Bol: The Death and Life of Safdar Hashmi*. New Delhi: LeftWord Books, 2020, p. 24.
  2. *Ibid.*, p. 25.
  3. *Ibid.*
  4. Quoted in pyotra.tumblr.com, Feb. 26, 2016.
  5. Shelley Walia, "The Luminous Life of Safdar Hashmi," *The Tribune India*, April 12, 2020.
  6. Sudhanva Deshpande, "Remembering Safdar Hashmi and the Play That Changed Indian Street Theatre Forever," January 3, 2017, at Scroll.in.
  7. Deshpande, *Halla Bol*, p. 28.
  8. *Ibid.*, p. 48.
  9. *Ibid.*, p. 53.
  10. *Ibid.*, p. 56.

Chapter 5

  1. Oscar Brockett and Robert Findlay, *Century of Innovation*. Englewood Cliffs, NJ: Prentice Hall, 1973, p. 87.
  2. *Ibid.*, p. 91.
  3. In Holz's equation, x represented the artist's subjectivity and the limitations of his medium.
  4. With plays based on social problems like *Society* (1865) and *Ours* (1866), Robertson had become Britain's foremost contributor to the realistic school.
  5. Brockett and Findlay, p. 110.
  6. *Ibid.*, p. 116.

Chapter 6

  1. Nick Worrall, *The Moscow Art Theatre*. London: Taylor and Francis, 1996, p. 36.
  2. S.D. Balukhaty, ed. *The Seagull Produced by Stanislavsky*. New York: Theatre Arts Books, 1952, pp. 40–41.

  3. Quoted in Worrall, p. 15.
  4. *Ibid.*, pp. 40–41.
  5. *Ibid.*, p. 42.
  6. *Ibid.*, p. 43.
  7. *Ibid.*, pp. 46–47.
  8. *Ibid.*, p. 48.

Chapter 7

  1. Chekhov 1920; Letter to A.F. Koni, Project Gutenberg.
  2. S.D. Balukhaty, ed., *The Seagull Produced by Stanislavsky*. New York: Theatre Arts Books, 1952, p. 25.
  3. *Ibid.*, p. 28.
  4. Jean Benedetti, ed., *Moscow Art Theatre Letters*. New York: Theatre Arts, 1991, p. 15.
  5. *Ibid.*, p. 16.
  6. *Ibid.*, p. 17.
  7. *Ibid.*
  8. Jean Benedetti, ed., *Dear Writer, Dear Actress: The Love Letters of Anton Chekhov and Olga Knipper*. Hopewell, NJ: Ecco Press, 1996, p. 5.
  9. His "directorial score" would later be published under the title *The Seagull Produced by Stanislavsky*.
  10. Balukhaty, p. 175.
  11. Jean Benedetti, *Stanislavsky: His Life and Art*, revised edition. London: Methuen, 1999, p.78.
  12. Quoted in *Ibid.*, p. 86.
  13. Both quotations are from Balukhaty, p. 77.
  14. *Ibid.*, p. 74.
  15. Sarah Grochala and Adam Rush, "The Seagull's Two Premieres," May 10, 2013, headlong.co.uk.
  16. Benedetti, *Dear Writer, Dear Actress*, p. 284.
  17. *Ibid.*, p. 291.

Chapter 8

  1. David A. Crespy, *Off-Off-Broadway Explosion*. New York: Back Stage Books, 2003, p.70.
  2. *Ibid.*, p. 69.
  3. "La Mama Experimental Theater," Wikipedia.
  4. Crespy, p. 72.
  5. *Ibid.*, p. 77.
  6. *Ibid.*, p. 78.

Chapter 9

1. Quoted in Rachel Knowles, "Drury Lane Theatre Burns Down 24 February 1809," https://www.regencyhistory.net/2020/02/drury-lane-theatre-burns-down-24.html.
2. Marc Baer, *Theatre and Disorder in Late Georgian London*. Oxford: Oxford Univ. Press, 1992, p. 22.
3. *Ibid.*
4. *Ibid.*, p. 19.
5. A shilling in 1809 was roughly the equivalent of eighteen U.S. dollars today.
6. Baer, p. 34.
7. *Ibid.*, p. 27.
8. *Ibid.*, p. 33.
9. Quoted in "Old Price Riots," Wikipedia.
10. Baer, p. 35.

Chapter 10

1. Gerald Bordman, *The Concise Oxford Companion to American Theatre*. Oxford: Oxford Univ. Press, p. 408.
2. Brander Matthews and Lawrence Hutton, eds., *Actors and Actresses of Great Britain and the United States*. London: Cassell, 1886, p.23.
3. William Toynbee, ed., *The Diaries of William Charles Macready, 1833–1851*, vol. 1. New York: Putnam's, 1912, p. 230.
4. All quotations in this paragraph from Toynbee, vol. 2, pp. 228–29.
5. Quoted in James Rees, *The Life of Edwin Forrest*. Philadelphia: T.B. Peterson, 1874, p. 130.
6. William Toynbee, ed., *The Diaries of William Charles Macready, 1833–1851*, vol. 2. New York: Putnam's, 1912, p. 226.
7. Toynbee, vol. 2, p. 327.
8. Quoted in Edward Ziter, *Macready, Booth, Terry, Irving: Great Shakespeareans*, vol. xi, Richard Schoch, ed. London: A&C Black, 2014, p. 48.
9. Toynbee, vol. 2, p. 404.
10. The poster can be seen at "Astor Place Riots," Wikipedia.

Chapter 11

1. Otto P. Schinnerer, "The History of Schnitzler's 'Reigen,'" in *PMLA*, no. 3 (Sept. 1931), pp. 839–859, p. 851.

2. *Ibid.*
3. Quoted in Carl R. Mueller, *Arthur Schnitzler: Four Major Plays*. Lyme, NH: Smith and Kraus, 1999, p. vi.
4. Quoted in Richie Robertson, *Arthur Schnizler: Round Dance and Other Plays*, J.M.Q. Davies ed. Oxford: Oxford Univ. Press, 2004, pp. ix–x.
5. *Ibid.*, xiii.
6. Mueller, p. 54.
7. Robertson, p. xv.
8. Mueller, p. viii.
9. Bruce Thompson, *Schnitzler's Vienna: Image of a Society*. London: Routledge, 1990, p. 1.
10. Robertson, p. x.
11. Schinnerer, p. 852.
12. Quoted at https://www.learnimprov.com/la-ronde.

Chapter 12

1. "Oh! Calcutta!" Wikipedia.
2. Kenneth Tynan et al., *Oh! Calcutta!* New York: Grove Press, 1969, p. 50.
3. *Ibid.*, p. 111.
4. Alexis Soloski, "'Oh! Calcutta!' At 50: Still Naked After All These Years," *New York Times*, June 17, 2019, nytimes.com/2019/06/17/theater/oh-calcutta-at-50.
5. *Ibid.*
6. *Ibid.*
7. *Ibid.*
8. *Ibid.*
9. *Ibid.*
10. "Oh! Calcutta!" Wikipedia.
11. Soloski.
12. *Ibid.*

Theater Quarrels

1. James Panera, "That Is to Say: Nowhere," in *The New Criterion*, vol. 40, no. 10, June 2022, newcriterion.com/issues/2003/9/that-is-to-say-nowhere.

Chapter 13

1. Michael James Foulkes, *The Reasons Behind La Querelle de l'Ecole des Femmes*. MA thesis, Durham University, 2012, p. 19.
2. *Ibid.*, p. 16.
3. *Ibid.*, p. 40.

4. *Ibid.*, pp. 53–55. I am indebted to Michael James Foulkes for his description of the action in "Zelinde."

5. *Ibid.*, p. 72.

6. *Ibid.*, p. 74.

7. For a more in-depth look at the quarrel, please see Michael James Foulkes, *The Reasons Behind La Querelle de l'Ecole des Femmes.* MA thesis, Durham University, 2012.

Chapter 14

1. A.S. Byatt, "Blaming Nora," *The Guardian*, May 2, 2009, theguardian.com/ stage/2009/may/02/ibsen-a-dolls-house.

2. I am indebted to "Henrik Ibsen," Wikipedia, for biographical information about Ibsen.

3. Sarah Schnebly, "Nora, Torvald, & Ibsen's Audience Through the Ages," huntingtontheatre.org.

4. Joan Templeton, "The *Doll House* Backlash," *PMLA*, vol. 104, no. 1 (January 1989), p. 29.

5. Byatt, "Blaming Nora."

6. H.L. Mencken, *The Collected Drama of H.L. Mencken: Plays and Criticism.* Lanham: Scarecrow Press, 2012, p. 185.

7. Bernard F. Dukore, "Karl Marx's Youngest Daughter and *A Doll's House,*" *Theatre Journal*, vol. 42, no. 3 (October 1990), pp. 308–321.

Chapter 15

1. "Ubu Roi," Wikipedia.

2. *Ibid.*

3. Keith Beaumont, *Alfred Jarry.* New York: St. Martin's Press, 1984, p. 99.

4. Nigey Lennon, *Alfred Jarry.* Los Angeles: Panjandrum, 1984, p. 48.

5. Dan Piepenbring, "An Inglorious Slop-pail of a Play," *The Paris Review*, September 8, 2015, theparisreview.org/ blog/2015/09/08/an-inglorious-slop-pail-of-a-play.

6. William Butler Yeats, *The Autobiography of William Butler Yeats.* New York: Macmillan, 1953, p. 210.

7. "Alfred Jarry," Wikipedia.

8. Martin Esslin, *The Theatre of the Absurd.* Garden City, NY: Doubleday, 1961, p. 255.

Chapter 16

1. Deborah Martinson, *Lillian Hellman: A Life with Foxes and Scoundrels.* New York: Counterpoint Press, 2005, p. 148.

2. *Ibid.*

3. "The Little Foxes," Wikipedia.

4. Martinson, p. 148.

5. Allen Ryskind, *Hollywood Traitors.* Washington, DC: Regnery, 2015, p. 332.

6. Boze Hadleigh, *Broadway Babylon.* New York: Backstage Books, 2007, p. 118.

7. Eleanor Mills, *Journalistas.* New York: Seal Press, 2005, p. 275.

8. Joel Lobenthal, *Tallulah.* New York: HarperCollins, 2004, p. 273.

9. William Wright, *Lillian Hellman.* New York: Simon & Schuster, 1986, p. 212.

10. Martinson, 148.

11. *Ibid.*, 147.

12. *Ibid.*, 148.

13. *Ibid.*, 147.

14. *Ibid.*, 148.

15. "Tallulah Bankhead," Wikipedia.

16. Jeffrey Carmer, *Tallulah Bankhead.* New York: Greenwood Press, 1991, p. 90.

17. Martinson, 152.

18. Andre Soares, "*The Little Foxes* Movie Review," *Alt Film Guide*, altfg.com/ film/the-little-foxes.

Chapter 17

1. Sophocles wrote other plays about the Oedipus myth, but they were not part of the trilogy with *Oedipus Tyrannus.*

2. "Eleutherae," Wikipedia.

3. Oscar Brockett, *History of the Theatre*, 10th edition, Boston: Allyn and Bacon, 2008, pp. 17–18.

4. I am indebted to "Dionysia," in Wikipedia, for its description of the City Dionysia.

5. "Sophocles," Wikipedia.

6. *Ibid.*

7. Donald William Lucas, *The Greek Tragic Poets.* London: Cohen and West, 1969, p. 128.

8. Edith Hall, "Introduction," *Sophocles: Antigone, Oedipus the King, Electra.* Oxford: Oxford Univ. Press, 1994, pp. xix–xxii.

9. Cedric H. Whitman, *Sophocles.* Cambridge, MA: Harvard Univ. Press, 1951, p. 123.

10. Sigmund Freud, *The Interpretation of Dreams*. New York: Empire, 2011, p. 296.

Chapter 18

1. "James Burbage," Wikipedia.
2. "Globe Theatre," Wikipedia.
3. "Allen v Burbage," shakespearedocumented.folger.ed.
4. Henry Wotton (2 July 1613) in Logan Pearsall Smith, ed., *The Life and Letters of Sir Henry Wotton*, vol. 2. Oxford: Clarendon, 1907, pp. 32–33.
5. Details of the archeological dig are provided in Simon McCudden, "The Discovery of the Globe Theatre," *London Archeologist*, vol. 6, no. 6 (1990), pp. 143–144.

Chapter 19

1. Leonard Doucette, *Theatre in French Canada: Laying the Foundations, 1606–1867*. Toronto: Univ. of Toronto Press, 1984, p. 7.
2. "Marc Lescarbot," Wikipedia.
3. Doucette, p. 4.
4. Quoted in Doucette, p. 5.
5. Kailin Wright, "Politicizing Difference: Performing (Post) Colonial Historiography in Le Théâtre de Neptune en la Nouvelle-France and Sinking Neptune," *Studies in Canadian Literature*, vol. 38, no. 1 (January 2013), p. 16. Retrieved from journals.lib.unb.ca/index.php/SCL/article/view/21446.
6. Beamish Murdoch, *A History of Nova Scotia*. Halifax: J. Barnes, 1865, p.34.
7. Wright, p. 20.

A Tale of Two Countries

1. William Archer, *About the Theatre*. London: T. Fisher Unwin, 1886, p. 97.
2. See Peter Brooks, *The Melodramatic Imagination*. New Haven, CT: Yale Univ. Press, 1976.

Chapter 20

1. Lady Jane Franklin, *As affecting the fate of my absent husband: Selected Letters of Lady Franklin Concerning the Search for the Lost Franklin Expedition*, edited by Erika Behrisch Elce. Montreal: McGill-Queen's University Press, 2009, pp. 25–26.
2. Jen Hill, *White Horizon*. Albany: SUNY Press, 2008, pp. 122–123.
3. Peter Ackroyd, *Dickens*. London: Sinclair-Stevenson, p. 772.
4. Quoted in Ackroyd, p. 773.
5. Quoted in Ackroyd, p. 776.
6. Queen Victoria, who had expressed a desire to see the play, offered Buckingham Palace as a venue, but Dickens politely turned her down.
7. Quoted in Ackroyd, p. 785.
8. Quoted in Ackroyd, p. 788.
9. Ackroyd, 790.
10. Quoted in Ackroyd, p. 792.
11. Ackroyd, p. 913–914.
12. Ackroyd, p. 1004.

Chapter 21

1. Laurence Irving, *Henry Irving: The Actor and His World*. London: Faber and Faber, 1951, p. 200.
2. Madeline Bingham, *Henry Irving and the Victorian Theatre*. London: George Allen and Unwin, 1978, p. 72.
3. *Ibid.*
4. *Ibid.*, p. 63.
5. Benedict Nightingale, "Great Moments in Theatre," *The Times*, March 11, 2011.
6. Quoted in Eric Jones-Evans, ed., *Henry Irving and The Bells: Irving's Personal Script of the Play*. Manchester: Manchester Univ. Press, 1980, p.6.
7. "Henry Irving," Wikipedia.
8. Russell Jackson,ed., *Victorian Theatre*. New York: New Amsterdam Books, 199, p. 119. "Effect" was the word used to describe any scene that created a sense of mood and atmosphere on the stage.
9. Louis S. Warren, "Buffalo Bill Meets Dracula: William F. Cody, Bram Stoker, and the Frontiers of Racial Decay," *The American Historical Review*, vol. 107, no. 4 (October 2002), pp. 1124–1157.
10. It would be another twenty-five years before a British actress was given a similar honor.
11. He and his wife later drowned in the 1914 sinking of the *Empress of Ireland* after a collision with a Norwegian collier in the St. Lawrence River.

Chapter 22

1. Quoted in Ann Marie Koller, *The Theater Duke: Georg II of Saxe-Meiningen and the German Stage*. Stanford: Stanford Univ. Press, 1984, p. 147.
2. I am indebted to "Georg II, Duke of Saxe-Meiningen," Wikipedia for much of the biographical information contained herein.
3. Koller, *The Theater Duke*, p. 152.
4. *Ibid.*, p. 152.
5. *Ibid.*, p. 157.
6. *Ibid.*, p. 153.
7. *Ibid.*, p. 152.
8. *Ibid.*, p. 157.
9. *Ibid.*, p. 158.
10. Ann Marie Koller, "Ibsen and the Meininger," *Educational Theatre Journal*, vol. 17, no. 2 (May 1965), pp. 101–110, p. 101.
11. Quoted in *Ibid.*, p.102.
12. Koller, *The Theater Duke*, pp. 213–214.
13. Stephen DeHart, *The Meininger Theater, 1776–1926*. Ann Arbor, MI: UMI Research Press, 1981, p.68.
14. Konstantin Stanislavsky, *My Life in Art*, trans. J.J. Robbins. Boston: Little, Brown and Co., 1938, p. 201.

Chapter 23

1. Frederic Spotts, *Bayreuth: A History of the Wagner Festival*. New Haven, CT: Yale Univ. Press, 1994, p. 67.
2. *Ibid.*
3. *Ibid.*, p. 64.
4. *Ibid.*, p. 31.
5. *Ibid.*, p. 33.
6. *Ibid.*, p. 29.
7. Oscar Brockett and Robert R. Findlay, *Century of Innovation*. Englewood Cliffs, NJ: Prentice Hall, 1973, p. 31.
8. Spotts, p. 63.
9. *Ibid.*, p. 68.
10. *Ibid.*, p. 72.
11. *Ibid.*, p. 71.
12. Brockett and Findlay, p. 31.
13. Spotts, p. 70.
14. Spotts, p. 1.
15. George R. Kernodle, "Wagner, Appia, and the Idea of Musical Design," *Educational Theatre Journal*, vol. 6, no. 3 (October 1954), p. 225.

Chapter 24

1. Quoted in Philip Glahn, *Bertolt Brecht*. London: Reaktion Books, 2014, p. 90.
2. *Ibid.*, p. 89.
3. *Ibid.*, p. 88.
4. *Ibid.*, p. 88.
5. "Bertolt Brecht and Kurt Weill's 'The Threepenny Opera' Premieres in Berlin," November 16, 2009, history.com.
6. Glahn, p. 91.
7. Quoted in John Willett, *Brecht in Context*. London: Methuen, 1998, p. 103 and in John Willett, *Art and Politics in the Weimar Period*. New York: De Capo Press, 1978, p. 72.
8. Bertolt Brecht, "A Short Organum for the Theatre," in John Willett, ed., *Brecht on Theatre: The Development of an Aesthetic*. London: Methuen, 1964, pp. 179–205.
9. J. Chris Westgate, "Brecht on Broadway," in *Brecht, Broadway and the United States*. Newcastle: Cambridge Scholars, 2007, p. xi.
10. Glahn, p. 205.
11. *Ibid.*, p. 91.
12. *Ibid.*, p. 88.

Chapter 25

1. Nayoung Aimee Kwon, "Conflicting Nostalgia: Performing *The Tale of Ch'unhyang* in the Japanese Empire," *The Journal of Asian Studies*, vol. 73, no. 1 (February 2014), pp. 113–141, p. 113.
2. I am indebted to "Tomoyoshi Murayama," Wikipedia for these biographical details.
3. Quoted in Kwon, p. 129.
4. *Ibid.*, p. 130.
5. *Ibid.*, p. 132.
6. *Ibid.*, p. 133.
7. *Ibid.*, p. 135.

Chapter 26

1. "Peter Weiss," Wikipedia.
2. Peter Weiss, *Marat/Sade, The Investigation and The Shadow of the Body of the Coachman*, edited by Robert Cohen. New York: Continuum, 1998, pp. xii–xiv.
3. *Ibid.*, p. xiv.
4. *Ibid.*, p. 58.
5. *Ibid.*, p. xv.
6. Quoted in Amanda Di Ponio, *The*

Early Modern Theatre of Cruelty and Its Doubles. Cham, Switzerland: Palgrave Macmillan, 2018, p. 223.

7. "Antonin Artaud," *Encyclopedia Britannica.*

8. Eric Bentley, *The Theory of the Modern Stage.* London: Penguin, 1992, p.66.

9. Peter Brook, *The Shifting Point.* London: Methuen, 1987, p. 47.

10. Di Ponio, p. 220.

11. Interview with Robert Langdon Lloyd, June 13, 2022.

12. Robert Langdon Lloyd, email to author, July 16, 2022.

13. Michael Coveney, "Marat/Sade," *The Independent,* October 4, 2011.

14. Interview with Robert Langdon Lloyd, June 13, 2022. Lloyd played the Priest in Brooks' production.

15. *Ibid.*

16. "Marat/Sade," encyclopedia.com.

17. *Ibid.*

18. Peter Brook, *There Are No Secrets: Thoughts on Acting and Theatre.* London: Methuen, 1993, p. 34.

19. Quoted in "Marat/Sade," encyclopedia.com.

Chapter 27

1. For this plot synopsis, I am indebted to Luca Somigli, "The Poet and the Vampire," *Italica,* vol. 91, no. 4 (Winter 2014), p. 575, jstor.

2. I am indebted to "Filippo Tomaso Marinetti," Wikipedia, for these biographical details.

3. David Ohana, *The Futurist Syndrome.* Brighton: Sussex Academic Press, 2010, p. 3.

4. Quoted in *Ibid.,* p. 3.

5. *Ibid.,* p. 58.

6. Quoted in *Ibid.,* p. 6.

7. *Ibid.,* pp. 2–3.

8. *Ibid.,* p. 60.

9. *Ibid.,* pp. 61–62.

10. *Ibid.,* p. 59.

11. Oscar Brockett and Robert R. Findlay, *Century of Innovation.* Englewood Cliffs, NJ: Prentice Hall, 1973, p. 291.

12. *New Zealand Evening Post,* June 2, 1909.

13. Fedele Azari, "Futurist Aerial Theatre," in *The Drama Review: TDR,* vol. 15, no. 1 (Autumn 1970), p. 129.

14. Ohana, p. 83.

15. Quoted in *Ibid.,* p. 87.

16. Much of the historical information for this essay was gleaned from Luça Somigli, "The Poet and the Vampire," *Italica,* vol. 91, no. 4, (Winter 2014), pp. 571–589, jstor.

Chapter 28

1. I am indebted to "Max Ernst," Wikipedia, for much of the biographical material in this essay.

2. Quoted in Carol Rumens, "Poem of the Week: 'Gadji Beri Bimba' by Hugo Ball," *The Guardian,* August 31, 2009, theguardian.com/books/booksblog/2009/aug/31/hugo-ball-gadji-beri-bimba.

Chapter 29

1. Williams' sister Rose had been lobotomized because of her erratic behavior during one of his several stints away at college.

2. Brooks Atkinson, *Broadway.* New York: Limelight Editions, 1985, pp. 37–38.

3. John Lahr, *Tennessee Williams: Mad Pilgrimage of the Flesh.* New York: W.W. Norton, 2014, p. 9.

4. *Ibid.,* p. 11.

5. *Ibid.,* p. 12.

6. Marc Vitali, "When 'Tennessee' Came to Chicago," December 18, 2014, https://news.wttw.com/2014/12/18/when-tennessee-came-chicago.

7. Lahr, p. 60.

8. All quotations from Robert Gottlieb, "The Greatest 'Menagerie,'" *The New Yorker,* October 18, 2013.

9. Lahr, p. 63.

Chapter 30

1. Alvin Klein, "Decades Later, the Quest for Meaning Goes On," *New York Times,* November 2, 1997.

2. Martin Esslin, *The Theatre of the Absurd.* New York: Anchor, 1961, p. xvii.

3. Harold Pinter, "Writing for the Theatre," in *Complete Works: Three.* London: Grove Press, 1977, p. 11.

4. I am indebted to "Samuel Beckett," Wikipedia, for these biographical details.

5. Jean-Paul Sartre, *What Is Literature?* trans. Bernard Frechtman. London: Methuen, 1950, p. 173.

6. Russell Dembin, "Nothing but Time: When 'Godot" Came to San Quentin," January 22, 2019, americantheatre.org.
7. Quoted in Esslin, *The Theatre of the Absurd*, p. xvi.
8. Quoted in Dembin, "Nothing but Time."
9. Quoted in Paige St. John, "Rick Cluchey, Ex-con, Playwright, and Samuel Beckett Collaborator, Dies at 82," *Los Angeles Times*, January 1, 2016, latimes.com/local/obituaries/la-me-rick-cluchey-20160103-story.
10. Lisa Armstrong, "The Power of Theater Performance in Prison," *Rolling Stone*, July 29, 2018.

Chapter 31

1. Dan Rebellatto, "An Introduction to *Look Back in Anger*," bl.uk. September 7, 2017.
2. Philip Hope-Wallace, "Prolix and Ugly but Original and Felt," *The Guardian*, May 9, 1956.
3. Samantha Ellis, "*Look Back in Anger*, May 1956," *The Guardian*, May 21, 2003.
4. *Ibid.*
5. Tynan's review appears online at bl.uk/20th-century-literature/articles/an-introduction-to-look-back-in-anger.
6. The original manuscript is online at bl.uk/20th-century-literature/articles/an-introduction-to-look-back-in-anger.
7. "Lord Chamberlain's Report and Correspondence About *Look Back in Anger*," bl.uk.
8. Quoted in "John Osborne," Wikipedia.
9. Royal Court Theatre website.
10. "*Look Back in Anger*," bl.uk.
11. "Dejavu," Wikipedia.

Chapter 32

1. Quoted in haroldpinter.org.
2. *Ibid.*
3. Much of this chapter is based on a telephone interview with Henry Woolf, recorded in May 2020.

Chapter 33

1. "A Raisin in the Sun," Wikipedia.
2. Lorraine Hansberry, *To Be Young, Gifted and Black*. New York: Signet, 1970, p. 52.
3. *Ibid.*, p. 51.

4. *Ibid.*, p. 125.
5. "Willie McGee (convict)," Wikipedia.
6. "Lorraine Hansberry," Wikipedia.
7. "Lorraine Hansberry," Wikipedia.
8. *Ibid.*
9. James Baldwin, "Sweet Lorraine," in Lorraine Hansberry, *To Be Young, Gifted and Black*. New York: Signet, 1970, p. xii.

True North

1. Gaëtan Charlebois and Ann Nothof, "Canadian Theatre History," *Canadian Theatre Encyclopedia*, canadiantheatre.com. I am indebted to Charlebois and Nothof for much of the historical information included in this introduction.

Chapter 34

1. Quoted in "Shakespeare Gets a New Home Town," *Macleans*, May 1, 2953, archive.macleans.ca/article/1953/5/1/shakespeare-gets-a-new-home-town.
2. Quoted in John Pettigrew and Jamie Portman, *Stratford: The First Thirty Years*, vol. 1. Toronto: Macmillan, 1985, p. 15.
3. Guthrie would eventually receive a knighthood in 1960, probably the result of pressure exerted from the office of Canada's Governor General Vincent Massey.
4. Pettigrew and Portman, p. 78.
5. Pettigrew and Portman, p. 62.
6. *Ibid.*, p. 5.
7. Robertson Davies, *Renown at Stratford*. Toronto: Clarke, Irwin, 1953, p. 43.
8. Pettigrew and Portman, p. 5.
9. Quoted in *Ibid.*, p. 8.
10. *Ibid.*, p. 4.
11. *Ibid.*
12. For more in-depth views of the Stratford (Canada) Festival, please see Robertson Davies, *Renown at Stratford*; Portman and Pettigrew, *Stratford: The First Thirty Years*; and Martin Knelman, *A Stratford Tempest*.
13. Davies, *Renown at Stratford*, p. 33.

Chapter 35

1. Don Rubin, "Creeping Toward a Culture: The Theatre in English Canada Since 1945." Guelph: Alive Press, 1972, p. 12. To

my knowledge, it was Rubin who first enunciated the importance of the year 1967, and of John Herbert, James Reaney, and George Ryga, in Canadian theatre history.

2. Gaëtan Charlebois and Ann Nothof note the importance of 1967 and of playwrights George Ryga, James Reaney, and John Herbert in the *Canadian Theatre Encyclopedia*, canadiantheatre.com/dict.pl?term=Canadian%20Theatre%20History.

3. "John Herbert," Wikipedia.

4. Anton Wagner, "Fortune and Men's Eyes," *Canadian Theatre Encyclopedia*, canadiantheatre.com.

5. George Bowering, "Why James Reaney Is a Better Poet (1) Than Any Northrop Frye Poet (2) Than He Used to Be," in *Northrop Frye's Canadian Literary Criticism and Its Influence*, edited by Branko Gorjup. Toronto: University of Toronto Press, 2009, pp. 111–121, p. 120.

6. Email from Moira Day to Dwayne Brenna, May 21, 2022.

7. Quoted in Colleen Krueger, *"Give Me Back the Real Me"; The Politics of Identity and the Ecstasy of Rita Joe, 1967–92*, Master's thesis, University of British Columbia, 2000, p. 11.

8. Quoted in *"The Ecstasy of Rita Joe,"* alllitup.ca/books/T/The-Ecstasy-of-Rita-Joe.

9. Moira J. Day, "Ryga, Miss Donohue, and Me," *Theatre Research in Canada*, vol. 38, no. 1 (2017), p 23.

10. Yvette Nolan, "A Prayer for Rita Joe," in *Performing Turtle Island: Indigenous Theatre on the World Stage*, edited by Jesse Rae Archibald-Barber, Kathleen Irwin and Moira J. Day. Regina, Canada: University of Regina Press, 2019, p. 118.

Chapter 36

1. Don Kerr, "History as a Six Pack," *The NeWest Review*, vol. 2, no. 9 (May 1977), p. 6.

2. Jean Macpherson, "Paper Wheat," *Saskatoon Star-Phoenix*, March 30, 1977, p. 58.

3. Alan D. Filewod, *Collective Encounters: Documentary Theatre in English Canada*. Toronto: University of Toronto Press, 1987, p. 99.

4. When he arrived in Saskatoon, Sprung decided to retain only Sharon Bakker and Michael Fahey from the original cast; he brought in David Francis, Skai Leja, and Lubomir Mykutiuk, all from Montreal, to play the remainder of the roles.

5. Jean Macpherson, "Paper Wheat," *Saskatoon Star-Phoenix*, September 30, 1977, p. 15.

6. Brian Freeman, "Saskatchewan Story Too Slow in Telling," *Toronto Star*, October 12, 1977, F1.

7. Ted Johns, *Toronto Theatre Review*, December 1977.

8. Michael Carroll, *Ottawa Review*, November 9–15, 1977.

9. Ray Conologue, "Dazzling Paper Wheat Inventive and Delightful," *Toronto Globe and Mail*, November 22, 1979, p. 19.

10. Arnold Edinborough, "A Fine Stage Harvest," *Financial Post*, September 15, 1979, p. 42.

11. Wayne Edmonstone, "Show Has Warmth and Honest Humour," *Vancouver Sun*, September 13, 1979, B5.

12. This chapter, with some modifications, first appeared in my book *Our Kind of Work: The Glory Days and Difficult Times of 25th Street Theatre*. Saskatoon: Thistledown Press, 2011.

Chapter 37

1. Jennifer Preston, "Weesageechak Begins to Dance," *Tulane Drama Review*, vol. 36, no. 1 (Spring 1992), p. 135.

2. Ann Nothof, "The Rez Sisters," *Canadian Theatre Encyclopedia*, canadiantheatre.com.

3. Preston, pp. 142–43.

4. Alan Filewod, "Receiving Aboriginality," *Theatre Journal*, vol. 46, no. 3 (October 1994), p. 367.

5. Julia Johnson, "In Conversation with Tomson Highway," *Macleans*, September 30, 2013.

6. June Scudeler, "This Show Won't Mean Anything Unless It Comes From 'the People,'" *Canadian Literature*, vol. 230, no. 31 (Autumn/Winter 2016), pp. 108–09.

7. "Native Earth Performing Arts' Donna-Michelle St. Bernard Steps Down as General Manager, Dec 2012," *Broadway World Toronto*, November 17, 2012, Broadwayworld.com.

Chapter 38

1. Andrew Dickson, "'The strange thing is we howled with laughter': Sara Kane's Enigmatic Last Play," *The Guardian*, May 11, 2016, theguardian.com/stage/2016/may/11/448-psychosis-sarah-kane-new-opera-philip-venables-royal-opera-house.
2. "Sarah Kane," Wikipedia.
3. Simon Hattenstone, "A Sad Hurrah (Part 2)," *The Guardian*, July 1, 2000.
4. *Ibid.*
5. *Ibid.*
6. *Ibid.*
7. "Sarah Kane," Wikipedia.
8. Dickson, "'The strange thing is....'"
9. Michael Billington, "How Do You Judge a 75-minute Suicide Note?" *The Guardian*, June 29, 2000.
10. Charles Spencer, "Sara Kane's Howl of Pain Is an Act of Artistic Heroism," *The Telegraph*, May 14, 2001.
11. Dickson, "'The strange thing is....'"

Chapter 39

1. Quoted in Eliot Nelson, "Mike Pence's 'Hamilton' Recollection Conflicts with Donald Trump's Take," *Huffpost*, November 23, 2016.
2. Lin-Manuel Miranda and Jeremy McCarter, *Hamilton: The Revolution*. New York: Grand Central Publishing, 2016, p.15.
3. *Ibid.*, p. 89.
4. *Ibid.*, p. 244.
5. Eric Bradner, "Pence: 'I wasn't offended' by Message of 'Hamilton,'" CNN, November 26, 2016, cnn.com/2016/11/26/politics/mike-pence-hamilton-message-trump.
6. All quotations from "Trump and Pence vs. 'Hamilton' Case: A Collision of Two Americas," *Washington Post*, November 19, 2016, washingtonpost.com/politics/trump-and-pence-vs-the-cast-of-hamilton.

Chapter 40

1. Joe Westerfield, "Uplifting 9/11 Musical 'Come From Away' Opens on Broadway," *Newsweek*, March 13, 2017.
2. *Ibid.*
3. Steven Suskind, "Aisle View: 38 Planes," *The Huffington Post*, December 3, 2017.
4. Johnny Oleksinski, "This Is Justin Trudeau's 'Hamilton,'" *The New York Post*, March 14, 2017.
5. *Ibid.*

Epilogue

1. Robert Cushman, "When Ustinov Was King," cushmancollected.com.
2. *Ibid.*
3. Ralph Berry, "Stratford Festival Canada," *Shakespeare Quarterly*, vol. 32, no. 2 (Summer 1981), p.177.
4. Martin Knelman, *A Stratford Tempest*. Toronto: McClelland and Stewart, 1982, p. 93.
5. *Ibid.*, p. 92.
6. *Ibid.*, p. 95.

Bibliography

Chapter 1

"Assassination of Abraham Lincoln," Wikipedia.

Freeman, Katie, "Letter Threatening Jackson's Life Determined to Be Written by Father of Man Who Killed Lincoln," knoxnews.com/news/2009/jan/25/letter-threatening-jacksons-life-determined-o-writte.

Goodwin, Doris Kearns, "The Night Abraham Lincoln Was Assassinated," *The Smithsonian*, April 18, 2015, smithsonianmag.com.

Lamon, Ward Hill, *Recollections of Abraham Lincoln, 1847–1865*. Washington, D.C.: Dorothy Lane Teillard, 1911.

Seymour, Samuel J., as told to Frances Spatz Leighton, "I Saw Lincoln Shot," *The American Weekly, Milwaukee Sentinel*, February 7, 1954.

Steers, Edward, Jr., *Blood on the Moon*. Lexington: Univ. Press of Kentucky, 2001.

Chapter 2

Gilloy, Dan, "The Murder of William Terriss," stagebeauty.com.

Jack-the-ripper-tour.com/generalnews/the-murder-of-william-terriss.

Johnson, Alice, "Examination of a Premonitory Case: Mr. Lane's dream of the death of Mr. Terriss," *Proceedings of the Society for Psychical Research* (Great Britain). London: Kegan Paul, 1899, pp. 309–316.

Millward, Jessie, *Myself and Others*. London: Hutchinson, 1923.

Rowell, George, *William Terriss and Richard Prince: Two Players in an Adelphi Melodrama*. London: Society for Theatre Research, 1987.

"William Terriss," Wikipedia.

"William Terriss (Ghost)," Paranormalist.fandom.com.

Chapter 3

Arechiga, Patricia, "Woman Made of Stone: The Murder of Albert Snyder," November 12, 2019, stmuhistorymedia.org.

Atkinson, Brooks, "The Play," *New York Times*, September 8, 1928.

"Machinal," Wikipedia.

MacKellar, Landis, *The "Double Indemnity" Murder: Ruth Snyder, Judd Gray, & New York's Crime of the Century*. Syracuse: Syracuse Univ. Press, 2006.

Maxwell, Perriton, "The Editor Goes to the Play." *Theatre Magazine*, November 1928.

"Ruth Snyder," Wikipedia.

"Sophie Treadwell," Wikipedia.

Chapter 4

Deshpande, Sudhanva, *Halla Bol: The Death and Life of Safdar Hashmi*. New Delhi: Left-Word Books, 2020.
Deshpande, Sudhanva, "Remembering Safdar Hashmi and the Play That Changed Indian Street Theatre Forever," January 3, 2007, scroll.in.
Pyotra.tumblr.com, Feb. 26, 2016.
Walia, Shelley, "The Luminous Life of Safdar Hashmi," *The Tribune India*, April 12, 2020.

Chapter 5

"André Antoine," Wikipedia.
Brockett, Oscar, *History of the Theatre*, 10th ed. Boston: Allyn and Bacon, 2008.
Brockett, Oscar and Robert R. Findlay, *Century of Innovation*. Englewood Cliffs, NJ: Prentice Hall, 1973.

Chapter 6

Balukhaty, S.D., *The Seagull Produced by Stanislavsky*. New York: Theatre Arts Books, 1952.
Brockett, Oscar, and Robert R. Findlay, *Century of Innovation*. Englewood Cliffs, NJ: Prentice Hall, 1973.
"Konstantin Stanislavsky," Wikipedia.
"Moscow Art Theatre," Wikipedia.
"Vladimir Nemirovich-Danchenko," Wikipedia.
Worrall, Nick, *The Moscow Art Theatre*. London: Taylor and Francis, 1996.

Chapter 7

Balukhaty, S.D., *The Seagull Produced by Stanislavsky*. New York: Theatre Arts Books, 1952.
Benedetti, Jean, ed., *Dear Writer, Dear Actress: The Love Letters of Anton Chekhov and Olga Knipper*. Hopewell, NJ: Ecco Press, 1996.
Benedetti, Jean, ed., *Moscow Art Theatre Letters*. New York: Theatre Arts, 1991.
Benedetti, Jean, *Stanislavsky and the Actor*. London: Methuen, 1998.
Benedetti, Jean, *Stanislavsky: His Life and Art*, revised ed. London: Methuen, 1999.
Chekhov, Anton 1920; Letter to A.F. Koni, Project Gutenberg.
Grochala, Sarah and Adam Rush, "The Seagull's Two Premieres," May 10, 2013, headlong.co.uk.

Chapter Eight

Crespy, David A., *Off-Off-Broadway Explosion*. New York: Back Stage Books, 2003.
"Ellen Stewart," Wikipedia.
"La Mama Experimental Theater," Wikipedia.

Chapter 9

Baer, Marc, *Theatre and Disorder in Late Georgian London*. Oxford: Oxford Univ. Press, 1992.
Knowles, Rachel, "Drury Lane Theatre Burns Down 24 February 24 1809," https://www.regencyhistory.net/2020/02/drury-lane-theatre-burns-down-24.html.
"Old Price Riots," Wikipedia.

Chapter 10

"Astor Place Riots," Wikipedia.

Bordman, Gerald, *The Concise Oxford Companion to American Theatre*. Oxford: Oxford Univ. Press, 1990.

Matthews, Brander, and Lawrence Hutton, eds., *Actors and Actresses of Great Britain and the United States*. New York: Leopold Classic Library, 2016.

Rees, James, *The Life of Edwin Forrest*. Philadelphia: T.B. Peterson, 1874.

Toynbee, William, ed., *The Diaries of William Charles Macready, 1833–1851*, vol. 1. New York: Putnam's, 1912.

Toynbee, William, ed., *The Diaries of William Charles Macready, 1833–1851*, vol. 2. New York: Putnam's, 1912.

Ziter, Edward, *Macready, Booth, Terry, Irving: Great Shakespeareans*, ed. Richard Schoch, vol. xi. London: A&C Black, 2014.

Chapter 11

"Arthur Schnitzler," Wikipedia.

Learnimprov.com

Mueller, Carl R., ed. *Arthur Schnitzler: Four Major Plays*. Lyme, NH: Smith and Kraus, 1999.

Robertson, Richie, *Arthur Schnitzler: Round Dance and Other Plays*, J.M.Q. Davies, ed. Oxford: Oxford Univ. Press, 2004.

Schinnerer, Otto P., "The History of Schnitzler's 'Reigen,'" in *PMLA*, no. 3 (Sept. 1931), pp. 839–859.

Thompson, Bruce, *Schnitzler's Vienna: Image of a Society*. London: Routledge, 1990.

Chapter 12

"Oh! Calcutta!" Wikipedia.

Soloski, Alexis, "'Oh! Calcutta' at 50: Still Naked After All These Years," *New York Times*, June 17, 2019, nytimes.com/2019/06/17/theater/oh-calcutta-at-50.

Tynan, Kenneth et al., *Oh! Calcutta!* New York: Grove Press, 1969.

Theater Quarrels

Panera, James, "That Is to Say: Nowhere," *The New Criterion*, vol. 40, no. 10 (June 2022), newcriterion.com/issues/2003/9/that-is-to-say-nowhere.

Chapter 13

Foulkes, Michael James, *The Reasons Behind La Querelle de l'Ecole des Femmes*. MA thesis, Durham University, 2012.

Panera, James, "That Is to Say: Nowhere," *The New Criterion*, vol. 40, no. 10 (June 2022), newcriterion.com/issues/2003/9/that-is-to-say-nowhere.

Chapter 14

Brockett, Oscar, and Robert R. Findlay, *Century of Innovation*. Englewood Cliffs, NJ: Prentice Hall, 1973.

Byatt, A.S., "Blaming Nora," *The Guardian*, May 2, 2009, theguardian.com/stage/2009/may/02/ibsen-a-dolls-house.

Dukore, Bernard F., "Karl Marx's Youngest Daughter and *A Doll's House*," *Theatre Journal*, vol. 42, no. 3 (October 1990), pp. 308–321.

"Henrik Ibsen," Wikipedia.

Mencken, H.L., *The Collected Drama of H.L Mencken: Plays and Criticism*. Lanham, MD: Scarecrow Press, 2012.

Schnebly, Sarah, "Nora, Torvald, & Ibsen's Audience Through the Ages," huntingtontheatre.org.

Templeton, Joan, "The *Doll House* Backlash," *PMLA*, vol. 104, no. 1 (Jan. 1989), p. 29.

Chapter 15

"Alfred Jarry," Wikipedia.

Beaumont, Keith, *Alfred Jarry*. New York: St. Martin's Press, 1984.

Esslin, Martin, *The Theatre of the Absurd*. Garden City, NY: Doubleday, 1961.

Lennon, Nigey. *Alfred Jarry*. Los Angeles: Panjandrum, 1984.

Piepenbring, Dan, "An Inglorious Slop-pail of a Play," *The Paris Review*, September 8, 2015, theparisreview.org/blog/2015/09/08/an-inglorious-slop-pail-of-a-play.

"Ubu Roi," Wikipedia.

Yeats, William Butler, *The Autobiography of William Butler Yeats*, New York: Macmillan, 1953.

Chapter 16

Carmer, Jeffrey, *Tallulah Bankhead*. New York: Greenwood Press, 1991.

Hadleigh, Boze, *Broadway Babylon*. New York: Backstage Books, 2007.

"Lillian Hellman," Wikipedia.

"The Little Foxes," Wikipedia.

Lobenthal, Joel, *Tallulah*. New York: HarperCollins, 2004.

Martinson, Deborah, *Lillian Hellman: A Life with Foxes and Scoundrels*. New York: Counterpoint Press, 2005.

Mills, Eleanor, *Journalistas*. New York: Seal Press, 2005.

Ryskind, Allen, *Hollywood Traitors*. Washington, D.C.: Regnery, 2015.

Soares, Andre, "*The Little Foxes* Movie Review," *Alt Film Guide*, altfg.com/film/the-little-foxes.

"Tallulah Bankhead," Wikipedia.

Wright, William, *Lillian Hellman*. New York: Simon & Schuster, 1986.

Chapter 17

Brockett, Oscar, *History of the Theatre*, 10th ed. Boston: Allyn and Bacon, 2008.

"Dionysia," Wikipedia.

"Eleutherae," Wikipedia.

Freud, Sigmund, *The Interpretation of Dreams*. New York: Empire Books, 2011.

Hall, Edith, "Introduction," *Sophocles: Antigone, Oedipus the King, Electra*. Oxford: Oxford Univ. Press, 1994.

Lucas, Donald William, *The Greek Tragic Poets*. London: Cohen and West, 1969.

"Sophocles," Wikipedia.

Whitman, Cedric H., *Sophocles*. Cambridge, MA: Harvard Univ. Press, 1951.

Chapter 18

"Allen v Burbage," shakespearedocumented.folger.ed.

"Globe Theatre," Wikipedia.

"James Burbage," Wikipedia.

McCudden, Simon, "The Discovery of the Globe Theatre," *London Archeologist*, vol. 6, no. 6, (1990), pp. 143–144.

Wotton, Henry (2 July 1613) in Logan Pearsall Smith ed, *The Life and Letters of Sir Henry Wotton*, vol. 2, Oxford: Clarendon, 1907.

Chapter 19

Doucette, Leonard, *Theatre in French Canada: Laying the Foundations, 1606–1867.* Toronto: Univ. of Toronto Press, 1984.
"Marc Lescarbot," Wikipedia.
Murdoch, Beamish, *A History of Nova Scotia.* Halifax: J. Barnes, 1865.
Wright, Kailin, "Politicizing Difference: Performing (Post) Colonial Historiography in Le Théâtre de Neptune en la Nouvelle-France and Sinking Neptune," *Studies in Canadian Literature*, vol. 38, no. 1 (January 2013), pp. 7–30, retrieved from journals.lib.unb.ca.

A Tale of Two Countries

Archer, William, *About the Theatre.* London: T. Fisher Unwin, 1886.
Brooks, Peter, *The Melodramatic Imagination.* New Haven, CT: Yale Univ. Press, 1976.

Chapter 20

Ackroyd, Peter, *Dickens.* London: Sinclair-Stevenson, 1990.
"Charles Dickens," Wikipedia.
Franklin, Lady Jane, *As affecting the fate of my absent husband: Selected Letters of Lady Franklin Concerning the Search for the Lost Franklin Expedition*, edited by Erika Behrisch Elce. Montreal: McGill-Queen's University Press, 2009.
Hill, Jen, *White Horizon.* Albany: SUNY Press, 2008.
"The Frozen Deep," Wikipedia.

Chapter 21

Bingham, Madeline, *Henry Irving and the Victorian Theatre.* London: George Allen and Unwin, 1978.
"Henry Irving," Wikipedia.
Irving, Laurence, *Henry Irving: The Actor and His World.* London: Faber & Faber, 1951.
Jackson, Russell, ed., *Victorian Theatre.* New York: New Amsterdam Books, 1999.
Jones-Evans, Eric, ed., *Henry Irving and The Bells: Irving's Personal Script of the Play.* Manchester: Manchester Univ. Press, 1980.
Nightingale, Benedict, "Great Moments in Theatre," *The Times*, March 11, 2011.
Warren, Louis S., "Buffalo Bill Meets Dracula: William F. Cody, Bram Stoker, and the Frontiers of Racial Decay," *The American Historical Review*, vol. 107, no. 4 (October 2002), pp. 1124–1157.

Chapter 22

DeHart, Stephen, *The Meininger Theater, 1776–1926.* Ann Arbor, MI: UMI Research Press, 1981.
"Georg II, Duke of Saxe-Meiningen," Wikipedia.
Koller, Ann Marie, "Ibsen and the Meininger," *Educational Theatre Journal*, vol. 17, no. 2 (May 1965), pp. 101–110.
Koller, Ann Marie, *The Theater Duke: Georg II of Saxe-Meiningen and the German Stage.* Stanford: Stanford Univ. Press, 1984.
Stanislavsky, Konstantin, *My Life in Art*, trans. J.J. Robbins. Boston: Little, Brown and Co., 1938.

Chapter 23

Brockett, Oscar, and Robert R. Findlay, *Century of Innovation*. Englewood Cliffs, NJ: Prentice Hall, 1973.
Kernodle, George R., "Wagner, Appia, and the Idea of Musical Design," *Educational Theatre Journal*, vol. 6, no. 3 (October 1954), pp. 223–230.
"Richard Wagner," Wikipedia.
"Ring Cycle," Wikipedia.
Spotts, Frederic, *Bayreuth: A History of the Wagner Festival*. New Haven, CT: Yale Univ. Press, 1994.

Chapter 24

"Bertolt Brecht," Wikipedia.
"Bertolt Brecht and Kurt Weill's 'The Threepenny Opera' Premieres in Berlin," November 16, 2009, history.com.
Brecht, Bertolt, "A Short Organum for the Theatre," in *Brecht on Theatre: The Development of an Aesthetic*, edited by John Willett. London: Methuen, 1964, pp. 179–205.
Glahn, Philip, *Bertolt Brecht*, London: Reaktion Books, 2014.
"Threepenny Opera," Wikipedia.
Westgate, J. Chris, "Brecht on Broadway," in *Brecht, Broadway and the United States*. Newcastle: Cambridge Scholars, 2007.
Willett, John, *Art and Politics in the Weimar Period*. New York: De Capo Press, 1978.
Willett, John, *Brecht in Context*. London: Methuen, 1998.

Chapter 25

Kwon, Nayoung Aimee, "Conflicting Nostagia: Performing *The Tale of Ch'unhyang* in the Japanese Empire," in *The Journal of Asian Studies*, vol. 73, no. 1, February 2014: 113–141.
"Tomoyoshi Murayama," Wikipedia.

Chapter 26

"Antonin Artaud," *Encyclopedia Brittanica*.
Bentley, Eric, *Theory of the Modern Stage*. London: Penguin, 1992.
Brook, Peter, *There Are No Secrets: Thoughts on Acting and Theatre*. London: Methuen, 1993.
Brook, Peter, *The Shifting Point*. London: Methuen, 1987.
Coveney, Michael, "Marat/Sade," *The Independent*, October 4, 2011.
Di Ponio, Amanda, *The Early Modern Theatre of Cruelty and Its Doubles*. Cham, Switzerland: Palgrave Macmillan, 2018.
Lloyd, Robert Langdon, email to Dwayne Brenna, July 16, 2022.
Lloyd, Robert Langdon, in interview with Dwayne Brenna, June 13, 2022.
"Marat/Sade," encyclopedia.com.
"Peter Weiss," Wikipedia.
Weiss, Peter, *Marat/Sade, The Investigation and The Shadow of the Body of the Coachman*, edited by Robert Cohen. New York: Continuum, 1998.

Chapter 27

Azari, Fedele, "Futurist Aerial Theatre," *The Drama Review: TDR*, vol. 15, no. 1 (Autumn 1970), pp. 128–130.
Brockett, Oscar, and Robert R. Findlay, *Century of Innovation*. Englewood Cliffs, NJ: Prentice Hall, 1973.
"Filippo Tomaso Marinetti," Wikipedia.

New Zealand Evening Post, June 2, 1909.

Ohana, David, *The Futurist Syndrome*. Brighton: Sussex Academic Press, 2010.

Somigli, Luca, "The Poet and the Vampire," *Italica*, vol. 91, no. 4 (Winter 2014), pp. 571–589.

Chapter 28

"Dada Early Spring," Wikipedia.

"Max Ernst," Wikipedia.

Rumens, Carol, "Poem of the Week: 'Gadji Beri Bimba' by Hugo Ball," *The Guardian*, August 31, 2009, theguardian.com/books/booksblog/2009/aug/31/hugo-ball-gadji-beri-bimba.

Chapter 29

Atkinson, Brooks, *Broadway*. New York: Limelight Editions, 1985.

"The Glass Menagerie," Wikipedia.

Gottlieb, Robert, "The Greatest 'Menagerie,'" *The New Yorker*, October 18, 2013.

Lahr, John, *Tennessee Williams: Mad Pilgrimage of the Flesh*. New York: W.W. Norton, 2015.

"Tennessee Williams," Wikipedia.

Vitali, Marc, "When 'Tennessee' Came to Chicago," December 18, 2014, https://news.wttw.com/2014/12/18/when-tennessee-came-chicago.

Chapter 30

Armstrong, Lisa, "The Power of Theater Performance in Prison," *Rolling Stone*, July 29, 2018.

Dembin, Russell, "Nothing but Time: When 'Godot' Came to San Quentin," January 22, 2019, americantheatre.org.

Esslin, Martin, *The Theatre of the Absurd*. New York: Anchor, 1961.

Klein, Alvin, "Decades Later, the Quest for Meaning Goes On," *New York Times*, November 2, 1997.

Pinter, Harold, "Writing for the Theatre," in *Complete Works: Three*. London: Grove Press, 1977.

St. John, Paige, "Rick Cluchey, Ex-con, Playwright, and Samuel Beckett Collaborator, Dies at 82," *Los Angeles Times*, January 1, 2016, latimes.com/local/obituaries/la-me-rick-cluchey-20160103-story.

"Samuel Beckett," Wikipedia.

Sartre, Jean-Paul, *What Is Literature?* trans. Bernard Frechtman. London: Methuen, 1950.

Chapter 31

"Dejavu," Wikipedia.

Ellis, Samantha, "*Look Back in Anger*, May 1956," *The Guardian*, May 21, 2003.

"John Osborne," Wikipedia.

"*Look Back in Anger*," bl.uk.

"Lord Chamberlain's Report and Correspondence About *Look Back in Anger*," bl.uk.

Hope-Wallace, Philip, "Prolix and Ugly but Original and Felt," *The Guardian*, May 9, 1956.

Rebellato, Dan, "An Introduction to *Look Back in Anger*," September 7, 2017, bl.uk/20th-century-literature/articles/an-introduction-to-look-back-in-anger.

Royal Court Theatre website.

Chapter 32

Haroldpinter.org.

Henry Woolf, in a telephone interview with Dwayne Brenna, May 2020.

Chapter 33

Baldwin, James, "Sweet Lorraine," in Lorraine Hansberry, *To Be Young, Gifted and Black*. New York: Signet, 1970.

Hansberry, Lorraine, *To Be Young, Gifted, and Black*. New York: Signet, 1970.

"Lorraine Hansberry," Wikipedia.

"A Raisin in the Sun," Wikipedia.

"Willie McGee-Convict," Wikipedia.

True North

Charlebois, Gaëtan, and Ann Nothoff, "Canadian Theatre History," *Canadian Theatre Encyclopedia*, canadiantheatre.com.

Chapter 34

Davies, Robertson, *Renown at Stratford*. Toronto: Clarke, Irwin, 1953.

Knelman, Martin, *A Stratford Tempest*. Toronto: McClelland and Stewart, 1982.

Pettigrew, John, and Jamie Portman, *Stratford: The First Thirty Years*. Toronto: Macmillan, 1985.

"Shakespeare Gets a New Home Town," *Macleans*, May 1, 1953, macleans.ca/article/1953/5/1/shakespeare-gets-a-new-home-town.

Chapter 35

Bowering, George, "Why James Reaney Is a Better Poet (1) Than Any Northrop Frye Poet (2) Than He Used to Be," in *Northrop Frye's Canadian Literary Criticism and Its Influence*, edited by Branko Gorjup. Toronto: University of Toronto Press, 2009, pp. 111–121.

Charlebois, Gaëtan, and Ann Nothoff, "Canadian Theatre History," in *Canadian Theatre Encyclopedia*, canadiantheatre.com.

Day, Moira, in an email to Dwayne Brenna, May 21, 2022.

Day, Moira, "Ryga, Miss Donohue, and Me: Forty Years of *The Ecstasy of Rita Joe* in the University," *Theatre Research in Canada*, vol. 38, no. 1 (2017).

"*The Ecstasy of Rita Joe*," alllitup.ca/books/T/The-Ecstasy-of-Rita-Joe.

"George Ryga," Wikipedia.

"James Reaney, Wikipedia.

"John Herbert," Wikipedia.

Krueger, Colleen, *"Give Me Back the Real Me"; The Politics of Identity and the Ecstasy of Rita Joe, 1967–92*, Master's thesis, University of British Columbia, 2000.

Nolan, Yvette, "A Prayer for Rita Joe," in *Performing Turtle Island: Indigenous Theatre on the World Stage*, edited by Jesse Rae Archibald-Barber, Kathleen Irwin and Moira J. Day. Regina, Canada: University of Regina Press, 2019.

Rubin, Don, "Creeping Toward a Culture: The Theatre in English Canada Since 1945." Guelph: Alive Press, 1974.

Wagner, Anton, "Fortune and Men's Eyes," *Canadian Theatre Encyclopedia*.

Chapter 36

Brenna, Dwayne, *Our Kind of Work*. Saskatoon: Thistledown Press, 2011.

Carroll, Michael, *Ottawa Review*, November 9–15, 1977.

Conologue, Ray, "Dazzling Paper Wheat Inventive and Delightful," *Toronto Globe and Mail*, November 22, 1979.

Edinborough, Arnold, "A Fine Stage Harvest," *Financial Post*, September 15, 1979.

Edmonstone, Wayne, "Show Has Warmth and Honest Humour," *Vancouver Sun*, September 13, 1979, B5.

Freeman, Brian, "Saskatchewan Story Too Slow in Telling," *Toronto Star*, October 12, 1977, F1.

Johns, Ted, *Toronto Theatre Review*, December 1977.

Kerr, Don "History as a Six Pack," *The NeWest Review*, vol. 2, no. 9 (May 1977), p. 6.

Macpherson, Jean, "Paper Wheat," *Saskatoon Star-Phoenix*, March 30, 1977, p. 58.

Macpherson, Jean, "Paper Wheat," *Saskatoon Star-Phoenix*, September 30, 1977, p. 15.

Chapter 37

Filewod, Alan, "Receiving Aboriginality," *Theatre Journal*, vol. 46, no. 3 (October 1994), pp. 363–373.

Johnson, Julia, "In Conversation with Tomson Highway," *Macleans*, September 30, 2013.

"Native Earth Performing Arts' Donna-Michelle St. Bernard Steps Down as General Manager, Dec 2012," *Broadway World Toronto*, November 17, 2012, Broadwayworld.com.

Nothoff, Ann, "The Rez Sisters," *Canadian Theatre Encyclopedia*, canadiantheatre.com.

Preston, Jennifer, "Weesageechak Begins to Dance," *Tulane Drama Review*, vol. 36, no. 1 (Spring 1992), pp. 135–159.

Scudeler, June, "This Show Won't Mean Anything Unless It Comes From 'the People,'" *Canadian Literature*, vol. 230, no. 31(Autumn/Winter 2016), pp. 108–122.

Chapter 38

Billington, Michael, "How Do You Judge a 75-minute Suicide Note?" *The Guardian*, June 29, 2000.

Dickson, Andrew, "'The strange thing is we howled with laughter': Sara Kane's Enigmatic Last Play," *The Guardian*, May 11, 2016, https://www.theguardian.com/stage/2016/may/11/448-psychosis-sarah-kane-new-opera-philip-venables-royal-opera-house

Hattenstone, Simon, "A Sad Hurrah (Part 2)," *The Guardian*, July 1, 2000.

"Sarah Kane," Wikipedia.

Spencer, Charles, "Sara Kane's Howl of Pain Is an Act of Artistic Herolism," *The Telegraph*, May 14, 2001.

Chapter 39

Bradner, Eric, "Pence: 'I wasn't offended' by Message of 'Hamilton,'" CNN, November 26, 2016, cnn.com/2016/11/26/politics/mike-pence-hamilton-message-trump.

Miranda, Lin-Manuel, and Jeremy McCarter, *Hamilton: the Revolution*. New York: Grand Central Publishing, 2016.

Nelson, Eliot, "Mike Pence's 'Hamilton" Recollection Conflicts with Donald Trump's Take," *Huffpost*, November 23, 2016.

"Trump and Pence vs. 'Hamilton' Case: A Collision of Two Americas," *Washington Post*, November 19, 2016, washingtonpost.com/politics/trump-and-pence-vs-the-cast-of-hamilton.

Chapter 40

Oleksinski, Johnny, "This Is Justin Trudeau's 'Hamilton,'" *The New York Post*, March 14, 2017.

Suskind, Steven, "Aisle View: 38 Planes," *The Huffington Post*, December 3, 2017.

Westerfield, Joe, "Uplifting 9/11 Musical 'Come From Away' Opens on Broadway," *Newsweek*, March 13, 2017.

Epilogue

Berry, Ralph, "Stratford Festival Canada," *Shakespeare Quarterly*, vol. 32, no. 2 (Summer 1981), pp. 176–180.

Cushman, Robert, "When Ustinov Was King," cushmancollected.com.

Knelman, Martin, *A Stratford Tempest*. Toronto: McClelland and Stewart, 1982.

Index